The Quintessence Of Nietzsche

Also from Westphalia Press
westphaliapress.org

The Idea of the Digital University

Dialogue in the Roman-Greco World

The Politics of Impeachment

International or Local Ownership?: Security Sector Development in Post-Independent Kosovo

Policy Perspectives from Promising New Scholars in Complexity

The Role of Theory in Policy Analysis

ABC of Criminology

Non-Profit Organizations and Disaster

The Idea of Neoliberalism: The Emperor Has Threadbare Contemporary Clothes

Donald J. Trump's Presidency: International Perspectives

Ukraine vs. Russia: Revolution, Democracy and War: Selected Articles and Blogs, 2010-2016

Iran: Who Is Really In Charge?

Stamped: An Anti-Travel Novel

A Strategy for Implementing the Reconciliation Process

Issues in Maritime Cyber Security

A Different Dimension: Reflections on the History of Transpersonal Thought

Contracting, Logistics, Reverse Logistics: The Project, Program and Portfolio Approach

Unworkable Conservatism: Small Government, Freemarkets, and Impracticality

Springfield: The Novel

Lariats and Lassos

Ongoing Issues in Georgian Policy and Public Administration

Growing Inequality: Bridging Complex Systems, Population Health and Health Disparities

Designing, Adapting, Strategizing in Online Education

Secrets & Lies in the United Kingdom: Analysis of Political Corruption

Pacific Hurtgen: The American Army in Northern Luzon, 1945

Natural Gas as an Instrument of Russian State Power

New Frontiers in Criminology

Feeding the Global South

Beijing Express: How to Understand New China

Demand the Impossible: Essays in History as Activism

The Quintessence
of Nietzsche

by J. M. Kennedy

WESTPHALIA PRESS
An Imprint of Policy Studies Organization

The Quintessence Of Nietzsche
All Rights Reserved © 2018 by Policy Studies Organization

Westphalia Press
An imprint of Policy Studies Organization
1527 New Hampshire Ave. NW
Washington, D.C. 20036
info@ipsonet.org

ISBN-13: 978-1-63391-714-9
ISBN-10: 1-63391-714-2

Cover design by Jeffrey Barnes:
jbarnesbook.design

Daniel Gutierrez-Sandoval, Executive Director
PSO and Westphalia Press

Updated material and comments on this edition
can be found at the Westphalia Press website:
www.westphaliapress.org

THE QUINTESSENCE
OF NIETZSCHE

FRIEDRICH NIETZSCHE.

THE QUINTESSENCE
OF NIETZSCHE

BY

J. M. KENNEDY

T. WERNER LAURIE
CLIFFORD'S INN
LONDON

OSCARO LEVY, M.D.

POST NIETZSCHIUM MORTUUM

PHILOSOPHIAE NOVAE

LUMEN OCCULTUM DUX CERTUS RECTOR CONSTANS

HUNC LIBRUM

GRATI ANIMI

ET

SINCERAE AMICITIAE

D. D. D.

AUCTOR

PREFACE

IT would be unreasonable to expect a Liberal Cabinet Minister to justify and apologise for the repeal of the Corn Laws ; it would be just as unreasonable to expect a new book about Nietzsche to be written in a justificatory and apologetic tone. This book, therefore, is explanatory ; and I have left Nietzsche to explain himself in his own words as far as possible. I have had the advantage over all previous writers of being able to study the philosopher in the pages of his autobiography (*Ecce Homo*), which was published only a few months ago ; and in the chapters that follow the English-speaking public is presented for the first time with an account of Nietzsche's posthumous works, including several quotations from the more important. In particular I would direct the attention of readers to the wonderful account of Inspiration, and the fragments on woman's suffrage, which I have translated from the *Ecce Homo* (p. 342

foll.).   The publication of the posthumous
works has also given me the opportunity of quoting some of Nietzsche's views on Socialism (p. 275
foll.).   Again, two of the aphorisms I have quoted
from the *Joyful Wisdom* (Nos. 68 and 71) show
that Nietzsche held a point of view concerning
women which English reviewers have not attributed to him, and one which compares favourably,
to say the least, with that held by several fathers
of the Church.

The chief authority for Nietzsche's life, of
course, is the bulky *Leben Friedrich Nietzsche's*,
by his sister, Mrs. E. Foerster-Nietzsche.   Other
information concerning his life is to be found in
Deussen's two books, *Die Wahrheit über Nietzsche*
and *Erinnerungen an Friedrich Nietzsche*, in Bernoulli's *Overbeck und Nietzsche*, and in many
other monographs which it is hardly necessary
to specify.   Criticisms on his philosophy are, it
need scarcely be said, extremely numerous; but,
until the publication of the revised text of the
Will to Power in 1906, the letters, several volumes
of which have appeared from 1900 onwards, and
the autobiography already referred to, it was
impossible to judge Nietzsche adequately.   I
have appended a short bibliography, giving the
names of only the more important books which

it is necessary for the reader to consult when he wishes to acquire a full detailed knowledge of Nietzsche and his philosophy.

My best thanks are due to Dr. Oscar Levy, editor of the first complete English translation of Nietzsche, who has kindly permitted me to make use of four volumes of his series * (all published at the time of writing), and two others which are as yet in proof.† All the other quotations given I have translated myself, and most of them have not hitherto appeared in English in any form.

I have said that this book is explanatory, which does not necessarily mean that it is innocuous. Nietzsche appears in the following pages, and, to adopt a homely simile never out of date, the pill may be difficult to swallow, and it is not sugared. Why should it be ? Here is a new philosophy, and " A new philosophy may be a more powerful enemy than all the navies in the world, and therefore well worth knowing." ‡

---

* Mr. Ludovici's translation of *Thoughts out of Season*, I ; Mr. Collins' translation of *Thoughts out of Season*, II ; *Beyond Good and Evil*, and *The Birth of Tragedy*.

† Mr. Common's version of *Thus Spake Zarathustra*, with Mr. Ludovici's Commentary thereon, and my own translation of *The Future of our Educational Institutions*.

‡ Dr. Oscar Levy in *The Revival of Aristocracy*, p. vi.

Nor think that this philosophy may be laid aside in favour of the much vaunted British common sense, for " Your common sense, dear Englishmen, is worth nothing compared with that uncommon sense you stand in need of so badly." * Put Mrs. Grundy and Stiggins aside for the time being, and try to concentrate your mind on facts —you are always asking for facts.

Stendhal says in *Julien Sorel*—one of the few really great novels of the nineteenth century, far outweighing the combined works of the Brontë family plus Anthony Trollope—that wit and genius lose twenty-five per cent of their value when imported into England. It is not pleasant to have this remark made about one's country, and I trust it will not hold good in the case of Friedrich Nietzsche. For Nietzsche is a dangerous weapon to be handled by those not accustomed to fight intellectual battles, and one must beware of him in an age when the land is suffering from nervous breakdown, when rumours of air-ships sailing for unknown destinations send tremors of fear through the once stolid John Bull, when wails and gnashing of teeth arise from all and sundry as the Kaiser reviews his troops. On top of all this comes Fried-

* *The Revival of Aristocracy*, Preface.

rich Nietzsche, roaring a terrifying message :
" The aim of my philosophy is, Who is to be
master of the world ?   My philosophy reveals
the triumphant thought through which all other
systems of thought must ultimately go under.
It is the great disciplinary thought : those races
that cannot bear it are doomed ; those that regard it as the greatest blessing are destined to
rule.   The refrain of my practical philosophy is,
Who is to be master of the world ? "

John Bull is a patient just now.   Nietzsche is
the only doctor who can help him, for his greatest
disease is Socialism, and all the evils that inevitably follow in the train of Socialism.   Dr.
Nietzsche either cures his patients radically—
or kills them.   In this case, which is it to be ?

J. M. KENNEDY.

CONTENTS

PAGE

PREFACE   vii

PART I

CHAPTER I

Early Life and Education   .   .   1

CHAPTER II

At Basel—The Franco-German War—*The Birth of Tragedy—Thoughts Out of Season*—Bayreuth   .   13

CHAPTER III

Travels—Later Works—Miss Andréas Salomé   .   27

CHAPTER IV

Mental Breakdown, Illness, and Death   .   40

PART II

CHAPTER I

Introductory — Religion — Christianity — Master and Slave Morality   51

CHAPTER II

Nietzsche and Politics—" Systems "—Sexuality—The Church of England—Socialism   .   .   73

CONTENTS

CHAPTER III

PAGE

Homer and Classical Philology—The Birth of Tragedy 106

CHAPTER IV

Minor Philologico-Philosophical Works—*The Future of our Educational Institutions* . . . 142

CHAPTER V

The Relationship of Schopenhauer's Philosophy to a German Culture — Philosophy in the Tragic Age of Greece—On Truth and Lying in an Amoral Sense—Thoughts Out of Season . . . 168

CHAPTER VI

Human—The Dawn of Day—The Joyful Wisdom . 261

CHAPTER VII

The Eternal Recurrence—Zarathustra . 289

CHAPTER VIII

Later Works : *Beyond Good and Evil—The Genealogy of Morals—The Will to Power—The Antichrist— The Twilight of the Idols*—Wagner once more— *Ecce Homo* 320

CHAPTER IX

Summary and Conclusion . . 345

BIBLIOGRAPHY . 355

INDEX . 357

PART I

THE QUINTESSENCE
OF NIETZSCHE

CHAPTER I

EARLY LIFE AND EDUCATION

NIETZSCHE was born in the little village of Röcken, near Lützen, in Saxony, on October 15th, 1844. His father, a clergyman, had been appointed to the living of Röcken a few years before by command of Frederick William IV, then King of Prussia, and he was, we are told, greatly delighted that his son should have been born on the birthday of his august patron. This coincidence led to the future philosopher's being christened Friedrich Wilhelm, in honour of the sovereign. In 1846 was born his sister, Elizabeth, of whom more will be heard in the following pages ; and in 1850 his brother Joseph was born, who, however, did not long survive.

There was an uncertain tradition in the family, which Nietzsche seems to have believed and endeavoured to investigate, that he and his people were descended from an aristocratic Polish family of the name of Nicki (pronounced Niëtsky). A member of this family was said to have had an earldom conferred upon him by Augustus the Strong, who secured the kingdom of Poland by bidding highest for the crown when it was put up for sale in 1697. When Augustus was deposed, and Stanislaus Leszcynsski crowned king in 1706, Nietzsche's ancestor became involved in a conspiracy and was sentenced to death. Taking flight, it seems that he was befriended by the Earl of Brühl, and here, for some time, the evidence was thought to end.

Before Nietzsche's breakdown at Turin he had begun to investigate this tradition closely; and some enthusiast even professed to have traced the ancestry, giving the results of a patient inquiry in an essay (now unfortunately lost) entitled " L'Origine de la Famille seigneurale de Nicki." The careful researches of the philosopher's sister within the last few years have, however, satisfactorily established the family's Polish origin.* It is undisputed that Nietzsche's parents and grandparents belonged to a cultured, higher middle-class circle, nor is there any doubt that, even early in life, Nietzsche showed a commanding, aristocratic nature, all his traits exhibiting

---

* The Poles, of course, were once the aristocrats of Eastern Europe, as the Italians now are of Western Europe; and such was their respect for individual opinion that a single dissentient vote in their upper House of Parliament was sufficient to throw out a bill.

that ideal of the " master " whom he was afterwards to describe in such vigorous languag-

It may be mentioned here that in Italy Nietzsche was generally referred to as " Il Polacco,"
and that when Peter Gast and a friend went to
call upon him at Bâle, after the publication of
The Birth of Tragedy, they were astonished
to find, not a benign, round-shouldered philosopher, buried amidst dry-as-dust " systems," but
a sturdily-built, strong-looking man with a fierce
moustache, resembling a colonel of grenadiers
rather than a student.   Gast was surprised, but
he was still further puzzled by Nietzsche's voice,
which was soft and low.   He afterwards learnt
that Nietzsche, like Stendhal, " wore a mask,"
and that, to counteract the effect of his military
appearance, he took pains to keep his voice at
a low pitch.   It is quite clear from the evidence
we possess that Nietzsche always looked what
he really was—a leader of men.

As the result of an accident Nietzsche's father
died in the summer of 1849.   In the following
year the family removed to Naumburg, where
they lived with the deceased clergyman's parents.
Nietzsche received his early education at Naumburg, and here again his instinctive aristocratic
nature showed itself.   He exhibited a horror of
vulgarity and of questionable companions, and
a moral and physical propriety which earned him
the nickname of " the little parson."   We learn
that he took a deep interest in the Crimean War,

and that he wrote a short military drama, *The
Gods on Olympus*. And it should especially be
noted that he endeavoured, above all, to be
alone. " From my very childhood I sought
solitude," he says in a short autobiography
written in his early teens, " and I was happiest
when I could find some secluded spot and give
myself up undisturbed to my own thoughts."*

In the autumn of 1858 the headmaster of the
celebrated Landes-Schule, Pforta, offered Mrs.
Nietzsche a scholarship for her son, tenable for
six years. Although Nietzsche's mother and
sister disliked the separation, it was decided to
accept the offer ; and to Pforta Nietzsche accordingly went in October, 1858.

Founded as a Cistercian abbey about the middle
of the twelfth century, Pforta, the German Eton,
has been for generations surrounded by an atmosphere of culture. The Cistercians, if they
did but little for the development of the sciences,
helped, at all events, to promote agriculture and
architecture ; but at the end of the fifteenth
century the Order had become wealthy and in-
dolent, and, like other Orders, its decay followed
as a matter of course. Maurice of Saxony turned
the monks out bag and baggage in 1543 to make
way (though he scarcely knew it at the time)
for the advance of Protestantism, for new ideas
and new ideals. The abbey was then changed
into the famous Landes-Schule, which, in Nietz-

* *Das Leben Friedrich Nietzsches*, I, 30.

sche's boyhood, was especially renowned for its historico-philological instruction. Like our own Eton, however, the school has within recent years fallen under the evil influence of Democracy, that political system in which, as Stendhal has happily remarked, men are not weighed, but counted.

The discipline of the school, although strict, was not severe, and Nietzsche seems to have spent a happy time at Pforta. He studied industriously, made several friends, devoted his spare moments to music and literature, and for the first time became familiar with some of Wagner's productions. One defect was the wine served out to the students on Sundays ; it appears to have .been so sour, says Mrs. Foerster-Nietzsche, that her brother looked upon wine with aversion all his life after.

The chief event of importance in Nietzsche's life at this time was the founding of the Germania club. The origin of this is partially explained in a series of lectures which Nietzsche long afterwards delivered in Bâle University " On the Future of our Educational Institutions."

" We resolved to found a small club," he says, " which would consist of ourselves and a few friends, and the object of which would be to provide us with a stable and binding organisation directing and adding interest to our creative impulses in art and literature ; or, to put it more plainly, each of us would be obliged to present an original piece of work to the club once a month—either a poem, a treatise, an architectural design, or a musical composition, upon which each of the others, in a friendly spirit, would have to pass free and unrestrained criticism. We thus hoped, by means of mutual correction, to be able both to stimulate and to chasten our creative impulses ; and, as a matter of fact, the success of the scheme was such that we always felt a sort of respectful attachment for the hour and the place at which it first took shape in our minds." *

A few additional particulars are given by Mrs. Foerster-Nietzsche : " It was in the summer of 1860, when my brother was one day walking on the banks of the Saale, that he thought of putting this intellectual intercourse upon a firm foundation through the medium of a literary and artistic club. The plan was first mooted to William Pinder and Gustav Krug, and heartily agreed to. Of course, the initial meeting had to take place at an out-of-the-way spot and with unusual solemnity ; and after some consideration the three fifteen-year-old boys carried their idea into effect on July 23rd, 1860. They bought a nine-penny bottle of Naumburg claret and walked gravely to the ruins of Schönburg, about an hour's journey away, clambered up the decayed steps leading to the watch-tower overlooking the beautiful valley of the Saale, and discussed

* *Educational Institutions*, Lecture I.

their lofty views on culture. . . . Finally they swore friendship to one another, baptised the club ' Germania,' and hurled the empty bottle over the battlements." The members of this club appear to have derived not a little benefit from it before it was broken up.

Many of the essays contributed by Nietzsche to the Germania Club papers, as well as several fragments jotted down during his school life,* show the philosophic bent of his mind at this early period. During his latter years at Pforta his favourite authors were Emerson, Shakespeare, the Edda, the Niebelungen, Tacitus, Aristophanes, Plato, and Æschylus. The Greek and Latin authors he read, of course, in the original, entering into their spirit with a fervour worthy of Macaulay at his best. Indeed, his zest for Greece and Rome, shown in several of his posthumous writings, remind us of many passages in Macaulay's diary. And it is pleasing to note that he frees himself from a heap of learned German lumber to take up a book which always remained his delight. " I have received the *Tristram Shandy*, and am now reading the first volume," he writes to his sister. " I read the book again and again. At first I did not understand the greater part of it, and I was even sorry that I had bought it at all. But now it attracts me wonderfully. I note all the striking thoughts ; and I have never yet met with a

* See Appendix to *Das Leben Friedrich Nietzsches*, Vol. I.

work that shows such an all-round knowledge of the sciences, or one that analyses the human heart so well."

Nietzsche left Pforta in September, 1864. As an original subject for the leaving examination he wrote a Latin essay on Theognis, the aristocratic philosopher of a democratic age, who influenced his after-life in many ways. From his leaving certificate we find that his conduct and industry were entirely satisfactory ; he is classed as " excellent " in Religion, German, and Latin ; " good " in Greek ; " fair " in Mathematics, French, History, and Hebrew.

Nietzsche's deep religious convictions are not without significance, and we shall have occasion to refer to them later in the second part of this work.*

Having rested at home for a few weeks, Nietzsche went to the university of Bonn. The splendid linguistic training he had received at Pforta induced him to devote himself principally to philology, but he also took up theology. At Bonn he studied under two of the most eminent philologists of the last century, Ritschl and Jahn. As the result of a quarrel between himself and Jahn, Ritschl left Bonn in the autumn of 1865 and went to the university of Leipzig. Nietzsche and several other students followed their favourite teacher to this university. In this year also Nietzsche first made Wagner's acquaintance,

* *Vide* p. 292 foll.

though their really intimate friendship did not begin until a few years later.

Nietzsche's studies at Leipzig between 1865 and 1867 were wide and deep. " The amount of work my brother succeeded in accomplishing during his student days seems almost incredible," writes Mrs. Foerster-Nietzsche. " When we examine his record for the years 1865-7 we can scarcely believe it refers to only two years' industry, for at a guess no one would hesitate to suggest four years at least. But in those days, as he himself declared, he possessed the constitution of a bear. He did not know what headaches or indigestion meant, and, despite his short sight, his eyes were able to endure the greatest strain without giving him the smallest trouble." Among his teachers were Curtius, the philologist; Roscher, the political economist; and Tischendorf, the orientalist.

Ritschl, who was a friend to Nietzsche as well as a teacher, suggested his forming a philological club at Leipzig; and an improved " Germania " was the outcome of the suggestion. Among the members was Erwin Rohde, with whom Nietzsche afterwards became very intimate. Ritschl, too, was more and more attracted to the young scholar when he read through his carefully thought-out essays on intricate questions of Greek and Latin philology; and Ritschl's influence was of great advantage to Nietzsche in securing many privileges for him in connection with the libraries and municipal archives of the city. In a MS. describing his university life, now preserved at the Nietzsche-Archiv, Nietzsche always speaks tenderly of his great teacher.

It was at Leipzig that Nietzsche first came upon a volume of Schopenhauer. He writes in his journal that he was wandering about aimlessly, in a somewhat depressed state of mind. " I happened to be near the shop of Rohn, the second-hand bookseller, and I took up *The World as Will and Idea*, glancing at it carelessly. I do not know what demon suggested that I should take the book home with me. Contrary to my usual practice—for I did not as a rule buy second-hand books without looking through them —I paid for the volume and went back home. Throwing myself on the sofa I gave myself up to the thoughts of that gloomy genius. From every line I heard the cry of renouncement, denial, and resignation ; I saw in the book a mirror in which the world, life itself, and my own soul were all reflected with horrifying fidelity. The dull, uninteresting eye of art looked at me ; I saw sickness and recovery, banishment and restoration, hell and heaven." *

As a result of Nietzsche's researches during his university course, he entered for a prize offered by the authorities of the university for an essay on the subject, " De Fontibus Diogenis Laertii." His treatise proved to be the best,

* *Das Leben Friedrich Nietzsches*, I, 232.

gained the prize, and was published, with a few of his earlier philological productions, in the *Rheinisches Museum*. While Nietzsche had read widely in English, French, Greek, and Latin, he seems to have paid particular attention to Theognis, Diogenes Laertius, and Democritus.

The next important event in Nietzsche's life was his military service of one year. He presented himself for examination, but was at first disqualified because, although healthy in every other respect, he was short-sighted. A new military regulation, however, decided that men who did not suffer from myopia to a very great extent should serve in the army, and Nietzsche took his place in the ranks shortly afterwards. He performed his duties to the complete satisfaction of his superiors, but an unfortunate accident compelled him to leave the colours before his term of service had expired. While mounting a restive horse, the animal suddenly reared, dashing the pommel of the saddle against his chest and throwing him to the ground. Nietzsche made a second attempt, and succeeded in mounting. He stuck manfully to his duties for the rest of the day, but the intense pain at length caused him to swoon, when it was found that he had severely strained the breast, the pectoral muscle, and the adjacent ribs. The wound became inflamed, and it was ultimately found necessary to consult a well-known specialist in Halle, Dr. Volkmann, who quickly set matters right.

One of the few great philosophers who have had the courage to mount a horse and take their place in the line of battle, Nietzsche was pleased with his military experiences. He was kept with a squad of artillery ; and this may have been in his mind when he remarked afterwards : " Like the old artillerist that I am, I have several shells in my ammunition locker which I have not yet exploded against Christianity, but I will shortly do so."

It was during Nietzsche's residence at Leipzig, owing to various causes which will be referred to later, that he gradually became estranged from Christianity, and fell to a great extent, though not entirely, under the influence of Schopenhauer.

CHAPTER II

NIETZSCHE'S University career was now drawing to a close. On returning to his studies in October, 1868, after having recovered from his illness, his intention was to get his doctoral degree as soon as possible, and then to visit France, Italy, and Greece. His philological essays published in the *Rheinisches Museum*, however, had attracted the attention of the authorities at Basel University. One of their number communicated with Ritschl, who gave a glowing account of Nietzsche's learning and abilities, saying : " Nietzsche is a genius ; he can do whatever he chooses to put his mind to." As a consequence the Board of Education had little hesitation in offering Nietzsche their vacant professorship of Classical Philology, although a cautious member of the board remarked : " If the proposed candidate is really such a genius, we had better not appoint him, for he would be sure to stay but a short time at the little university of Basel."

This unexpected offer was naturally looked upon as a great honour, for Nietzsche was but a few months over twenty-four years of age when it was made. Although it meant that his trips abroad would have to be postponed, he accepted the position, and the university of Leipzig immediately granted him his doctoral degree without further examination—another mark of honour.

Nietzsche delivered his inaugural address at the university of Basel on May 28th, 1869, and it came as a revelation to all who were interested, not merely in the teaching of Latin and Greek, but in the whole life of antiquity. The title of his address was " Homer and Classical Philology," * but the new professor made it clear that he used the word " Philology " in a very broad sense ; he showed that the science was not concerned merely with variant readings and grubbing among faded MSS. ; and that the great object of a philologist should not be to decide who wrote this or that, whom a particular allusion in some obscure author referred to, or which one of a dozen or more different readings and emendations was to be preferred. His aim was expressed in a sentence of Seneca which he thus turned backwards : " Philosophia facta est quæ

* " Philologie " has a somewhat narrower meaning than " Philology," and would correspond more to the English word " scholarship " ; but Nietzsche's wide conception of the science justifies the translation I have given.

philologia fuit " ; i.e. he wished the philologist to include the philosopher, just as he contended that philology itself was made up of history, natural science, and æsthetics. His firm grasp and delicate handling of the subject, his insight into the very soul of antiquity, and his enthusiastic references to the glories of ancient Greece—almost, as it were, presenting the beautiful Hellenic world to the eyes of those present—held the audience spellbound ; and we can well imagine how his young students would be roused into enthusiasm by the inspiring words which concluded a portion of the lecture : " And as the Muses descended upon the dull and tormented Bœotian peasants, so Philology comes into a world full of gloomy colours and pictures, full of the deepest, most incurable woes, and speaks to men comfortingly of the beautiful and godlike figure of a distant, rosy, and happy fairyland." Little wonder that the cautious member of the Board of Education exclaimed that they had indeed caught a rare bird, and that it was acknowledged on all sides that Ritschl's account of his young friend was not exaggerated.

Nietzsche's appointment had made it necessary for him to become a naturalised Swiss subject. When the Franco-German war broke out, however, the philosopher felt himself urged on to help his own countrymen in the struggle. Being a Swiss he could not now serve in the ranks, but he was enabled to accompany the hospital corps. Nietzsche brought all his energy to his new work, and as a result his health became undermined. Some of the soldiers he was tending were suffering from diphtheria and dysentery, and Nietzsche caught the latter disease himself. He was relieved from his duties, and went away to recuperate ; but, instead of waiting until he had fully recovered, he took up his work in Basel University before the effects of his illness had passed away. It is to this fact that his sister ascribes Nietzsche's stomach trouble and the other complaints from which he suffered during the rest of his life.

When the war was over the worst side of the conquerors showed itself. Nietzsche had seen the practical part of the war, and was ready to admit that the " honest German bravery " had won the day. But every Teuton insisted that German culture had had a large share in this victory, and German schools were pointed to with pride as being the real training-ground of the conquerors. Not only had German muscle achieved a remarkable triumph, but the German intellect was said to have vanquished the Latin intellect ; Teutonic ideals had vanquished Latin ideals ; in Germany alone was culture to be found. Nietzsche saw with alarm and sorrow that a spirit of snobbery and Philistinism had been awakened among the Germans by the successful outcome of the war, and when this became worse and worse every day his indignation knew no bounds. He first sought to combat it by giving a series of public lectures in Basel " On the Future of our Educational Institutions." It is in these lectures that his profound psychological insight and light humour first became manifest. But they are also noteworthy for something else, for in them we trace the embryo of the superman, a figure which had not yet taken definite shape in his mind. Already, however, he had a subconscious perception that his task in the world was to do all in his power towards elevating the type man ; and at this period of his life he thought this ideal would be practicable by the careful training of men of genius. Hence his fierce, bitter indictment of the German schools of the age—purely materialistic institutions, where the boys were taught how to " get on," how to turn themselves into money-making machines, how to be useful to the State—schools where culture was at first despised, then neglected, and finally lost sight of. Nietzsche's aim at this time was to point out the magnificent standards of the Greeks, and to try to instil an artistic conception of life into his self-satisfied countrymen. To endeavour to work upon the vulgar with fine sense is like attempting to hew blocks with a razor, said Pope, and it is to be feared that the razor-like satire of the modern prose Dunciad was blunted against very tough blockheads indeed. Nietzsche's lectures certainly influenced a few thinking spirits, but on the vast Philistine population they produced but little effect.

The essence of the five lectures and the introduction which Nietzsche afterwards prefixed to them may be summed up thus : There are plenty of institutions for teaching how to succeed in life, how to take part in the struggle for existence ; and such instruction is undoubtedly necessary for the majority. But such an education will turn a nation into a race of semi-civilised barbarians if it is not counteracted by artistic ideals. There must therefore be some men of genius—leaders—and such men must be carefully selected from the vulgar herd and trained in a special institution away from the restless bustle of commercial life. These geniuses must be nurtured on Hellenism—adapted in some respects to modern times—for it is only in the ancient Hellenic world that we can find the lofty principles, the high aims, and good taste which are necessary for leaders. But how is this ancient world introduced into our school curricula ? It is submerged in a flood of irrelevant facts. Goethe's dictum that the only value of history lies in the enthusiasm which it inspires is entirely forgotten ; and, instead of entering into the spirit of ancient Greece, scholars are dulled by abstruse questions about variant readings and similar trifles—a mere beating of the air. The teachers are as dull as the pupils ; and the pupils, or most of them, will in their turn become dull teachers.

The thoughts contained in the whole series of
lectures are just as applicable to-day as they
were in 1872, for Germany has not abated one
jot of her Philistinism.   They are, however, applicable in some degree to our English schools,
where scholars are taught either to take part in
the commercial battle of life or to be useful to
the State, but where culture *per se* is not deemed
much of an ideal, even after the passionate protests of Matthew Arnold.

If the lectures are applicable to both Germany
and England, they are even more applicable to
the United States of America, probably the most
Philistine country in the world.   This heterogeneous agglomeration of eighty million Philistines stands badly in need of a Nietzsche at the
present moment, and as the country is not likely
to produce one—its schools and colleges turn
out mere standardised money-making machines
—we can only hope that these lectures will be
thoughtfully studied there by the few who
have not been drawn into the commercial
vortex.

These lectures were delivered in 1872, and in
January of the same year was published Nietz-
sche's first important work, *The Birth of Tragedy*.
In her preface to the latest edition of this book,
Mrs. Foerster-Nietzsche writes : " *The Birth of
Tragedy* is really only a portion of a much greater
work on Hellenism which my brother had always
in view from the time of his student days.   But

even the portion it represents was originally designed upon a much larger scale than the present one, the reason probably being that Nietzsche desired only to be of service to Wagner [who was now living at Triebschen, and whom Nietzsche frequently visited]. When a portion of the projected work on Hellenism was ready under the title *Greek Cheerfulness*, my brother happened to call on Wagner in 1871, and found him very low-spirited in regard to his mission in life. My brother was very anxious to take some decisive step to help him, and, laying the plans of his great work on Greece aside, he selected a small portion from the already completed MS., a portion dealing with one distinct side of Hellenism—its tragic art. He then associated Wagner's music with it, and the name Dionysus."

This work was composed from 1869 onwards, and its publication aroused much enthusiasm among musicians. Professed philologists, however, perceived that Nietzsche was rising above their heads, and they received their fellow-professor's book coldly, to say the least. Nietzsche's old friend Ritschl wrote to express his mild disapproval ; and a philologist who is well known at the present day, Wilamowitz-Moellendorf, wrote a fiery pamphlet against the book. His ill-temper left him open to attack in several places, and his pamphlet was answered in an equally severe fashion by Nietzsche's friend

Rohde. It was generally admitted that the
victory rested with Rohde, although Wilamowitz-
Moellendorf wrote a second pamphlet, somewhat
feebler than the first. This attack, however,
had done Nietzsche some harm, and he had no
philological pupils during the winter term of
1872-3. Nietzsche's co-professors were willing
to acknowledge his philological talents, but they
could not forgive him for flying to heights beyond
their own reach—the ethereal regions of æsthetics
and philosophy.*

Nietzsche's mind, however, had now begun to
develop : he perceived that his high ideal could
not be attained by philology alone, and the
philologist within him gradually began to give
place to the poet and philosopher. He was beginning to find himself, to " be himself," and as
a consequence he was forced to discard some of
his old ideals. Hellenism still retained its hold
on him, but his estimation of Schopenhauer and
Wagner diminished.

Indeed, as we know from Nietzsche's diaries,†
he had not at first perceived the true characteristics of Wagner or Schopenhauer. His attitude towards them is bound up to some extent with his
sexual feelings, which were by no means normal.
It will suffice to say here that he idealised both

* See Chapter **XXXVIII** of *Zarathustra* : "On Scholars."
† See also Mr. Ludovici's preface to his translation of
Thoughts out of Season, Vol. I., and Mr. Adrian Collins's
preface to the same work, Vol. II.

of them as a lover does his mistress, and, again like the lover, he saw all his own good qualities reflected in them. When the veil was lifted from his eyes, however, he was genuinely astonished at what he saw before him. He recognised the ultimate consequences of Schopenhauer's pessimism, and he saw that Wagner was fast becoming a decadent Christian. Schopenhauer's despair could not withstand Nietzsche's Dionysian outlook. As for Wagner : " What I heard, as a young man, in Wagnerian music had absolutely nothing to do with Wagner ; when I described Dionysian music I described only what *I* had heard, and I thus translated and transfigured all that I bore in my own soul into the spirit of the new art. The strongest proof of this is my essay, *Richard Wagner in Bayreuth ;* in all the decidedly psychological passages in this book the reader may simply read my name, or the name ' Zarathustra,' wherever the text contains the name of Wagner." *

The essay here referred to forms one of the four *Thoughts out of Season.* The first, *David Strauss,* published in 1873, is almost a continuation of the lectures on Educational Institutions, specifically directed against David Strauss as representing the Philistinism of the period, especially in his book, *The Old Faith and the New.* Nietzsche's blows had some effect this time, and a loud outcry was raised in some quar-

* *Ecce Homo,* p. 68.

ters against the daring philologist. The noise had hardly died down when Nietzsche attacked modern German historians in a second "Thought," *The Use and Abuse of History*, which, however, did not give rise to so great a clamour as the first. This second "Thought" was published in 1874, and in the same year appeared the third, *Schopenhauer as Educator*. The fourth "Thought," the *Richard Wagner in Bayreuth* referred to above, came out in 1876. While apparently a panegyric on Wagner, the careful student of Nietzsche will have no difficulty in recognising the passages in which it is evident that any influence Wagner may have at one time exercised on him is now at an end. It is noteworthy that neither these books, nor Nietzsche's later works, received the attention they merited in his own country. He could say years afterwards : " I have now written fifteen books, and I have never yet seen an honest German review of one of them."

While writing these *Thoughts out of Season* Nietzsche suffered greatly from stomach trouble and occasional headaches, due, amongst other causes, to overwork. He spent his holidays at various places in Switzerland and Italy, and his sister came to keep house for him ; but Nietzsche was too restless to settle down to a quiet, regular mode of existence. The performance of Wagner's *Ring of the Niebelungs* at the Bayreuth theatre disgusted him completely, and put the finishing

touch to his relations with Wagner. They saw
each other some time afterwards at Sorrento,
but the meeting was purely formal, and when
Nietzsche published his next book, *Human,
All-too-human*, their intercourse came to an
end.

An interesting description of Nietzsche as he
appeared at this time is given by E. Schuré in
the *Revue des Deux Mondes* (August 15, 1895),
and is quoted by Mrs. Foerster-Nietzsche in
Vol. II of her biography.

" I met Nietzsche at Bayreuth in 1876, when
the *Ring of the Niebelungs* was first performed.
If those memorable scenic events indicate a
turning-point in the history of dramatic art, it
may perhaps be that they were also the secret
origin of Nietzsche's new evolution. While
speaking to him I was struck by the superiority
of his mind and the strangeness of his physiog-
nomy. He had a massive forehead, with short
hair well brushed back, and the prominent cheek-
bones of the Slav. His heavy moustache and
bold type of countenance would have made him
resemble a cavalry officer but for something else
in his appearance not easily describable—a mixture of haughtiness and nervousness. His musical
voice and slow speech gave evidence of his artistic
feelings ; his discreet and thoughtful bearing
indicated the philosopher. Nothing could have
been more deceptive than the apparent calmness
of his expression. The fixed eye revealed the

sad work of the thinker—it was at once the eye
of a keen observer and of a fanatic visionary.
This two-fold characteristic gave it the appearance of something restless and disquieting, more
especially as it always appeared to be concentrated
on one particular point. When he began to talk
for any length of time, his face assumed a look
of dreamy sweetness, but it soon became hostile
again. . . . At the time he first met Wagner,
Nietzsche had placed himself on a footing of
equality with his master. To him he dedicated
his first book—*The Birth of Tragedy*—with a reference to his ' sublime protagonist.' Perhaps he
conceived of the reformation of Germany by a
school of philosophy, æsthetics, and morals, of
which Schopenhauer would be the honoured
ancestor, Wagner the artist and manager, while
he, Nietzsche, would be the prophet and supreme
law-giver. . . . Nietzsche was present, but without enthusiasm, at the grandiose scenes of *Wal-
kyrie*, *Siegfried*, and the *Twilight of the Gods*,
which he had looked forward to with so much
pleasure. When we came away together, no
criticism, no word of blame, fell from his lips ;
he showed only the sad resignation of a conquered man. I well remember the expression of
weariness and dejection with which he spoke of
the master's next work : ' He told me he wanted
to re-read the *Universal History* before writing
his *Parsifal !* '—this with the smile and the accent
of ironical indulgence, the hidden meaning of

which might be : ' Those are the illusions of these poets and musicians, who think they can make the universe enter into their phantasmagorias, and only enter in themselves, after all ! ' "

CHAPTER III

FRIENDSHIP played a prominent part in Nietzsche's life, as may be noted from a chapter in the *Zarathustra*. It is beyond all doubt that he lavished more affection on Wagner than on any one else ; and the rupture at Bayreuth was a severe blow to the philosopher. About this time, as we learn from Mrs Foerster-Nietzsche's biography, Nietzsche was thinking of giving up his professorship at Basel and retiring to some quiet spot to meditate, living on the interest derived from a capital of some fifteen hundred pounds. He finally decided, however, that this would scarcely be sufficient to meet his expenses, for he always had a craving for travel. Readers of his autobiography *Ecce Homo* will note the importance he ascribed to the effect of a residence on his thoughts, and how Basel is pointed to as one of the plague spots. Nevertheless, he determined to retain his professorship for some time longer, and busied himself between 1874 and 1877 in preparing a draft of *Human, All-too-human*.

Failing health necessitated his obtaining leave of absence for a time ; and in 1878 he had to give up part of his duties. In the same year, just at the time of the Bayreuth festivals, *Human, All-too-human* was published. Nietzsche sent a presentation copy to Wagner, which crossed a copy of *Parsifal* that Wagner had just forwarded to Nietzsche. Neither acknowledged the other's work, and the rupture was complete.

In the next year, 1879, failing health, coupled with a desire to have all his time at his own command, induced Nietzsche to resign his professorship. The university authorities granted him a retiring allowance of three thousand francs a year, and wrote him a letter expressing their warm thanks for his ten years' faithful service at the University.

Nietzsche immediately took his departure from Basel, spending a few weeks first at Berne, then at Zürich, and afterwards at St. Moritz in the Oberengadin. He was delighted with this district, and used to remark: "Oberengadin restored my life to me." This holiday improved his general health very considerably; but his stomach trouble still continued.

The winter of 1879–80 was spent by Nietzsche at his mother's home in Naumburg; and at this time his health was at its very lowest ebb.[*] He found the town dull and the climate unhealthy, and his mother does not seem to have been a very comforting companion for him. In fact, both mother and sister used to wail despairingly: "Oh, Fritz, Fritz, if you had only stuck to your Greeks!"

* *Das Leben Friedrich Nietzsches*, II, 348.

In February, 1880, however, he was visited by a friend of his, Dr. Rée; and shortly afterwards he went to Venice in company with his lifelong friend, Peter Gast.* Gast was probably the only disciple Nietzsche ever had during his lifetime; and after his master's death he, rendered valuable service in putting Nietszche's MSS. in order and preparing the collected edition of his works and letters.

In October, 1880, we find the ever-restless Nietzsche at Genoa. The second part of *Human, All-too-human* had appeared the year before; but the public received it without over-much enthusiasm. In July, 1881, appeared *The Dawn of Day*, which likewise met with a cold reception, although it was in some respects a turning-point in Nietzsche's philosophy. Broadly speaking, his former works had been destructive, and in this one the constructive element began to appear. Like the public, however, Nietzsche's friends did not regard the work with any great interest.

When composing the *Human, All-too-human*, Nietzsche had altogether shaken off the influence exercised upon him by Schopenhauer and Wagner. Through them he had found himself; he now proceeded to follow the path of his own mind.

In the *Human, All-too-human*, Nietzsche rapidly surveys the history of the moral sentiments, the religious life, the inner minds of artists and authors, man, the State, woman and child. This was his first real attempt to grapple with the

* Gast's real name is Heinrich Köselitz.

problem of the origin of morals. The results of his investigations are contained in a series of aphorisms, long and short ; and the book is one of the most pleasing to read of Nietzsche's earlier works : for in it he shows his growing command over his own language ; in it he is just beginning to attain that style which renders his later works so delightful from a literary point of view. In this work, too, we can perceive a brilliancy of thought and a depth of insight into moral problems which shows us that Nietzsche has raised himself far above the heads of all his European contemporaries.

In England, where a certain theological view of morality has been taken for granted for century after century, it is only to be expected that the startling views enunciated by Nietzsche in this volume—and, of course, in his later works also—will at first be treated with incredulity and derision, and that their author will be looked upon as nothing less than an *advocatus diaboli.** The conservative nature of the Englishman, too, will make it all the more difficult for him to absorb these strange views. It must nevertheless be clearly understood that morals are as much subject to change as anything else, and if they

* In this passage (and in many others throughout this book, except where a distinction is specifically made) " England " may be used in a broad sense to stand for English-speaking people i.e., Great Britain, the British Colonies, and the U. S. A. Americans are even more conservative than Englishmen in matters of morality.

threaten to endanger life itself they must be up-
rooted. The effects of an intellectual revolution
on the Continent of Europe may take years to
reach this country ; but they must reach it eventually and undermine the old hierarchy. Although England is an island, its inhabitants
belong to the Continent by race, religion, and
history. The reactionary century which has just
closed—reactionary so far as culture is concerned
—was noted in England for utilitarian inventions
and improvements in every direction ; but it was
left to an aristocratically-minded Slavonic German
to carry discoveries in morals to a height never
attained before or since. And never let, it be forgotten that Nietzsche's improvements in the
sphere of morals outweigh all the English and
American discoveries in engineering or similar
practical fields. The curse of Puritanism—
Christianity carried to its logical extremes—
which gave rise to the orgies of the Restoration,
called forth the sharp invectives of Macaulay, and
almost drove Matthew Arnold into despair, is
still with us, and our only antidote is Nietzsche.
Let the reader who is in doubt as to the merits or
demerits of Puritanism look for proof in the
literature of, say, three generations ago ; let him
look at the types, by no means mere caricatures,
delineated by the pens of Dickens and Thackeray ;
let him consider the hypocrisy engendered by
the code of morals contained in an interminable
number of Thou-shalt-nots ; and let him further

consider the staggering mental and moral perversities which have inevitably accompanied such a code. Where but in England could Morton have found material for his Mrs. Grundy; where else could we have had a decadent novel like Farrar's *Eric, or Little by Little* ?—to mention only two instances out of thousands that could be adduced. Small wonder that Mr. Ludovici, lecturing on Nietzsche at London University, proclaimed to an applauding audience that the British Empire had been built up, not with the help of Christianity, but in spite of it.

For several years in succession Nietzsche spent his summers at the little Swiss village of Sils-Maria. The solitude of the quiet spot, far from the beaten track of the average tourist until quite recently, and the lovely scenery, charmed him very much. It was here that the doctrine of the Eternal Recurrence took possession of him, and that he first wrote down a few notes which later on developed into *Thus Spake Zarathustra*.

Nietzsche went back to Genoa in the autumn of 1881, and, if we may judge from his letters, this was one of the happiest periods of his life. He was slowly beginning to get the better of his stomach complaint, and he felt strong enough to walk about for at least six hours every day. He spent the next few months in preparing a volume of aphorisms which was intended to supplement *The Dawn of Day*, but he afterwards gave the work a new title and published it as *The Joyful Wisdom*.

Early in 1882 Nietzsche and his friend, Dr. Paul Rée, took a trip to Monaco. Nietzsche felt nervous and shaken after the journey, and a physician he consulted recommended him to proceed to Messina by sailing vessel as a means of improving his health. Driven from Messina by the Sirocco, he proceeded to Grunewald, on the outskirts of Berlin, as it was thought that the climate and surroundings would suit him. Although the climate agreed with him, he could not stand the Berliners : for even in Germany Berlin is despised as a city without culture. It has never given birth to anything noteworthy in art, science, or literature ; and when the very inhabitants themselves acknowledge (or boast) that their city is the European Chicago, what stronger condemnation could be wished for ? Nietzsche left in disgust, as may well be imagined, and went to Naumburg, afterwards travelling to Tautenburg (Thüringen). Here he completed four parts of *The Joyful Wisdom*, which appeared in September, 1882. He added a fifth part in the second edition, published in 1886.

At Tautenburg took place one of the most peculiar episodes in Nietzsche's life. Hungering, as he had been for years, for some one who would be partly a disciple and partly a secretary for him, he was greatly pleased when an old lady friend of his, Malvida von Mysenbug, acting in conjunction with Dr. Paul Rée, sent a Miss Salomé to call on him, stating that she had taken a deep interest in his works, and would be found a fit companion for him. We can judge how little Nietzsche's friends really knew him when we examine the circumstances of this case; for assuredly the natures of the philosopher and the young lady were diametrically opposed. It requires some mental effort to comprehend how ill-assorted the man and woman were; but if the reader can conceive of Eliza Cook, with all her estimable qualities, proposing to act as private secretary and adviser to Napoleon, he will have some idea of the relationship it was intended to set up between Nietzsche and Miss Salomé. The philosopher bored the disciple; the disciple worried the philosopher. Miss Salomé (a vivacious Russian Jewess) committed her woes to paper, and sent letters to her friends such as Fanny Burney might have sent from Windsor in the fourth year of her service with Queen Charlotte. The philosopher hurried away to Leipzig, followed, however, by the disciple. But Dr. Rée became concerned for his protégée, and some correspondence passed between them. The upshot of an episode, which has had more consideration than it deserved, was a series of quarrels between Nietzsche, his sister, Miss Salomé, and Dr. Rée. The latter's friendship for Nietzsche cooled considerably, and he referred to the philosopher afterwards in bitter terms ; Miss Salomé, who of course had never understood her master, wrote the most unreliable book about him which has ever appeared in print ; and Nietzsche himself, disgusted with the turn affairs had taken, and vexed by his repeated failures to find a true disciple, left Leipzig and went to Genoa. Here he lived for some months, working hard at the first part of the *Zarathustra*, which was published in May of the following year, 1883.

About this time Nietzsche was troubled with insomnia, and he began to take chloral as a relief. When the first part of *Zarathustra* was published he went to Rome, rather downcast, as his latest book seemed to be as much misunderstood as his earlier ones. At Rome he wrote some of the second part of *Zarathustra ;* but the hot weather caused his health to break down once more. Having abandoned a plan of going to Ischia (which was afterwards almost entirely destroyed by an earthquake), he returned to Sils-Maria. With the change of scene and climate his health was soon restored, and in less than a fortnight he had completed the second part of *Zarathustra*, which was published in September, 1883.

Urged by his sister to secure another professorial chair, Nietzsche entered into half-hearted negotiations with the authorities of Leipzig University, but the matter fell through,

partly owing to Nietzsche's own indifference.
Shortly after this a breach occurred between
his sister and him. Elizabeth wanted to marry
Dr. Foerster, which would necessitate her accom-
panying him to Paraguay. Old Mrs. Nietzsche
opposed the marriage, and her son joined in
the protest. Lying tongues whispered that Dr.
Foerster had spoken slightingly of Nietzsche's
books. Irritated to some extent by this, but
principally by the fact that Dr. Foerster seemed
to be only a dreamy German idealist, with a
suspicious hatred of Semites, Nietzsche endeavoured to break off the match. In this he
was unsuccessful, and no correspondence passed
between him and his sister for some time.

After this painful incident Nietzsche left
Naumburg and proceeded to Nice via Genoa.
Here he thought out the third part of *Zarathustra*,
and wrote it down, as usual, in less than two
weeks. Published early in 1884, it met with
the usual cold reception.

Nietzsche now, as always, led the life of a
Spartan. The greater part of his income of
two hundred pounds a year went in paying
for the production of his own books, and in
travelling expenses. As a consequence, his
lodgings were chosen with a view to economy,
and furnished accordingly—very often he had
no stove in his rooms during the cold Italian
winter.

The spring of 1884 found Nietzsche at Venice,

where he had gone to see his friend Peter Gast.
After a short stay here he went to his beloved
Sils-Maria, making the acquaintance of Baron
Heinrich von Stein on the way. In the autumn
Nietzsche happened to be in Zürich, where he
met and became reconciled to his sister. He
spent several weeks in Germany with her,
writing many poems during this time ; and in
the winter he proceeded to Mentone. While
at Zürich and Mentone, and later at Nice, he
finished the fourth part of *Zarathustra* early in
1885. A legal action with his publisher resulted
in Nietzsche's printing only forty copies of this
part at his own expense. The matters out-
standing were settled later on, when the publication of Nietzsche's works was taken over
by C. G. Naumann, who made a huge profit
out of them as Nietzsche gradually became
better known.

The lonely philosopher left Nice early in
1885, and visited Peter Gast at Venice. Here
he planned *Beyond Good and Evil*, which he
intended to be a commentary on his *Zarathustra*.
Spending most of 1885-6 in Venice and Nice,
Nietzsche passed his time in editing all his
hitherto published works, from *The Birth of
Tragedy* to the *Zarathustra*. He made but
few changes in the text, but the value of his
works was greatly enhanced by the thoughtful
critical and explanatory prefaces he added.
In the midst of this work he rushed off to Leipzig

on a visit to Rohde, the friend of his college days who had taken part in the Wilamowitz-Moellendorf controversy. The differences between the two men, however, were now very marked. Nietzsche's contempt for Germany and the Germans did not meet with Rohde's approval, and the divergent views of the two men resulted in a quarrel. Saddened by the thought that he had now lost another friend, Nietzsche went back to Nice.

Beyond Good and Evil now appeared. Unfavourable criticisms came in one after another, and only two men, Burckhardt and Taine, recognised the merits of the work.

About this time Nietzsche set about gathering his philosophy into one homogeneous work. The title of this was to be *The Will to Power*, but Nietzsche unfortunately did not live to carry his plan entirely into effect. At the end of 1906, however, Mrs. Foerster-Nietzsche was able to publish a fairly complete version from her brother's MSS. (An incomplete version appears in the large German edition of Nietzsche's works, published 1895–1900; from this the standard French translation was published in 1903.)

In the autumn of 1886, just after the publication of *Beyond Good and Evil*, Nietzsche went to the Riviera, and afterwards to Nice. It is no easy matter, nor is it, indeed, very important, to trace Nietzsche on all his wanderings. There was no Boswell at hand, with ever-ready notebook and pencil, to write down a list of all the houses the philosopher had lived in. Having left Nice again, we find Nietzsche at Zürich and two or three other holiday resorts, and the spring of 1887 sees him once more at Sils-Maria, working at *The Will to Power*.

This scheme was constantly interrupted by smaller books, of which Nietzsche wrote a great many at this time. Moving from Sils-Maria to Venice, and from Venice to Nice, he wrote *The Genealogy of Morals*, a comparatively short book, intended to act as a commentary on *Beyond Good and Evil*, just as this in its turn had been a commentary on *Thus Spake Zarathustra*. His finances were now looked after by an old friend at Basel, Professor Overbeck, from among whose papers several of Nietzsche's letters were afterwards recovered, as well as several letters from Rohde to Overbeck, throwing light on Nietzsche's habits.

CHAPTER IV

MENTAL BREAKDOWN, ILLNESS, AND DEATH

WHEN Nietzsche took a big task in hand,
it seemed fated to be interrupted, and
his efforts in connection with *The Will to Power*
were no exception. The philosopher left Sils-
Maria early in 1888, and took up his abode in
Turin. Wagnerism had again become the rage,
and Nietzsche's wrath was kindled against
the followers of the decadent musician. He
stopped work on his great book to write a short
pamphlet, *The Case of Wagner*. The views in
this naturally aroused the anger of Wagnerians ;
but it stirred up no emotion in any other quarter.
Nietzsche put all the more zest into this attack,
as he had not long before heard with joy and
wonder a representation of *Carmen*. " Hurrah ! "
he writes to Peter Gast, " a happy find ! An
opera by some one called Georges Bizet (who
can he be ?), *Carmen*. It goes like one of Meri-
mée's novels ; witty, strong, moving. A true
French talent, and one not led astray by Wagner.
. . . I am not far from thinking that *Carmen* is
the best opera at present existing ; so long as
we live it will form an item in every European
répertoire."

Nietzsche went to Sils-Maria this summer as usual—his last visit. In the autumn he returned to Turin. Here he wrote *The Twilight of the Idols*, a parody of Wagner's *Twilight of the Gods*, and this book was published early in 1889.

When in Turin Nietzsche applied himself diligently to *The Will to Power*. Only one section of it, however, was actually completed here, viz. *The Antichrist*. At this time also he wrote most of his autobiography, which was not published until the end of 1908, and another pamphlet summing up his views on Wagner, entitled *Nietzsche contra Wagner*. And Turin was the scene of the saddest event in Nietzsche's life, and one which has drawn forth book after book from eminent continental physicians—his intellect broke down, and he became insane.

It is unnecessary to weary the reader with all the hypotheses which have been put forward to account for this breakdown. The most important medical data remain to be published; for Doctors Breiting, Binswanger, and Wille, all of whom attended Nietzsche, have not yet published their observations. Let it therefore suffice to say that early in January, 1889, Nietzsche's manner was seen to be strange. An apoplectic fit was the first intimation that something was seriously wrong; for it rendered him unconscious for two days.

On recovering from his stupor his manner became more and more eccentric ; he talked vaguely, bought insignificant trifles and paid for them with gold, and wrote many peculiar letters to his friends. Overbeck, somewhat alarmed by one of these communications, hurried from Basel to Turin. There being no doubt that Nietzsche was no longer responsible for his actions, Overbeck took him back to Basel. Nietzsche's mother being informed of her son's condition, she had him removed to Binswanger's psychiatric institution at Jena, and in the spring of 1890 he was deemed sufficiently improved to be taken to her home at Naumburg.

All our present evidence goes to show that Nietzsche's final breakdown was due principally to his arduous intellectual life, in addition to which must be mentioned his constant stomach trouble, and the mental irritation brought on by his inward and outward struggles. Again, it has been remarked on a preceding page that Nietzsche was in the habit of taking chloral to relieve his insomnia, and this, in conjunction with the other matters mentioned, may have had some effect on his mental condition. At all events, there is no ground for assuming that because Nietzsche finally went mad any of his works were produced when he was in an unsound state of mind. This theory was advanced some years ago on the Continent ; but it has now been abandoned there in the face of the evidence against it. As it is an excuse frequently urged in England for not studying Nietzsche's works, it is only referred to here that it may be refuted.

It must be clearly pointed out that this stroke of insanity came very suddenly. From the year 1882 Nietzsche's health had been steadily improving, and he was, generally speaking, in a happy frame of mind and a sound state of body. In 1888 he produced a large amount of work, in no part of which can any traces of madness be found by even the most sceptical inquirer. All the letters he wrote up to the end of 1888 are in quite a usual strain. On January 4th, 1889, however, he sent a letter to the celebrated Danish critic, Brandes, which was unmistakably written by a madman. It was in very large handwriting on a sheet of ruled paper, signed *Der Gekreuzigte*, the crucified one. So far as it is worth while deciphering its incoherence, we are led to suppose from it that Nietzsche identifies himself with Jesus Christ, of whom he imagines himself to be the successor and the " best enemy." His breakdown, then, took place with appalling suddenness between January 1st and 4th, 1889. A letter sent to Rohde on the 7th also shows distinct traces of insanity.

Nietzsche's sister Elizabeth, who had married Dr. Foerster and gone to Paraguay with him, returned a widow in 1893. Nietzsche was sufficiently recovered to meet her when she arrived at Naumburg ; but his mind was still weak, and his complete recovery was regarded as hopeless. In 1897 his aged mother died, and Nietzsche and his sister now removed to a villa at Weimar. Here Nietzsche used to sit on the verandah overlooking the city and the neighbouring hills. He took great delight in music, as he had always done, and his friends, particularly Peter Gast, often came and played to him. He did not, as a rule, welcome visitors, but when they called on him, he was able to enter into conversation.

In 1898 and 1899 Nietzsche was seized with apoplectic fits. And then came the final attack. " On August 21st [1900]," writes Mrs. Foerster-Nietzsche,* " he fell ill suddenly with a bad cold, accompanied with fever and difficulty in breathing, the symptoms being those of inflammation of the lungs. In a few days, however, with the help of the family physician, the disease seemed to be overcome ; in fact, the doctor thought that his further attendance was unnecessary. Afterwards, about noon on the 24th, as I was sitting opposite to him, I saw his whole expression change all of a sudden, and he sank back unconscious, as if seized with paralysis. A frightful thunderstorm was raging at the time, and it seemed as if this mighty spirit were to depart from the world amidst thunder and lightning. But he rallied again, recovered consciousness

* *Das Leben Friedrich Nietzsches*, Vol. II, part ii, *ad fin.*

later in the evening, and tried to speak. I went
into his room at two o'clock the following morning to give him a refreshing drink, and as I pulled
the lamp-shade to one side so that he could see
me he cried joyfully : ' Elizabeth ! ' which led
me to think that the danger was over. He slept
for several hours after this, which I thought
would help his recovery. But his face changed
more and more ; his breathing became ever more
difficult : the shadow of death fell over him.
Again he opened those wonderful eyes of his.
' He moved uneasily, opened his mouth, and
shut it again, as if he had something to say and
hesitated to say it. And it seemed to those who
stood around that his face slightly reddened
thereat.' Then a light shudder ; a deep breath—
and softly, silently, with one final majestic look,
he closed his eyes for ever.

" ' Thus it happened, that Zarathustra departed.' "

Nietzsche died on August 25th, 1900, and was
buried in his native village, Röcken. The
thunderstorm referred to by Mrs. Nietzsche as
taking place the day before her brother died, may
remind us of the respect paid by Nietzsche and
other exceptional men to astrological and other
elemental warnings. One involuntarily thinks of
Napoleon when his attendants at St. Helena told
him they had seen a comet flashing across the sky.

" You have seen a comet ?   Then I am going to die.   A comet appeared just before Julius Cæsar died."   And his death did take place not long afterwards.

An address was pronounced over Nietzsche's grave by his friend, Peter Gast, which, although at the first reading it may seem too stately and ceremonious, deserves to be quoted in full :

" And now that thy body, after the majestic Odyssey of thy mind, has returned to its mother earth, I, as thy disciple, and in the name of all thy friends, deliver unto thee our heartfelt thanks in memory of thy great past.

" How *could* we be thy friends ?   Only because thou didst value us too highly !

" What thou wast as a world-moving spirit is plain for all eyes to see ;   and what thy heart was is shown in the trend of thy thoughts.   For the stamp of greatness lies over all thou hast thought —and all great thoughts come, as Vauvenargues says, from the heart.

" We, however, who had the infinite good fortune to be near thee in daily life :   we know only too well that the charm of thy person can never be adequately conceived from the thoughts in thy books.   This has now left us for ever.

" What was said by the glance of thine eye, or by that remarkable mouth, was full of beauty and goodness ;   it was a *concealment* of thy majesty :   thou wouldst fain (to use one of thine own most tender phrases) thou wouldst fain

spare us from shame. For who can show us
another example of the wealth of thy spirit and
the impulse of thy heart to do good unto others ?

" Thou wast one of the noblest and purest men
that ever trod this earth.

" And although this is known to both friend
and foe, I do not deem it superfluous to utter this
testimony aloud at thy tomb. For we know the
world ; we know the fate of Spinoza ! Around
Nietzsche's memory, too, posterity may cast
shadows ! And therefore I close with the words :
Peace to thy ashes ! Holy be thy name to all
coming generations ! "

PART II

PART II

CHAPTER I

INTRODUCTORY—RELIGION—CHRISTIANITY— MASTER AND SLAVE MORALITY

"NIETZSCHE had one very definite and un-
altered purpose, ideal, and direction,"
writes Mr. Ludovici,* "and this was ' the elevation of the type man.' He tells us in *The Will to
Power* : ' All is truth to me that tends to elevate
man.' To this principle he was already pledged
as a student at Leipzig ; we owe every line that
he ever wrote to his devotion to it, and it is the
key to all his complexities, blasphemies, prolixi-
ties, and terrible earnestness. All was good to
Nietzsche that tended to elevate man ; all was
bad that kept him stationary or sent him backwards."

To any one who has made a thorough study of
Nietzsche's writings, it is clear that from his
youth on he had this great aim steadily in view.
It is greatly to be regretted, however, that up
to the present his works have been presented to
the English reading public only in a spasmodic
and irregular form. An attempt to produce a
complete English version was begun in 1896,
which, by first of all publishing two or three of

* Translator's preface to *Thoughts out of Season*, I.

Nietzsche's latest, most abstruse, and most violent works, was doomed to failure from the start. For several years, therefore, those who read English only were forced to be content with about one-sixth of the philosopher's writings, and it is hardly to be wondered at that most of the Anglo-Saxon conceptions of him are rather hazy. Needless to say, the same indifference was not shown in other countries. A fairly satisfactory French version of the works was begun in 1893, although single volumes had previously been translated. A Spanish edition was completed in 1907 ; and nearly every other European country possesses translations of at least the most important works. As yet, however, the twelve volumes of posthumous works and letters can be read only in the original.

Again, Nietzsche's scintillating, finely-chiselled aphorisms are eminently quotable, and by taking them at haphazard from his books and stringing them together it is possible to give his views almost any trend desired. This has naturally called forth strong protests from those who are better informed, as, for example, James Huneker's : " Thanks to the conception of some writers, Nietzsche and the Nietzschians are gigantic brutes, a combination of Genghis Khan and Bismarck, terrifying apparitions wearing mustachios like yataghans, eyes rolling in frenzy, with a philosophy that ranged from pitch-and-toss to manslaughter, and with consuming

atheism as a side attraction. Need we protest
that this is Nietzsche misled, Nietzsche butchered
to make a stupid novelist's holiday ? " *

Many accusations brought against Nietzsche
will doubtless be found refuted in the quotations
given in the following chapters ; and it is only
necessary to refer here to the three chief objec-
tions made to the man or his philosophy.

In the first place, then, nothing is commoner
than to hear the view expressed that Nietzsche
was an anarchist of anarchists : a man who
desired to upset all hitherto established law and
order, not only in politics and the ordinary
relations between man and man ; but also in
art, using the word in its widest sense. Hence
hundreds of romanticists and even Socialists, all
of whom Nietzsche would have spurned away
with indignation and contempt, have boldly
proclaimed themselves his followers, and contributed their share to his misrepresentation.
How far Nietzsche was from being an anarchist
may be seen in *Beyond Good and Evil*, to mention
only one book ; in fact, a correspondence on this
very point appeared not long ago in *The Outlook*.†
" Nietzsche preaches unrestrained liberty, will,
egoism, and primitive energy," wrote a corre-
spondent, concisely summing up the opinion of
Nietzsche held by hundreds of well-educated
men ; " he is the hater of all organisation. . . .

* *Egoists : A book of Supermen*, p. 256.
† *The Outlook*, May 22nd and 29th, and June 12th, 1909.

To him all law is an interference with the rights and liberty of the individual man. . . . Liberty is for him lawlessness. . . . The fact is that Nietzsche, like Schopenhauer, Spinoza, and many other philosophers, was by instinct and temperament an artist."

This letter was followed up by two others from well-known Nietzschian lecturers and critics, Mr. A. M. Ludovici and Mr. Thomas Common. " It is readily admitted," wrote Mr. Ludovici, " that the artist as he appears to day . . . has much of the anarchist in his constitution." Mentioning examples of anarchy in various branches of art, the writer proceeds : " But all this, though it is characteristic of the modern artist, is absolutely foreign to the genuine artist. For what distinguishes him from other men is precisely his orderliness. Tired of the disorder and chaos of Nature, whether in regard to its sounds or its kaleidoscopic pictures, we as laymen crave for order and rhythm. . . . The artist steps in and gives us what we require—that is his mission on earth. By being disorderly or anarchical, by being, that is to say, realistic or ' true to Nature,' he defeats his own ends, he forfeits his only justification in our midst." To prove that Nietzsche was a genuine artist, an artist in the true sense, Mr. Ludovici quotes a few sentences from aphorism 188 of *Beyond Good and Evil*, which is given in full on p. 321 of this work. Mr. Ludovici justly concludes by saying :

" Genius is essentially order and obedience to law ; and Nietzsche's highest aim, his loftiest aspiration, was to re-establish that law and order without which genius may fail to make its appearance in the future."

Nietzsche's political anarchy was refuted by Mr. Common. " Nietzsche believed in slavery (see sections 257–8 of *Good and Evil*,* and many other passages) which is the opposite of ' unrestrained liberty ' ; he believed also in judicious altruism (see ' The Bestowing Virtue,' † in *Zarathustra*, and many other passages) which is the opposite of ' egoism ' ; he believed in a thoroughly organised system of society, such as that of ancient India (*v.* section 57 of *The Antichrist* ‡ and many other passages), he therefore is not the hater of all organisations and civilised institutions ; he speaks favourably of theocracies, states, and governments, like those of ancient India, Greece, Rome, Venice, Russia, etc., in many passages which one could readily cite ; he did not therefore consider ' all law as a vicious interference with the individual ' ; he is also quite incorrectly described as an individualist (see *Das Leben Nietzsches*, p. 760, and other passages), while instead of favouring anarchy he is quite opposed to it (see ' The Tarantulas,' § in *Zarathustra*, and many other passages). . . .

* Quoted on pp. 61 and 325 of this book.
† *Vide* apposite passages quoted on p. 303.
‡ *Vide* p. 333.   § *Vide* p. 303.

Nietzsche always contemplates as his ideal a state of society which would ultimately involve one law for the meritoriously rich, and another law for the deservedly poor—far greater liberty than at present for the worthy classes of society, and far less liberty than at present for the unworthy."

The second objection made to Nietzsche is that he is a selfish egoist, and this accusation will be found sufficiently refuted in the quotations that follow. The third relates to his views on morality. It is somewhat surprising, and not a little irritating, that when this word is uttered English men and women immediately think of sexual relationships : a subject which, even now, it is not thought quite proper to discuss audibly. The British silence on this point is certainly curious, and a fit subject for the amusement of the more enlightened Latin races. The manner in which it is hedged about in England naturally gives rise to speculation. Is it that generations of hard, tiring labour have rendered us incapable of appreciating and paying due attention to anything else ?—that the men of the country are impotent ?—and that amative (or shall we say philoprogenitive ?) ἀπάθεια (in the Stoic sense) is to be added to the list of feminine shortcomings as the natural result of two or three generations of unduly severe and aimless education which was absolutely unsuited to the female brain ? Partly ; but it would probably be nearer the truth to say that morals (in the narrow English and North American sense of the word) are so bad in England that a high standard has to be set up as a sop to the wonderful English conscience. Never a very " moral " country from a purely Christian standpoint, England now seems to be inhabited chiefly by nymphs and satyrs. English morals may be compared to a brake on the wagon of English life. When the wagon is being driven down a slight incline, the brake— our moral standards—need not be often resorted to ; but when, as at present, the wagon threatens to rush headlong down a steep slope, the brake must be applied to the greatest possible extent. The nation would fain blink the fact that its morals are so bad ; hence the high standard of morality : and hence also, I imagine, the unwillingness to discuss moral problems observable in every section of society, to the no small astonishment of our continental neighbours. No doubt it is not edifying to bring one's family skeletons out of the cupboard.

Now, Nietzsche undoubtedly does touch upon this aspect of the problem of morality ; but the word has a broader significance for him. He takes morality to mean the whole table of values in accordance with which we live ; in accordance with which we do our deeds and think our thoughts. Accordingly, therefore, when the word " immoralty " occurs in connection with Nietzsche's philosophy, it must be remembered that it represents what is, in his opinion, a bad table of values : for every epoch or civilisation possesses what Nietzsche calls its hierarchy of values—it decides that one specific action is preferable to another ; that truth, for example, is better than lying. The drawing up of this table, and, in particular, the determining of the highest values, is a weighty matter ; since such a table will determine the conscious or unconscious acts of every individual, and influence all his judgments. An examination of our present European morality, as determined by Christianity, led Nietzsche to those startling conclusions which have given rise to so much discussion on the Continent during the last twenty years.

To assure ourselves that Nietzsche, whatever may be thought to the contrary, was really a deeply religious man, we have but to read through almost any one of his works. Take these two quotations, for instance :

For those who are strong and independent, destined and trained to command, in whom the skill and judgment of a ruling race is incorporated, religion is an additional means for overcoming resistance in the exercise of authority—as a bond which binds rulers and subjects in common, betraying and surrendering to the former the conscience of the latter, their inmost heart, which would fain escape obedience. And in the case of the unique natures of noble origin, if by virtue of superior spirituality they should incline to a more retired and contemplative life, reserving to themselves only the more refined forms of government (over chosen disciples or members of an order), religion itself may be used as a means of obtaining peace from the noise and trouble of managing *grosser* affairs, and for securing immunity from the *unavoidable* filth of all political agitation.

[To some] religion offers sufficient incentives and temptations to aspire to higher intellectuality, and to experience the sentiments of authoritative self-control, of silence, and of solitude. Asceticism and Puritanism are almost indispensable means of educating and ennobling a race which seeks to rise above its hereditary baseness and work itself upward to future supremacy. And finally, to ordinary men, to the majority of the people, who exist for service and general utility, and are only so far entitled to exist, religion gives valuable contentedness with their lot and condition, peace of heart, ennoblement of obedience, additional social happiness and sympathy, with something of transfiguration and embellishment, something of justification of all the commonplaceness, all the meanness, all the semi-animal poverty of their souls. Religion, together with the religious significance of life, sheds sunshine over such perpetually harassed men, and makes even their own aspect endurable to them ; it operates upon them as the Epicurean philosophy usually operates upon sufferers of a higher order, in a refreshing and refining manner, almost *turning* suffering *to account*, and in the end even hallowing and vindicating it. There is, perhaps, nothing so admirable in Christianity and Buddhism as their art of teaching even the lowest to elevate themselves by piety to a seemingly higher order of things, and thereby to retain their satisfaction with the actual world in which they find it difficult enough to live— this very difficulty being necessary.*

But when considering a religion Nietzsche has something else in view than its mere power to make men happy and contented with their lot on earth. He sees two lines of life : the ascending and the descending, and he subjects all religions to a searching examination in order to find out which line they follow. When Nietzsche's theory of morality is clearly understood, the importance of a religion will at once be recognised. His fundamental distinction between men, obtained by separating them into the divisions of masters on the one hand and slaves on the other, with their two radically different standards of morality, is the stupendous addition to human knowledge with which Nietzsche's name will always be associated.

In a tour through the many finer and coarser moralities which have hitherto prevailed or still

* *Beyond Good and Evil*, Chap. III.

prevail on the earth, I found certain traits recurring regularly together, and connected with
one another, until finally two primary types
revealed themselves to me, and a radical distinction was brought to light. There is master-
morality and slave-morality ; I would at once
add, however, that in all higher and mixed
civilisations, there are also attempts at the
reconciliation· of the two moralities ; but one
finds still oftener the confusion and mutual misunderstanding of them—even in the same man,
within one soul. The distinctions of moral
values have originated either in a ruling caste,
pleasantly conscious of being different from the
ruled—or among the ruled class, the slaves and
dependents of all sorts. In the first case, when
it is the rulers who determine the conception
" good," it is the exalted, proud disposition
which is regarded as the distinguishing feature,
and that which determines the order of rank.
The noble type of man separates from himself
the beings in whom the opposite of this exalted,
proud disposition displays itself : he despises
them. Let it at once be noted that in this first
kind of morality the antithesis " good " and
" bad " means practically the same as " noble "
and " despicable " ;—the antithesis " good "
and " *evil* " is of a different origin. The cowardly,
the timid, the insignificant, and those thinking
merely of narrow utility are despised ; moreover, also, the distrustful, with their constrained

glances, the self-abasing, the dog-like kind of
men who let themselves be abused, the mendi-
cant flatterers, and above all the liars. . . . It
is obvious that everywhere the designations of
moral value were at first applied to men, and
were only derivatively and at a later period applied to actions ; it is a gross mistake, therefore,
when historians of morals start with questions
like : "Why have sympathetic actions been
praised ?" The noble type of man regards
himself as a determiner of values ; he does not
require to be approved of ; he passes the judgment : "What is injurious to me is injurious in
itself " ; he knows that it is he himself only who
confers honour on things ; he is a *creator of
values*. He honours whatever he recognises in
himself : such morality is self-glorification. In
the foreground there is the feeling of plenitude
of power, which seeks to overflow, the happiness
of high tension, the consciousness of a wealth
which would fain give and bestow : the noble
man also helps the unfortunate, but not—or
rarely—out of pity, but rather from an impulse
generated by the superabundance of power.
The noble man honours in himself the powerful
one, him also who has power over himself, who
knows how to speak and how to keep silence,
who takes pleasure in subjecting himself to
severity and hardness, and has reverence for all
that is severe and hard.*

* *Beyond Good and Evil*, Aphorism 257.

In other words, the man of prey, the aristocrat, can determine for himself the values of men
and things, as Lichtenberger has concisely
summed the matter up : what is useful or harmful to him is good or bad in itself. " Good " is
whoever is his equal ; the noble, the master ;
" bad " is whoever is his inferior, the man of
lower rank, the despised slave. Thus his " good "
is the aggregation of those physical and moral
qualities which he values in himself and his
equals. He is strong and powerful, he is able to
control himself and others, and these are qualities he respects. It follows that he despises the
contraries of such qualities—humility, flattery,
baseness, fear, and above all, lying. He cares
little for pity or disinterestedness, qualities
which he thinks should not be found in a ruler.
Strength, audacity, deceit, and cruelty meet
with his approval, for these are qualities that
lead to success in war. Furthermore, he is convinced that he is under no obligation except to
his equals : he believes that he may act towards
slaves and strangers exactly as he thinks fit.
These noble ones, feeling themselves to be a
minority encamped in the midst of a hostile
multitude, do all in their power to maintain the
integrity of their caste and thus uphold the
qualities which have led them to power. Hence
they are rigorous in their treatment of their
children, severely punishing marriage with any
member of a lower caste ; and all their other

customs are calculated with a view to preserving their race in as pure a form as possible.

Very different, to quote Lichtenberger's summary again, is the morality of the weak, the slaves, the conquered. While the prevailing feeling in the masses is pride, the joy of living, the slaves look upon life as pessimists; they mistrust it; and they have in particular an instinctive hatred of the powerful nobles, whom they come to look upon as terrible monsters. Thus the strong and powerful man, the " good " man of the master-morality, becomes the " evil " man of the slave-morality. " Bad " from the standpoint of the weak is everything violent, hard, terrible; all that inspires fear. " Good," on the other hand, includes all those virtues, despised by the masters, which make life easier for the oppressed, the suffering: pity, gentleness, humility, patience—the " good " powerful warrior of the master-morality becoming, in the slave-morality, a quiet, easy-going, good-natured soul: somewhat contemptible, even, just because he is so inoffensive !

As Nietzsche's sympathy lies entirely with the masters, and as it is the aim of his whole philosophy to raise the masters to ever higher degrees of perfection, it is easy to understand why he attacked Christianity, which is primarily the religion of the weak. The great virtues inculcated by Christianity: charity, pity, equality, love of peace, stringent moral laws, the Thou-shalt-not

This and That, would, in Nietzsche's opinion, inevitably lead to the degeneration of the race if they became universal. He did not object to Christianity, of course, for certain classes of people, such as women and children and weak men, and all those whom Mr. Ludovici calls the "physiologically botched"; but Christianity, as Nietzsche (and others before him, e.g. Gibbon) had pointed out, had arisen among slaves and downtrodden beings. He therefore wished it to be retained for such people, but not to be made compulsory upon men for whom an entirely different type of morality is required.

Christianity denies life. The jealous God of the Jews—a privileged race—was transformed by the Christians into a pitying Deity who sacrificed his son for the benefit of the poor and lowly. To note the immediate effects of this momentous change, the reader has merely to turn to the works of historians dealing with the Roman Empire, especially Gibbon, Hertzberg, Lecky, and Duruy. The degenerate Romans of the period were only too glad to adopt some form of religion that assured them and their descendants of a happier existence, no matter at what cost to the human race. As the crowd of slavish degenerates greatly outnumbered the aristocratic few, it is not to be wondered at that the new faith spread like a prairie fire. Hence we find this religion summarised in the New Testament as the faith of the downtrodden. The happy aristocrat, enjoying the delights of this earth, aroused the envy of those who were incapable of enjoyment—the Nonconformists of the ancient world, with the New Testament as their combined *Daily News* * and *British Weekly*. The editorial policy, so to speak, was decidedly hostile to the world and this life in general. " Love not the world, neither the things that are in the world. If any man loves the world the love of the Father is not in him." " He that loveth life shall lose it, and he that hateth life in this world shall keep it unto life eternal." " Blessed are the poor in spirit : for theirs is the kingdom of heaven." " Blessed are they that mourn : for they shall be comforted." " Blessed are the peacemakers : for they shall be called the children of God." And, to crown all : " Blessed are the meek : for they shall inherit the earth." This last prophecy has almost literally come true ; for the weak have not done at all badly in this regard, at all events, so far as Europe is concerned. They have certainly inherited many parts of England, if we may judge from the death-like stillness that surrounds everything on a Sunday : the sanctimonious faces of the people as they slowly wend their way to church (worse

* I intend no discourtesy by this remark: all I object to in connection with the literary side of this newspaper is the strangely narrow-minded attitude adopted towards the greatest philosopher of the nineteenth century. Surely this is not "liberal"? Words fail to convey my appreciation of the political and general policy of the paper, with its splendid sixty years' record of Christian propaganda.

still, to the tabernacles of the Plymouth Brethren); the mournful gait of paterfamilias as he leads the family procession at a funeral pace up the aisle ; the vague, puzzled expression of children who begin their career of degeneration in the Sunday-schools ; the satanic attempt, which succeeds only too often, to do away with anything likely to remind one of *Life*. Everything that elevates Life, that stimulates Life, is kept carefully out of sight. The shadow of death hangs over all.

The Christians took the Jewish religion and ideals and caricatured them. In the Old Testament Jehovah's commands are transmitted to the noblest spirits of the chosen people—to priests and high dignitaries of the church. But the resentful natures of the decadents go to the opposite extreme, and make God's son born of a carpenter's wife. The glorification of the weak over the strong thus begins at the very commencement of the book, and continues to the end. The " physiologically botched " have it all their own way : woe to the happy, full-blooded aristocrat who takes delight in the pleasures of this world ! Mental and physical cripples will overpower him by sheer force of numbers. Furthermore, they will invent a hell for him, a place for eternal torment. The Judaic notion of sin is caricatured into original sin : he learns that he is condemned even at birth, and that, unless he chooses to enter the rank and file of the degener-ate herd, he is doomed to suffer for ever in the flames of hell. Little wonder that Nietzsche wrote :

In the Jewish " Old Testament," the book of divine justice, there are men, things, and sayings on such an immense scale, that Greek and Indian literature has nothing to compare with it. One stands with fear and reverence before those stupendous remains of what man was formerly, and one has sad thoughts about old Asia and its little out-pushed peninsula Europe, which would like, by all means, to figure before Asia as the " Progress of Mankind." To be sure, he who is himself only a slender, tame house-animal, and knows only the wants of a house-animal (like our cultured people of to-day, including the Christians of " cultured " Christianity), need neither be amazed nor even sad amid these ruins—the taste for the Old Testament is a touchstone with respect to " great " and " small " : perhaps he will find that the New Testament, the book of grace, still appeals more to his heart (there is much of the odour of the genuine, tender, stupid beadsman and petty soul in it). To have bound up this New Testament (a kind of *rococo* of taste in every respect) along with the Old Testament into one book, as the " Bible," as " The Book in Itself," is perhaps the greatest audacity and " sin against the spirit " which literary Europe has upon its conscience.*

* Beyond Good and Evil, Aphorism 52.

Hence, too, he wrote :

Will some one look down into the secret of the way [Christian] *ideals* are *manufactured* on earth ? Who has the courage to do so ? Up ! Here you can see into the gloomy workshop. But wait a moment, good Sir Paul Pry and dare-devil : your eye must first get accustomed to this false and uncertain light—that's it! Enough ! Now speak ! What's going on down below ? Tell me what you see, man of most dangerous curiosity ! I am now the listener.

" I see nothing ; I hear the more. There is a prudent, knavish, suppressed whispering in every nook and corner. They lie, it seems to me : a sugary mildness cleaves to every sound. Weakness is to be falsified into merit, there is no doubt of that ; you were quite right in that respect."

Go on !

" And impotence which doth not retaliate is to be falsified into ' goodness ' ; timorous base-ness into ' humility ' ; submission to those they hate into obedience (i.e. to some one who, they say, commands this obedience, ' God ' they call him). The inoffensiveness of the weak, coward-ice itself—of which they possess more than their share—their standing-at-the-door, the unavoid-able necessity of their waiting—these are called by good names here : such as ' patience ' ; they even call it *the virtue of virtues*. Not-to-be-able-to-take-revenge is called Not-to-wish-to-take-revenge, perhaps even forgiveness ('for *they* know not what they do ; we alone know what *they* do '). Then they talk of love of one's enemy, and sweat in doing so."

Go on !

" They are wretched, no doubt of that, all these mutterers and underground counterfeiters, though they huddle warmly against one another. But they say that their wretchedness is a choice and distinction of God, that the best-liked dogs are whipped ; and that perhaps their wretchedness may be a preparation, a trial, a schooling ; perhaps even more—something which at some future time will be requited and paid for with huge compound interest in gold : no ! in happiness. This they call ' bliss.' "

On !

" Now they tell me that they are not only better than the powerful ones, the lords of the earth, whose spit they must lick (*not* from fear : no ; not at all from fear ! but because God commands them to respect authority)—that they are not only better, but will certainly be even ' better off ' some day. But enough, enough ! I cannot stand it any longer. Bad air ! Bad air ! This workshop in which *ideals are manufactured* — meseems it stinks from prevarication."

No ! just one minute more. You have said nothing about the master-stroke of these necromancers, who make milk-white innocence out of every black. Didn't you notice what the very perfection of their *raffinement* is—their keenest, finest, subtlest, falsest, artistic stroke ? Give heed ! Those cellar animals, sated with hatred and revenge—what do they make out of hatred and revenge ? Did you ever hear those words before ? Going merely by what they say, would it occur to you that you were among so many men of *ressentiment ?*

" I understand. I open my eyes again (oh ! ah ! and *shut* my nose). Now I can distinguish what they have been saying so often : ' We, the good—*we are the just.*' What they demand, they do not call retribution, but ' the triumph of *justice* ' ; what they hate is not their enemy, no ! They hate ' *injustice* ' and ' ungodliness.' What they believe in and hope for, is not the hope of revenge, the intoxication of sweet revenge (' sweeter than honey ' Homer called it long ago *) ; but ' the triumph of God, the *just* God, over the Godless.' What remains for them to love on earth is not their brethren in hatred, but their ' brethren in love,' as they call them ; all the good and the just on earth."

And what name do they give that which serves them as a consolation in all the sufferings of life—their phantasmagoria of anticipated future bliss ?

* *Iliad*, xviii, 107 foll. If the reader feels inclined to retort, Καὶ γὰρ καὶ μέλιτος τὸ πλέον ἐστὶ χολή, I may be allowed to anticipate his objection by saying with Plato : Καὶ δὶς γὰρ τοι καὶ τρὶς φασι καλὸν εἶναι τὰ καλὰ λέγειν τε καὶ ἐπισκοπεῖσθαι.

"What ?   Do I hear aright ?   They call it ' the last judgment,' the coming of *their* kingdom, the ' kingdom of God ' !   Meanwhile, however, they live ' in faith,' ' in love,' ' in hope.' "

Enough !   Enough ! *

* *Genealogy of Morals*, Bk. I, 14.

CHAPTER II

IT was perhaps fortunate for the world at large that the religion of love and pity and turning the other cheek to the smiter gradually gave rise to the bloodiest wars recorded in history. The battles—whether of bitter controversy or powder and shot—waged round the words *consubstantiation, impanation,* and *transubstantiation,* and all the auxiliary dogmas of the Christian faith have merely a casual interest for us at the present day, now that dogma *per se* is practically extinct. All religions and moralities, of course, are merely something to aid nations and races in the struggle for power, and it has been pointed out ere this how, if Christianity were carried to its logical conclusions, it would lead to utter nihilism, the extinction of the species.* A healthy sign of the times is the

---

* It would certainly lead to the death of a nation. Speaking at Caxton Hall on July 27th, 1908, Dr. Horton said: "It is the function of a Christian State to conciliate the world not by being prepared for war, but by frankly not being prepared—(cheers)—and by making it plain that as a country it had decided to suffer rather than to fight or even to contemplate fight." And this in the face of the recorded

de-Christianising, if I may use the word, of the Church of England. Charity, pity, help to the oppressed—the first virtues of Christianity— are clearly absent in the Established Church of this country. A few isolated clergymen de- plore the manner in which the Church is " getting out of touch with the people," i.e. they deplore the fact that the Church is assuming a saner, more pagan, and hence more beautiful aspect, like the Roman Catholic Church in Italy at the time of the Renaissance—our clergy in- stinctively feel that they simply cannot degrade themselves by coming into contact with the populace. All the protests of a few low church parsons cannot force the great body of the Church proper to take an interest in " the masses," who, in many cases, are to-day working under worse conditions of labour than the slaves of ancient Rome, Greece, and Judea. The world can be justified only as an æsthetic phenomenon ; and the more the Church of England becomes like the Church of Rome the nearer we shall be to realising the Greek ideal of beauty ; for it would be childish to pretend that the Roman Catholic Church does not appeal to the æsthetic suscepti- bilities of its followers. What Dr. Sera says on this subject is instructive :

history of nearly two thousand years of Christianity! Dr. Horton and those who cheered his foolish speech are con- sistent and pious Christians, which fact accounts for the grotesque statement.

The continual occupation of Nietzsche's thought was religion, in which he saw the great corruptress, the most dangerous deceiver, the origin of all the seductions that menace man. So firmly was he impressed with this thought that he desired to compose his last work (which was not completed) especially against religion.

Much has been said in regard to the anti-religious criticism of Nietzsche and his hatred for Christianity, and I have no wish to repeat what is already well known. I shall make only one observation, which I do not think is out of place. Was it Christianity as a positive and exterior religion, having its culminating point in Roman Catholicism, or the Christian spirit in its original pureness and its restoration as carried out by the reformers, that Nietzsche had in mind when he spoke of Christianity as being the religion of the conquered, of the weak ?

In my opinion he had Protestantism specially in view, that hard, abstractive, and rationalist movement ; that mind, fierce and bitter in its unreal aspirations, which banished the beautiful images of Christ and of the Virgin, which banished solemn architecture and magnificent temples, and which permitted only music, the most abstract and least sensual of arts, to accompany religious feeling. It was not Roman Catholicism that he accused, with

its altars, sometimes odd-looking, but more
often ornamented with masterpieces of art ;
not Catholicism, with its memory of smoking
sacrifices in the censers, with its solemn rites
in which candles blazed and rich chasubles,
precious, many-coloured pluvials, and bejewelled
chalices glittered ; but what he did accuse was
the bitter, dry, and fanatic Reformation, with
its hatred for art and for anything attractive
to the senses, and with its rationalistic and
democratic foundation.

Roman Catholicism was an adaptation of
primitive Christianity to the spirit of peoples
who, by race, the climate in which they lived,
and for other reasons, had remained pagans,
and it was therefore a radical transformation
of it. The primitive Christian spirit was for
Catholicism the rough but solid foundation
upon which the latter erected its splendid
palace, and constituted the nucleus of belief
for the people and for its most humble priests,
that is to say, for the inferior minds ; but for
the higher minds the Church was gradually
separated from its original design, and this
primitive Christian spirit lost ground to make
way for the ancient dominating spirit of the
Latin race. This is why the religious sentiment
had its palingenesis in Germany and the northern
races, in which, sociality having been more developed, there is likewise a greater vigour of
interior life, a greater development of altruistic

tendencies, of emotions, of sympathy, pity, and solidarity.

We must here, however, note another point which characterised the Reformation : the hatred with which it persecuted the manifestations of sexual life was a true hatred of the north towards the south, one of those many historical aspects in which was once more revealed that ever-present antagonism between northerners and southrons.*

Again :

Sexual inhibition, which in cold countries is a physical fact, and as such more certain, must have been imposed by means of formulæ and commands, that is, by psychological means, in the more southern countries, at a time when, for many different reasons, the necessity for production was felt to a greater degree than formerly.

And hence arises the finer, more delicate, and more conscious nature of southern morality, which took its special colouring from the Roman Catholic religion. The morality of this religion, especially in respect to love, is a masterpiece of perfect knowledge of men and their needs—at least, in times past. If we moderns now find ourselves ill at ease in our religion—as the northern nations did before the Reformation—it is because we have made some pro-

* *On the Tracks of Life*, p. 190-1.

gress on the path of sociality, and have now
become, in a certain sense, more northern.

Roman Catholic sexual morality was that
which suited nations inclined to pleasure,
to the pagan conception of life, to amorous
ease ; and its anti-sexual character is perfectly
commensurate with the necessity for repressing
a strong tendency.   It may be remembered that
one of the first acts of the Reformers was to
proclaim freedom of love and marriage for
clergymen, and that the ex-Catholic monk,
Martin Luther, got married to the ex-nun, Bona,
an act which is apparently hardly capable of
setting an example of good manners and customs,
but which was an effectual return to chastity.*

The continually increasing tendency in the
High Church of England to adopt Roman
Catholic rites, and the number of Nonconformist
secessions to Romanism, are two indications
which lead us to hope that a new impetus will
be given to English literature, art, and morals ;
and perhaps in another quarter of a century
we shall begin to realise that Matthew Arnold's
protests were not made in vain.†

The Church of England, then, despises the
masses, inwardly, and very often outwardly ;
but it nevertheless has an outlet for its energies.
Where ?   Among the aristocratic classes ; among

* *On the Tracks of Life*, p. 103.
† *Vide* his works *passim*, especially *Culture and Anarchy*
and the *Essays in Criticism*.

the members of that caste peculiar to England,
the " gentlemen." It is to the English High
Church party, represented in politics, broadly
speaking, by the House of Lords and the Conservative members, that we must look to take
up the study of Nietzsche and the propagation
of his doctrines throughout the Empire. I would
lay special stress on what is generally recognised
as an important fact : the Church, politics,
and the Empire itself have reached a critical
point in our history. The " hush " * which
a cultured statesman recently referred to may
be the prelude to a fierce world-struggle, when
the older European nations, under the influence
of socialistic and democratic opium, have sunk
into a state of humanitarian torpor, and the
united younger races, in whose land Nietzsche
was born, begin (as they have done) to put the
cruellest side of their Master's teaching into
practice. The ideals sought by Mr. Masterman †
and the " new way of life " recommended by
Mr. St. Loe Strachey cannot be found—need
I say it ?—in out-of-date superstition, in reliance
upon a higher power (for, though a higher power,
let it be called God or Nature, exists in some form,
it does not come to our assistance in a miraculous
fashion), nor yet can they be found in universal
suffrage, State nationalisation of everything,
votes for women, or any of the other means

* Lord Rosebery at the Press Banquet, June 5th, 1909.
† See his *Condition of England.*

recommended in the hoarse Socialistic claptrap shouted ungrammatically into the patient air from thousands of inverted soap-boxes and *Clarion* vans ; they can be found only in the thorough grasp of the writings of one of the greatest philosophical geniuses that ever lived— Friedrich Nietzsche.

To Nietzsche, then, the philosopher of intellectual and physical aristocracy, we must turn. The future allows no room for what is somewhat ineptly called " Liberalism." We must now be governed either by the cultured aristocratic few or by the uncouth, boorish, democratico-socialistic many. And it will be borne in mind that the uncultured cannot be changed into the cultured merely by going through a course of board-school education.

Does Nietzsche, then, give us a " System " ? some one may inquire ; only to be referred to that passage in the philosopher's works where he says he distrusts all systematisers. And we may well ask ourselves, Of what use is a philosopher who calmly sits down in his study to build up an artificial system for the world to follow ? Of no use whatsoever. No man who composed his " philosophy " without a knowledge of the world—without a knowledge of *Life*—ever survived for long in the minds of men. What knowledge of Life, for example, had Kant or Hegel, and what knowledge of Life have the dull professors who still expound their works in obscure universities? The answer is easy. But with Nietzsche the case is vastly different. He has nothing in common with the pseudo-philosophers who know nothing of Life but what they glean from books, students' lectures, or daily newspapers, and the greatest events of whose existence are occasional visits to the theatre (if the play is a moral one, and meets with the approval of Mrs. Grundy, the censor, the County Council, or the Watch Committee), and their transference from one dull, stately college to another dull, stately college. Nietzsche, a master of several languages, and, better still, with a thorough appreciation of the manners and customs of the nations that spoke them; with a keen, penetrating insight into humanity; an artist-musician; a fighter, who had borne an honourable part in one of the most strenuous campaigns of modern times; a traveller; a teacher; a lecturer who held audiences entranced by the magic of his wonderful voice; a man of letters; a man of the world; a *genius*; how is it possible for a moment to compare him with the Kants, the Hegels, and the Fichtes— men who bear all the traces of those whom he contemptuously designated as "moles"? * And the secret of Nietzsche's grip on his reader is

* In *Homer and Classical Philology*, his inaugural address at Basel University.

this : he wrote his books with his blood ; he impressed the stamp of his intellect on every line of his works ; his very sexual feelings, instead of being directed in the usual channel, were directed to his writings, and are reflected in them ; * for we can say on the authority of Deussen, his lifelong friend, *mulierem nunquam attigit*. In a word, Nietzsche attained a combination which was not attained even by the greatest philosophers of Greece—a combination of poetry and philosophy. And if the literary history of two thousand years has proved anything, it has surely proved this : that true poetry (in the widest sense of the word), and poetry alone, is eternal and immutable. Who would read through the smooth Greek of Plato, for example, or the rocky Greek of Aristotle, but as a matter of historic interest, if it were not for the poetical style appearing here and there ? How many thousands of readers has Bacon had for his essays for a single one who has struggled through the *New Organon* or the *De Augmentis ?* Do we read the *Essay on Man* for the sake of its rather shallow philosophy or for the sake of Pope's harmonious couplets, with those felicitous lines here and there which are known by heart wherever English is read ? And what has now become of all the portentous artificial systems discharged upon a weary world from the time of Vishnu and Siva to the time of

* Cf. Otto Weininger's *Geschlecht und Charakter.*

Kant and Hegel ? For assuredly the two Indian
deities did not arrogate to themselves any higher
claims than the two German " moles." The only
writer we can compare with Nietzsche is Lucretius,
but for whose magnificent poem we should know
little or nothing of the Epicurean philosophy.
But Nietzsche's philosophy is of infinitely more
importance than that of Epicurus, and it is expressed not only with all the fervour of Lucretius,
but also with all the poetic devices at the command of the greatest names of antiquity ; with
the grandeur and sublimity of Homer, with the
sting of Juvenal, with the short, sharp eloquence
of Demosthenes, with long drawn out Ciceronian
periods, with the suave politeness of Horace,
or the coarseness of Martial, whichever he deemed
most suitable. With the single exception of
Heine, there is no other German prose writer,*
not even Goethe or Lessing, to be compared
with him as a stylist. He proudly boasted that
he had brought his native tongue to a pitch of
perfection hitherto unattained. I make no exaggerated claims in his behalf ; let any cultured
reader with a sound knowledge of the language
compare Nietzsche's works with the heavy,
lumbering prose of other German writers, and
he will recognise the truth of this assertion.
The poetical expression is always apparent ;

* See Dr. William Barry's amusing comparison of German
prose to a ploughed field, soaked with rain. *Heralds of
Revolt*, art. Nietzsche.

but to say that Nietzsche has no sense of humour (a statement made by a recent German critic) is to show a gross misunderstanding of the philosopher. Aristotle's best hits, as Professor J. W. Mackail has justly said,* are nearly always in a parenthesis, and Nietzsche, in his earlier works, has a number of parenthetical Aristotelian sarcasms, while parts of his later works almost seem to roar with Homeric laughter. In short, we may apply to him the high praise he himself bestowed upon certain French moralists : his works, if translated into Greek, would have been understood by the Greeks.

Nietzsche's attitude towards women is usually mistaken. Far from despising the whole sex, as he is usually made out to do, he expresses his regard for women over and over again. But what he did decidedly object to—and who can blame him ?—was the type of de-womanised woman engendered by modern civilisation : the lady clerk, the lady doctor, the lady journalist (a most reprehensible breed, this)—the lady man, we might say, and be done with it ; the women who have renounced all the qualities which go to make up the charm and glory of their sex, and who are physically and mentally incapable of acquiring others which could endear them in the eyes of men. For there are, as every one

* In his *History of Latin Literature*, art. Quintilian.

knows, radical intellectual and bodily distinctions between the sexes ; and it is the aim of our levelling, democratising " socialistic fools and shallow-pates " to make the sexes equal, not only before the law, but in every other way possible for human ingenuity to devise. Nietzsche believes, on the contrary, as every reflecting man does, that the sharp distinctions between the sexes should be accentuated rather than smoothed down ; thus making a woman into a true woman and a man into a true man. Not even the foolish demagogues who have thrown over Christianity to " live by reason " (which is ten times worse, inasmuch as it withdraws them from poetry altogether—see Mill's mournful complaints) will deny that women are not improved in appearance when they are compelled to assume an awkward stoop as the result of poring over books, when a long course of high-school or college training makes their cheek-bones more prominent, their eyes red, their foreheads wrinkled, and finally drives away the last vestige of physical charm which it should be a woman's first duty to preserve. But few women are left as they should be after a severe educational training (I do not, of course, refer to their natural subjects, e.g. music and singing), and even when they do retain their good looks, they bore us to death with their pseudo-intellectuality. Who has not met the passionless, children-hating woman ? e.g. the Muriel of Mr.

Hamilton Fyfe's play, *A Modern Aspasia?*
What can we say of such a creature but *écrasez
l'infâme?* The feminist movement has gone
far enough ; and it is but right that Nietzsche's
protests should partly be quoted.

Woman wishes to be independent, and therefore she begins to enlighten men about " woman
as she is "—*this* is one of the worst developments
of the general *uglifying* of Europe. For what
must these clumsy attempts of feminine scientificality and self-exposure bring to light ! Woman
has so much cause for shame ; in woman there
is so much pedantry, superficiality, school-
masterliness, petty presumption, unbridledness,
and indiscretion concealed—study only woman's
behaviour towards children !—which has really
been best restrained and dominated hitherto by
the *fear* of man. Alas, if ever the " eternally
tedious in woman"—she has plenty of it !—is
allowed to venture forth ! if she begins radically
and on principle to unlearn her wisdom and art
of charming, of playing, of frightening-away-
sorrow, of alleviating and taking-easily ; if she
forgets her delicate aptitude for agreeable
desires ! Female voices are already raised,
which, by Saint Aristophanes ! make one
afraid : with medical explicitness it is stated in a
threatening manner what woman first and last
requires from man. Is it not in the very worst
taste that woman thus sets herself up to be

scientific? Enlightenment hitherto has fortunately been men's affairs, men's gift—we remained therewith " among ourselves " ; and in the end, in view of all that women write about " woman," we may well have considerable doubt as to whether woman really *desires* enlightenment about herself—and *can* desire it. If woman does not thereby seek a new *ornament* for herself—I believe ornamentation belongs to the eternal feminine?—why, then, she wishes to make herself feared : perhaps she thereby wishes to get the mastery. But she does not *want* truth—what does woman care for truth ! From the very first nothing is more foreign, more repugnant, or more hostile to woman than truth —her great art is falsehood, her chief concern is appearance and beauty. Let us confess it, we men : we honour and love *this* very art and *this* very instinct in woman : we who have the hard task, and for our recreation gladly seek the company of beings under whose hands, glances, and delicate follies, our seriousness, our gravity, and profundity appear almost like follies to us. Finally, I ask the question : Did a woman herself ever acknowledge profundity in a woman's mind, or justice in a woman's heart ? And is it not true that on the whole " woman " has hitherto been most despised by woman herself, and not at all by us ? We men desire that woman should not continue to compromise herself by enlightening us ; just as it was man's care and the consideration for woman, when the church decreed : *mulier taceat in ecclesia.* It was to the benefit of woman when Napoleon gave the too eloquent Madame de Staël to understand : *mulier taceat in politicis !*—and, in my opinion, he is a true friend of woman who calls out to women to-day : *mulier taceat de muliere !* *

Woman has hitherto been treated by man like birds, which, losing their way, have come down among them from an elevation : as something delicate, fragile, wild, strange, sweet, and animating—but as something also which must be cooped up to prevent it from flying away.†

To be mistaken in the fundamental problem of " man and woman," to deny here the profoundest antagonism and the necessity for an eternally hostile tension, to dream here perhaps of equal rights, equal training, equal claims and obligations : that is a typical sign of narrow-mindedness ; and a thinker who has proved himself shallow at this dangerous spot—shallow in instinct !—may generally be regarded as suspicious, nay, more, as betrayed, as discovered ; he will probably prove too "short" for all fundamental questions of life, future as well as present, and will be unable to descend into *any* of the depths. On the other hand, a man who has depth of spirit as well as of desires,

* *Beyond Good and Evil,* Aphorism 232.
† *Ibid.,* Aphorism 237A.

and has also the depth of benevolence which is capable of severity and harshness, and easily confounded with them, can only think of woman as Orientals do : he must conceive of her as a possession, as confinable property, as a being predestined for service and accomplishing her mission therein—he must take his stand in this matter upon the immense rationality of Asia, upon the superiority of the instinct of Asia, as the Greeks did formerly ; those best heirs and scholars of Asia—who, as is well known, with their *increasing* culture and amplitude of power, from Homer to the time of Pericles, became gradually *stricter* towards woman, in short, more Oriental. *How* necessary, *how* logical, *how* humanely desirable this was, let us consider for ourselves ! *

The weaker sex has in no previous age been treated with so much respect by men as at present—this belongs to the tendency and fundamental taste of democracy, in the same way as disrespectfulness to old age—what wonder is it that abuse should be immediately made of this respect ? They want more, they learn to make claims, the tribute of respect is at last felt to be wellnigh galling ; rivalry for rights, indeed actual strife itself, would be preferred : in a word, woman is losing modesty. And let us immediately add that she is also losing taste. She is unlearning to *fear* man :

* *Beyond Good and Evil*, Aphorism 238.

but the woman who " unlearns to fear " sacrifices her most womanly instincts. That woman should venture forward when the fear-inspiring quality in man—or more definitely, the *man* in man—is no longer either desired or fully developed, is reasonable enough and also intelligible enough; what is more difficult to understand is that precisely thereby—woman *deteriorates*. This is what is happening nowadays : let us not deceive ourselves about it ! Wherever the industrial spirit has triumphed over the military and aristocratic spirit, woman strives for the economic and legal independence of the clerk : " woman as clerkess " is inscribed over the portal of the modern society which is in course of formation. While she thus appropriates new rights, aspires to be " master," and inscribes " progress " of woman on her flags and banners, the very opposite realises itself with terrible obviousness : *woman retrogrades*. Since the French Revolution, the influence of woman in Europe has *declined* in proportion as she has increased her rights and claims ; and the " emancipation of woman," in so far as it is desired and demanded by women themselves (and not only by masculine shallow-pates), thus proves to be a remarkable symptom of the increased weakening and deadening of the most womanly instincts. There is *stupidity* in this movement, an almost masculine stupidity, of which a well-reared woman—who is always a sensible woman—

might be heartily ashamed. To lose the intuition as to the ground upon which she can most
surely achieve victory ; to neglect exercise in
the use of her proper weapons ; to " let herself
go " before man, perhaps even " to the book,"
where formerly she kept herself in control and in
refined artful humility ; to neutralise with her
virtuous audacity man's faith in a *veiled*, funda-
mentally different ideal in woman, something
eternally, necessarily feminine ; to dissuade
man loquaciously and emphatically from the
idea that woman must be preserved, cared for,
protected, and indulged, like some delicate,
strangely wild, and often pleasant domestic
animal ; the clumsy and indignant collection of
everything of the nature of servitude and bondage which the position of woman in the hitherto
existing order of society has entailed and still
entails (as if slavery were a counter-argument,
and not rather a condition of every higher culture, of every elevation of culture) : what does
all this betoken, if not a disintegration of
womanly instincts, a defeminising ? Certainly,
there are enough of idiotic friends and corrupters
of woman amongst the learned asses of the
masculine sex, who advise woman to defeminise
herself in this manner, and to imitate all the
stupidities from which " man " in Europe, European " manliness," suffers,—who would like to
lower woman to " general culture," indeed, even
to newspaper reading and meddling with politics.

Here and there they wish even to make women into free spirits and literary workers : as if a woman without piety would not be something perfectly obnoxious or ludicrous to a profound and godless man ; almost everywhere her nerves are being ruined by the most morbid and dangerous kind of music (our latest German music), and she is daily being made more hysterical and more incapable of fulfilling her first and last function, that of bearing robust children. They wish to " cultivate " her in general still more, and intend, as they say, to make the " weaker sex " *strong* by culture : as if history did not teach in the most emphatic manner that the " cultivating " of mankind and his weakening— that is to say, the weakening, dissipating, and languishing of his *force of will*—have always kept pace with one another, and that the most powerful and influential women in the world (and lastly, the mother of Napoleon) had just to thank their force of will—and not their schoolmasters !—for their power and ascendency over men. That which inspires respect in woman, and often enough fear also, is her *nature*, which is more " natural " than that of man, her genuine, carnivora-like, cunning flexibility, her tiger-claws beneath the glove, her *naïveté* in egoism, her untrainableness and innate wildness, the incomprehensibleness, extent, and deviation of her desires and virtues. That which, in spite of fear, excites one's sympathy for the dangerous

and beautiful cat, " woman," is that she seems
more afflicted, more vulnerable, more necessi-
tous of love and more condemned to disillusion-
ment than any other creature.   Fear and
sympathy : it is with these feelings that man has
hitherto stood in the presence of woman, always with one foot already in tragedy, which
rends while it delights.   What ?   And all that is
now to be at an end ?   And the *disenchantment*
of woman is in progress ?   The tediousness of
woman is slowly evolving ?   Oh, Europe !
Europe ! *

It is a favourite argument with socialistic
writers that the present political system tends
to crush down men of genius and talent, or, at
any rate, to reward them in a way very disproportionate to their abilities.   Under Socialism,
so we are given to understand, men of superior
intellectual gifts would find a better outlet for
their powers than they do at present.   When
we turn to the writings and speeches of ultra-
democrats, however, it is impossible to avoid
taking cognisance of one notable fact :   their
blind, abject, we might almost say superstitious
adoration of reason.   The influence of instinct
on mankind seems to be entirely neglected ;
and yet instinct is by far the stronger force,
the only force ; for it is pleasing to be able to
chronicle that no one has yet been able to live

* *Beyond Good and Evil*, Aphorism 239.

by mere reason alone. The name of Socrates, that interrogation-mark incarnate, at once occurs to us—probably one of the most uninviting figures in history ; and as we gradually come to know Socrates through Plato's dialogues and Xenophon's *Apology*, we wonder that the Athenians tolerated him as long as they did. Yet Socrates is surely the type of man who would be dear to democrats of every kind. Poetry and the instincts are looked upon with suspicion ; logic and reason are everything. From Mr. W. L. Courtney's admirable book,* *The Idea of Tragedy*, taken in conjunction with Nietzsche's *Birth of Tragedy*, it is not difficult to see how Socratian dialectics exercised a maleficent influence on Euripides, and ruined the Greek drama ; and from Socrates to the Goddess of Reason of the French revolutionists is but a single step, however long the historical interval may be. It is natural that democrats should worship logic and reason ; for it is only by means of subtle, Aquinas-like argument that they can " prove " their pros and brush aside the contras. Let us hear Nietzsche apropos of this.

" With Socrates Greek taste swerves round in favour of dialectics ; what really happens then ? The result is that the *superior* taste is overcome ; and the vulgar herd achieves the

* Although Mr. Courtney, if a theological expression be permitted, is " not sound " on Nietzsche as yet, he merits nothing but praise for anything he has written dealing with Greece.

victory by the use of dialectics. Previously
to Socrates dialectical manners were looked at
askance in good society ; they were considered
as bad manners ; they dissembled. Young men
were warned against them. Again, men who
put forth their arguments in this fashion were
distrusted. Honest things, like honest men, did
not carry their reasons in their hands like this.
That which requires to be proved is of little
value. All over, where authority is still an integral part of good customs—where one commands and does not ' demonstrate '—the dialectician is regarded as a buffoon ; no one takes
him seriously. Socrates was a buffoon—*who
got himself taken seriously*. What happened
then ? . . . We choose dialectics when we have
no other means : we know it gives rise to suspicion
and does not convince. Nothing is more easily
brushed aside than the effect of a dialectician ;
this is proved by the experience of every as-
sembly where speeches are made. It can only
be a last resource in the hands of such as have
no other weapon left." *

Thus, as Mr. Ludovici remarks, Nietzsche
held that to prove is to plead, to plead is to beg,
and he, at all events, did not wish to be a beggar.†

Obviously, then, the men of " intellect " who
would come to the front under Socialism would
be the intellectual descendants of Socrates—

* *Twilight of the Idols :* The Problem of Socrates, ss. 5 and 6.
† *Who is to be Master of the World?* p. 7.

men who, to use Nietzsche's scornful expression, would have nothing to bestow—nothing, at any rate, but an unending series of hairsplitting quibbles.   Under the Socialistic régime we should have no Nietzsches, no Goethes, no Drydens, nothing but an interminable family of Kants, Hegels, and Herbert Spencers.   Herbert Spencer, indeed, is just the type of man to be chief professor at a Socialist university ; a man who has nothing to bestow but a huge artificial " system." It is no part of my plan—I am thankful to say— to criticise Spencer's philosophy in detail ; but a generation that greedily absorbs a *Clarion* pamphlet once a fortnight, and permits Mr. G. K. Chesterton's unique talents to be confined to unappreciative Nonconformists in the pages of a Radical newspaper once a week, may well be content to listen to a few words on Spencer by a well-known Italian philosopher, Giovanni Papini :

I am very sorry indeed that Prichard, the English railway contractor, laid his plans for the Northampton-Worcester line before the parliamentary commission in such a hurry. I am sorry in the first place because Prichard, being denied the necessary authority, let a good contract slip through his fingers ; but I am still more sorry in the second place because it resulted in Herbert Spencer's having to give up his honourable calling as an engineer.

At that time, about 1848, Spencer had begun to make his mark in the railway world. In 1837 he had entered the service of the Charles Fox Railway Company, and in the same year had taken part in the survey of the auxiliary Chalk Farm Railway. In May, 1838, at Wembly, he audited the contractor's accounts, and in September of the same year he was promoted to be draughtsman at the Worcester station of the Gloucester-Birmingham line. But higher rewards were in store. March, 1840, saw him engineering secretary to Captain Moorsom at Powick, and when holding this position he built a bridge at Bromsgrove, and experimented with American locomotives. In April, 1841, he left the Fox Company, and it was doubtless the boredom of his lack of work which drove him to write *Letters on the Proper Sphere of Government*. The out-of-work engineer was turning into a philosopher. But the change was not lasting. In 1844 he accepted the invitation of Hughes, the engineer, and again entered the service of a railway company, working enthusiastically on the Stourbridge-Wolverhampton line. In 1845 he went to the London offices of the company; but, quarrelling with his superiors, he entered Prichard's employment. But Prichard, as already stated, had pushed his projects forward too hurriedly; the company was dissolved, and Spencer found himself out of a job once more.

Later on, in 1859, Spencer thought he could make himself useful to England in a manner suited to his tastes. He looked for a situation with the East India Company ; sought a post as collector ; and asked to be nominated as the governor of a gaol. He did not succeed, however, in getting himself smuggled in anywhere ; so in the following year, 1860,—now lost for ever to railways and business houses—he published his plans for a course of synthetic philosophy. The out-of-work engineer revenged himself on the world by threatening it with a system.

Surely he could have consoled himself in some other way. He might have emigrated to the United States ; he could have got a situation in some office ; or he could have given lessons in mathematics, as he had done in his early youth ; or, again, if it came to the worst, he could have married a rich woman. Instead of this, urged on by I do not know what inopportune advice, he made up his mind to be a philosopher—the grandson of Aristotle, and the son of Comte—and to bestow upon mankind the synthesis of the visible and invisible world.

And the threat was carried out. But Spencer, in becoming a philosopher, could not erase from his mind the traces of those primitive instincts which had guided his nascent activities to mathematics and physics. He could let himself be infected with the philosophical bacillus ; he could acquire a professional " twist " or

" bent " ; but he could never shake off the qualities he already possessed, and it is for this reason that the Spencerian philosophy presents itself to us as undeniably the patient and untiring labour of an out-of-work engineer. . . . I even think that I am dealing gently with Spencer in calling him an engineer at all. For, in reality, he has no right to this title, at once so elegant and ironical. *

And the Italian philosopher goes on to point out in what respects a capable engineer has the advantage over Spencer, whose scientific studies were never pursued with regularity and precision.

And Spencer's is the type of intellect that would succeed under Socialism.

The antithesis of Herbert Spencer, a man who would very likely not amount to very much under a levelling system of ultra-democracy—for his works are on a high plane, and above the comprehension of the mob—is Mr. A. J. Balfour. Having struggled through Spencer's dreary plebeianism, it is a relief to turn to the works of a cultured intellectual aristocrat, to the *Defence of Philosophic Doubt* or the *Foundations of Belief*— the latter one of the most important and fascinating philosophical works of the nineteenth century. Mr. Balfour's *Essays and Addresses*, with their parenthetical Aristotelian irony, contain some really charming passages (all the more so when

* G. Papini: *Il Crepuscolo dei Filosofi*, art. Nietzsche.

contrasted with Spencer's dullness) and not a few real additions to our stock of knowledge. In some respects they might be compared to Stendhal's novels, nor is the comparison—as regards their psychological insight, we mean—so far-fetched as might be imagined. Indeed, a remark in the *Essays and Addresses* might well be applied to the Hegels and Kants : " True dullness is seldom acquired ; it is a natural grace, the manifestations of which, however modified by education, remain in substance the same " (p. 10). The *Foundations of Belief* is a truly *deep* work : the preface to the eighth revised edition is in itself a stimulating essay, and the date at the foot of it is a silent eulogy of its author, when we consider that it was written in what was probably the busiest year of his life. Furthermore, Mr. Balfour fulfils another requirement which Nietzsche has hinted at in a few scattered passages as being necessary for the truly cultured man, viz. a tradition of culture on both sides of the family.

This juxtaposition of Spencer and Balfour may be thought long ; but it will not be out of place if it stimulates the reader to a further investigation of the type of intellect likely to arise under Socialism and the type likely to be engendered if Nietzsche's views were carried out. Take one final comparsion : place portraits of Nietzsche, Spencer, and Balfour side by side. The eager face of the German philosopher and the calm features of the British statesman stand out in marked contrast to the lower primate cast of Herbert Spencer.*

The spread of Socialism among certain sections in the Church of England has naturally given rise to some comment, and yet the reason is not very recondite. Christianity being the religion of the weak, the poor, and the lowly, and Socialism being the political system exactly suited to—and in fact devised by—the mean, the impotent, and the " physiologically botched," it is not surprising that the two should have sooner or later come together. This is as Nietzsche would have wished. He knew that a higher caste of men must be based on slavery, and further, that it would be necessary for the slaves to have a religion to enable them to forget and become reconciled to their miserable lot on earth. They might posit a hell for their enemies : what would it matter ? England is fortunate in having the close connection between Socialism and Christianity thus made apparent at what may be the beginning of a long class warfare. On the Continent matters are reversed. The French Revolution caused the lower classes all over the Continent to throw religion overboard to live by their " reason," and aristocratic politicians, with votes in view, have perforce adopted the despised Christian religion

* The combination of statesman, theological thinker, and philosopher has evidently puzzled Monsieur J. Rey, who begins his *La Philosophie de M. Balfour* with the words: " L'Angleterre est le pays de surprises: les hommes d'Etat y sont aussi théologiens."

to secure the support of the middle classes. It is time that some bold statesman clearly pointed out the connection between the religion of the weak and the political system of the impotent, and relieved the upper classes of this country from the burden of an exotic slave creed. The lower classes, on the other hand, must be more and more impressed with Christianity and encouraged to adopt it. A hell in the distant future is better than annoying revolutions at the present day. Christianity is designed for the lower orders ; it is their natural heritage, and in the vast library of Christian books they will surely find enough comfort to sustain them in their rough passage through life. Sermons, as Dr. Johnson justly remarked, form a not inconsiderable portion of English literature ; and, he might have added, contain some of the finest passages in the language. We still feel the charm of Jeremy Taylor ; Hooker can still extort our reverence and Barrow our admiration. *Holy Living*, the *Ecclesiastical Polity*, and hundreds of similar books, have not yet lost their power to fascinate, and there seems to be no reason why they should not be studied in Socialistic Sunday-schools. On the other hand, the aristocratic youth of the country would have to be brought up on aristocratic works, or works tending to an aristocratic state of mind—e.g. Nietzsche's own writings, and the men he specifically mentions as his " predecessors " — Empedocles, Heraclitus,

Spinoza, and Gœthe, together with all the classics which have come down to us from Greece and Rome—with the possible exception, however, of Vergil, who was the first to introduce a note of pity into the otherwise perfect Latin literature. The famous *sunt lacrimæ rerum* passage in the *Ænead* * is a significant indication of the degenerate state of Rome which paved the way for Christianity. And it will be recollected that stern Christians who view the literary masterpieces of the two best-known ancient worlds with disfavour have made an exception in favour of Vergil as being a Christian rather than a pagan writer.†

Is it clearly realised what consequences may follow from the adoption of Socialism by the European races ?. It may seem but a trifling change to suggest that the State—i.e. the whole nation, including the weak, the impotent, and the physiologically botched—should own the means of production and distribution instead of private capitalists ; but, though the financial change may be small, the moral results would be far-reaching. Just as Christianity paralysed all higher natures, and perverted our moral and physical organism, so would Socialism set the coping-stone on this edifice of the weak and do for our intellect what Christianity did for our morals. Is it not enough that we have been

* Book I, 462. This passage is undoubtedly genuine.
† *Vide* for example Mr. Gosse's *Father and Son.*

living under a system of religious anarchy for two thousand years ?   Must we now look forward to political anarchy as well ?   If Socialism were carried into effect, the answer would undoubtedly be in the affirmative, and the lambs might be left in peace for a century or so.   Then would come the awakening.   The descendants of gifted leaders, for whom life in such an unhealthy atmosphere would be intolerable, would be found in the armies of those nations where democracy is still an unknown word and a proper system of castes prevails.   The Turks, let us hope, would act the part of the Zarathustrian eagle and swoop down upon their helpless prey.   Let us hope, too, that the historians of those times would have to record bloodier massacres than any hitherto described in history.   After this—with Christians and Socialists in their proper places at the very bottom of the political pyramid—we should have a *true* Renaissance :   Judeo-Mahommedan in religion, perhaps ;   Greek in art ;   Turco-Roman in its political system : a Trinity beside which the Christian Trinity would sink into insignificance ; a nation from which would be generated a true superman : the real Master of the World.

We have done away with the " true world " : what world is left to us ?   The " world of appearances," perhaps ? . . . But no !   When abolishing the " true world " we also abolished the " world of appearances " !

(Noon; the instant of the most fleeting shadow; end of the longest error; humanity's apogee : INCIPIT ZARATHUSTRA !) *

And this ruthless slaughter of a degenerate society doubtless forms part of the " mission " referred to in *Beyond Good and Evil :* †

The *universal degeneracy* of mankind to the level of the " man of the future "—as idealised by the Socialistic fools and shallow-pates—this degeneracy and dwarfing of man to an absolutely gregarious animal (or as they call it, to a man of " free society "), this brutalising of man into a pigmy with equal rights and claims, is un-doubtedly *possible !* He who has thought out this possibility to its ultimate conclusions knows *another* loathing unknown to the rest of mankind —and perhaps also a new *mission !*

* *Twilight of the Idols:* "How the 'true world' at last became a fable."
† Aphorism 203, *ad fin.*

CHAPTER III

IN addition to the works mentioned in the preceding pages, Nietzsche wrote several others between 1869 and 1889 which remained in MS. for many years. These unpublished works were found to be almost equal in bulk and importance to those published during Nietzsche's lifetime ; and after his death in 1900 they were carefully edited by his sister, Peter Gast, Dr. Koegel, Raoul Richter, and others. The standard text of these posthumous works, including the complete version of *The Will to Power*, is to be found in the Taschenausgabe or pocket edition of Nietzsche's works, published in 1905–7. In this edition, too, all the works were arranged for the first time in chronological order. The set does not include his early philological writings for the *Rheinisches Museum*, which are of a somewhat technical character, though of great interest to the philological student. *The Case of Wagner*, *Nietzsche contra Wagner*, and the *Ecce Homo* have not yet been included in this set. To give the reader a clear conception of Nietzsche's views, it

will be convenient to lead him through the works
as they appear in this edition, taking the text
of the other works from the large library edition.
The posthumous works are specifically referred
to as such.

Homer and Classical Philology, Nietzsche's
inaugural address at Basel University,* produced
an impression on his audience which has been
previously mentioned (*v.* pp. 14 and 15). The
young philologist was even at this early age
beginning to show traces of the philosopher and
a desire to penetrate beneath the surface of the
Hellenic world. After a short comparison between
science and art, and a glance at ancient Greece,
we come to the question of Homeric personality.

It is a common occurrence for a series of striking signs and wonderful emotions to precede an
epoch-making discovery. Even the experiment
I have just referred to [historico-cultural
criticism based on personality] has its own attractive history ; but it goes back to a surpris-
ingly ancient era. Friedrich August Wolf has
exactly indicated the spot where Greek antiquity dropped the question. The zenith of the
historico-literary .studies of the Greeks, and
hence also of their point of greatest importance
—the Homeric question—was reached in the age
of the Alexandrian grammarians. Up to this
time the Homeric question had run through the

* The text was published posthumously.

long chain of a uniform process of development, of which the standpoint of those grammarians seemed to be the last link, the last, indeed, which was attainable by antiquity. They conceived the *Iliad* and the *Odyssey* as the creations of *one single* Homer ; they declared it to be psychologically possible for two such different works to have sprung from the brain of *one* genius, in contradiction to the Chorizontes, who represented the extreme limit of the scepticism of a few detached individuals of antiquity rather than antiquity itself considered as a whole. To explain the different general impression of the two books on the assumption that *one* poet composed them both, scholars sought assistance by referring to the seasons of the poet's life, and compared the poet of the *Odyssey* to the setting sun. The eyes of those critics were tirelessly on the look out for discrepancies in the language and thoughts of the two poems ; but at this time also a history of the Homeric poem and its tradition was prepared, according to which these discrepancies were not due to Homer, but to those who committed his words to writing and those who sang them. It was believed that Homer's poem was passed from one generation to another *viva voce*, and faults were attributed to the improvising and at times forgetful bards. At a certain given date, about the time of Pisistratus, the poems which had been repeated orally were said to have been collected in manu-

script form ; but the scribes, it is added, allowed themselves to take some liberties with the
text by transposing some lines and adding others
here and there. This entire hypothesis is the
most important in the domain of literary
studies that antiquity has exhibited ; and the
acknowledgment of the dissemination of the
Homeric poems by word of mouth, as opposed to
the habits of a book-learned age, shows in
particular a depth of ancient sagacity worthy of
our admiration. From those times until the
generation that produced Friedrich August Wolf
we must take a jump over a long historical
vacuum ; but in our own age we find the argument left just as it was when the power of controversy departed from antiquity, and it is a
matter of indifference to us that Wolf accepted
as certain tradition what antiquity itself had set
up only as a hypothesis. It may be remarked as
most characteristic of this hypothesis that, in
the strictest sense, the personality of Homer is
treated seriously ; that a certain standard of
inner harmony is everywhere presupposed in
the manifestations of the personality ; and that,
with these two excellent auxiliary hypotheses,
whatever is seen to be below this standard and
opposed to this inner harmony is at once swept
aside as un-Homeric. But even this distinguishing characteristic, in place of wishing to recognise the supernatural existence of a tangible
personality, ascends likewise through all the

stages that lead to that zenith, with ever-increasing energy and clearness. Individuality is ever more strongly felt and accentuated ; the psychological possibility of a *single* Homer is ever more forcibly demanded. If we descend backwards from this zenith, step by step, we find a guide to the understanding of the Homeric problem in the person of Aristotle. Homer was to him the flawless and untiring artist who knew his end and the means to attain it ; but there is still a trace of infantile criticism to be found in Aristotle—i.e. in the naïve concession he made to the public opinion that considered Homer as the author of the original of all comic epics, the *Margites*. If we go still further backwards from Aristotle, the inability to create a personality is seen to increase ; more and more poems are attributed to Homer ; and every period lets us see its degree of criticism by how much and what it considers as Homeric. In this backward examination, we instinctively feel that away beyond Herodotus there lies a period in which an immense flood of great epics has been identi-fied with the name of Homer.

Let us imagine ourselves as living in the time of Pisistratus : the word " Homer " then com-prehended an abundance of dissimilarities. What was meant by " Homer " at that time ? It is evident that that generation found itself un-able to grasp a personality and the limits of its manifestations. Homer had now become of small consequence. And then we meet with this weighty question : What lies before this period ? Has Homer's personality, because it cannot be grasped, gradually faded away into an empty name ? Or had all the Homeric poems been gathered together in a body, the nation naïvely representing itself by the figure of Homer ? *Was the person created out of a conception, or the conception out of a person ?* This is the real " Homeric question," the central problem of the personality.

The difficulty of answering this question, how-ever, is increased when we seek a reply in another direction, from the standpoint of the poems themselves which have come down to us. As it is difficult for us at the present day, and necessi-tates a serious effort on our part, to understand the law of gravitation clearly—that the earth alters its form of motion when another heavenly body changes its position in space, although no material connection unites one to the other—it likewise costs us some trouble to obtain a clear impression of that wonderful problem which, like a coin long passed from hand to hand, has lost its original and highly conspicuous stamp. Poetical works, which cause the hearts of even the greatest geniuses to fail when they en-deavour to vie with them, and in which un-surpassable images are held up for the admira-tion of posterity—and yet the poet who wrote them with only a hollow, shaky name, whenever we do lay hold on him ; nowhere the solid kernel of a powerful personality. " For who would wage war with the gods ; who even with the one god ? " asks Goethe even, who, though a genius, strove in vain to solve that mysterious problem of the Homeric inaccessibility.

The conception of popular poetry seemed to lead like a bridge over this problem—a deeper and more original power than that of every single creative individual was said to have become active : the happiest people, in the happiest period of its existence, in the highest activity of fantasy and formative power, was said to have created those immeasurable poems. In this universality there is something almost intoxicating in the thought of a popular poem : we feel, with artistic pleasure, the broad, over-powering liberation of a popular gift, and we delight in this natural phenomenon as we do in an uncontrollable cataract. But as soon as we examine this thought at close quarters, we involuntarily put a poetic *mass of people* in the place of the poetising *soul of the people :* a long row of popular poets in whom individuality has no meaning, and in whom the tumultuous movement of a people's soul, the intuitive strength of a people's eye, and the unabated profusion of a people's fantasy, were once powerful : a row of original geniuses, attached to a time, to a poetic genus, to a subject-matter.

Such a conception justly made people sus-

picious. Could it be possible that that same
Nature who so sparingly distributed her rarest
and most precious production—genius—should
suddenly take the notion of lavishing her gifts
in one sole direction ? And here again the
thorny question made its appearance : Could
we not get along with one genius only, and explain the present existence of that unattainable
excellence ? And now eyes were keenly on the
lookout for whatever that excellence and
singularity might consist of. Impossible for it
to be in the construction of the complete works,
said one party, for this is far from faultless ; but
doubtless to be found in single songs : in the
single pieces above all ; not in the whole. A
second party, on the other hand, sheltered
themselves beneath the authority of Aristotle,
who especially admired Homer's " divine "
nature in the choice of his entire subject, and the
manner in which he planned and carried it out.
If, however, this construction was not clearly
seen, this fault was due to the way the poems
were handed down to posterity, and not to the
poet himself—it was the result of re-touchings
and interpolations, owing to which the original
setting of the work gradually became obscured.
The more the first school looked for inequalities,
contradictions, perplexities, the more energetically did the other school brush aside what
in their opinion obscured the original plan, in
order, if possible, that nothing might be left

remaining but the actual words of the original epic itself. The second school of thought of course held fast by the conception of an epoch-making genius as the composer of the great works. The first school, on the other hand, wavered between the supposition of one genius plus a number of minor poets, and another hypothesis which assumed only a number of superior and even mediocre individual bards, but also postulated a mysterious discharging, a deep, national, artistic impulse, which shows itself in individual minstrels as an almost indifferent medium. It is to this latter school that we must attribute the representation of the Homeric poems as the expression of that mysterious impulse.

Nietzsche then enters upon a luminous discussion as to the differences between the characteristics of a man of genius and the characteristics of the poetical soul of a whole people. He proceeds in the assumption that the combined individual wills of a whole people were greater than the power of an isolated individual—an opinion which, as he saw afterwards, undeservedly favoured the masses to too great an extent, and which he accordingly retracted. Applying certain principles to the criticism of the Homeric poems, he goes on to say :

Since literary history first ceased to be a mere collection of names, people have attempted to grasp and formulate the individualities of the poets. A certain mechanism forms part of the method : it must be explained—i.e., it must be deduced from principles—why this or that individuality appears in this way and not in that. People now study biographical details, environment, acquaintances, contemporary events, and believe that by mixing all these ingredients together they will be able to manufacture the wished-for individuality. But they forget that the *punctum saliens*, the indefinable individual characteristics, can never be obtained from a compound of this nature. The less there is known about the life and times of the poet, the less applicable is this mechanism. When, however, we have merely the works and the name of the writer, it is almost impossible to detect the individuality, at all events, for those who put their faith in the mechanism in question ; and particularly when the works are perfect, when they are pieces of popular poetry. For the best way for these mechanicians to grasp individual characteristics is by perceiving deviations from the genius of the people ; the aberrations and hidden allusions : and the fewer discrepancies to be found in a poem the fainter will be the traces of the individual poet who composed it.

All these deviations, everything dull and below the ordinary standard which scholars think they perceive in the Homeric poems, were attributed to tradition, which thus became the scapegoat. What was left of Homer's own individual works ? Nothing but a series of beautiful and prominent passages chosen in accordance with subjective taste. The sum total of æsthetic singularity which every individual scholar perceived with his own artistic gifts, he now called Homer.

This is the central point of the Homeric errors. The name of Homer, from the very beginning, has no connection either with the conception of æsthetic perfection or yet with the *Iliad* and the *Odyssey*. Homer as the composer of the *Iliad* and the *Odyssey* is not a historical tradition, but an æsthetic judgment. . . . The *Iliad* is not a garland, but a bunch of flowers. As many pictures as possible are crowded on one canvas ; but the man who placed them there was indifferent as to whether the grouping of the collected pictures was invariably suitable and rhythmically beautiful. He well knew that no one would ever consider the collection as a whole ; but would look at the individual parts. But that stringing together of some pieces as the manifestations of a grasp of art which was not yet highly developed, still less thoroughly comprehended and generally esteemed, cannot have been the real Homeric deed, the real Homeric epoch-making event. On the contrary, this design is a later product, far later than Homer's celebrity. Those, therefore, who look for the " original and perfect design " are looking for a mere phantom ; for the dangerous path of oral tradition had reached its end just as the systematic arrangement appeared on the scene ; the disfigurements which were caused on the way could not have affected the design, for this did not form part of the material handed down from generation to generation.

The relative imperfection of the design must not, however, prevent us from seeing in the designer a different personality from the real poet. It is not only probable that everything which was created in those times with conscious æsthetic insight, was infinitely inferior to the songs that sprang up naturally in the poet's mind and were written down with instinctive power : we can even take a step further. If we include the so-called cyclic poems in this comparison, there remains for the designer of the *Iliad* and the *Odyssey* the indisputable merit of having done something relatively great in this conscious technical composing : a merit which we might have been prepared to recognise from the very beginning, and which is in my opinion of the very first order in the domain of instinctive creation. We may even be ready to pronounce this synthetisation of great importance. All those dull passages and discrepancies—deemed of such importance, but really only subjective, which we usually look upon as the petrified remains of the period of tradition—are not these perhaps merely the almost necessary evils which must fall to the lot of the poet of genius who undertakes a composition virtually without a parallel, and, further, one which proves to be of incalculable difficulty ?

Let it be noted that the insight into the most diverse operations of the instinctive and the conscious changes the position of the Homeric problem ; and in my opinion throws light upon it.   We believe in a great poet as the author of the *Iliad* and the *Odyssey—but not that Homer was this poet*.

The decision on this point has already been given.   The generation that invented those numerous Homeric fables, that poetised the myth of the contest between Homer and Hesiod, and looked upon all the poems of the epic cycle as Homeric, did not feel an æsthetic but a material singularity when it pronounced the name " Homer."   This period regards Homer as belonging to the ranks of artists like Orpheus, Eumolpus, Dædalus, and Olympus, the mythical discoverers of a new branch of art, to whom, therefore, all the later fruits which grew from the new branch were thankfully dedicated.

And that wonderful genius to whom we owe the *Iliad* and the *Odyssey* belongs to this thankful posterity : he, too, sacrificed his name on the altar of the primeval father of the Homeric epic, Homēros.

The address is brought to a close by an impassioned protest in favour of Philology, a science which, in 1869, was looked upon with some contempt not only by the people in general, but also by those learned men who happened to be interested in other subjects.

You honour the immortal masterpieces of the Hellenic mind in poetry and sculpture, and think yourselves so much more fortunate than preceding generations, which had to do without them ; but you must not forget that this whole fairyland once lay buried under mountains of prejudice, and that the blood and sweat and arduous labour of innumerable followers of our science were all necessary to lift up that world from the chasm into which it had sunk. We grant that Philology is not the creator of this world, not the composer of this immortal music ; but is it not a merit, and a great merit, to be a mere virtuoso, and let the world for the first time hear that music which lay so long in obscurity, despised and undecipherable ? Who was Homer previously to Wolf's brilliant investigations ? A good old man, known at best as a " natural genius," at all events the child of a barbaric age, replete with faults against good taste and good morals.

Before we proceed to *The Birth of Tragedy*, we may, for convenience sake, mention the three periods into which Nietzsche's works are generally divided. All such divisions—and many have been formed, according to the taste of the critic —are entirely arbitrary—" the elevation of the type man " is the thread leading through the maze of Nietzsche's mind ; but there is no harm in adopting the classification most generally given. The first period is from 1869 to 1876, when Nietzsche was partly under the influence of Schopenhauer and Wagner. He was not a blind follower of either ; but of Dionysus, and this may be referred to as his Dionysian period, when Hellenism exercised an almost unbounded sway over his mind. This period is represented by the books or lectures from *Homer and Classical Philology* to *Wagner in Bayreuth*.

1876 to 1883 may be called his Appollonian period, represented by the books from *Human, All-too-human* to *The Joyful Wisdom*. During this time his mind is that of a philosopher, strictly so-called, whereas in the former period he was simply a philologist of very broad views, with philosophical traces appearing here and there. In this second period he appears to have investigated Positivism closely ; but, though he had a fairly high opinion of Comte, the great Frenchman's system of philosophy did not appeal to him. This period, too, is noteworthy for his onslaught against current morality.

The third period is from 1883 to 1889. It comprises the works from *Zarathustra* onwards, and is marked by Nietzsche's prophetic and poetical style. It is important to note that this period is especially rich in the constructive element of Nietzsche's philosophy. A patient study of *Zarathustra* and *Good and Evil* in particular will help to unravel many complexities.

How *The Birth of Tragedy* came to be published has already been stated (p. 19). It appeared in January, 1872, and the preface was added in 1886 (see p. 37).

In this preface Nietzsche seems to express doubts as to the views contained in the work itself, as well as his method of presenting them. However, as Mrs. Foerster-Nietzsche says, " the kernel of its thought he always recognised as perfectly correct ; and all he deplored in later days was that he had spoiled the grand problem of Hellenism, as he understood it, by adulterating it with ingredients taken from the world of modern ideas." Mrs. Foerster-Nietzsche has also given us some explanatory notes which her brother wrote in 1886 concerning this book : *

The Birth of Tragedy—a book consisting of mere experiences relating to pleasurable and unpleasurable æsthetic states, with a meta-physico-artistic background. At the same time the confession of a romanticist (*the sufferer feels the deepest longing for beauty—he begets it*) ; finally, a product of youth, full of youthful courage and melancholy. Fundamental psychological experiences : the word 'Apollonian '

---

* *Taschenausgabe*, I, xxxiii foll.

stands for that state of rapt repose in the presence of a visionary world, in the presence of the world of *beautiful appearance* designed as a deliverance from *becoming*: the word ' Dionysos,' on the other hand, stands for strenuous becoming, grown self-conscious, in the form of the rampant voluptuousness of the creator, who is also perfectly conscious of the violent anger of the destroyer. . . .

Deep antagonism to Christianity. Why? The degeneration of the Germanic spirit is to be ascribed to its influence.

Any justification of the world can only be an *æsthetic* one. Profound suspicions about morality (it is part and parcel of the world of appearance).

The happiness of existence is only possible as the happiness derived from appearance. ("*Being" is a fiction invented by all those who suffer from becoming.*)

The Dionysian and the Apollonian, two names recurring through all Nietzsche's works, have already been touched upon. Faguet, in his work *En lisant Nietzsche*, sums them up concisely: " There was once a race which loved only beauty and life. It especially loved life, strong and superabundant, puissant and joyous, exalted and triumphant. This is what might be called its Dionysian soul. But it also loved beauty, purity of race, the majestic brow, and serenity of look.

This is what might be called its Apollonian soul. These two aspirations are to some extent united and combined in the conception of Olympia. Olympia is the meeting-place of higher beings, both powerfully living and nobly beautiful, exalted in the joy of life and in the will to live; immortal : a word which, having been repeated too often, has lost its signification : immortal, that is to say, insatiable of life, desiring it for eternity ; beings also who are pleased to be beautiful, who realise their beauty, and endeavour to realise it ever more and more. The Olympian is the higher being who unites within himself the Dionysian and the Apollonian state."

Nietzsche speaks of himself in the preface to *The Birth of Tragedy* as " wrestling under the walls of Metz * with the notes of interrogation he had set down concerning the alleged ' cheerfulness ' of the Greeks and of Greek art. . . . The birth of tragedy from the spirit of *music* †—from music ? Greeks and the art-work of pessimism ? "

Is pessimism *necessarily* the sign of decline, of decay, of failure, of exhausted and weakened instincts ?—as was the case with the Indians, as is, to all appearance, the case with us " modern " men and Europeans ? Is there a pessi-

---

* i.e., during the Franco-German War.
† The book was first published under the title *The Birth of Tragedy from the Spirit of Music ;* this was afterwards changed to *The Birth of Tragedy, or Hellenism and Pessimism.*

mism of *strength?* An intellectual predilection for what is hard, awful, evil, problematical in existence, owing to well-being, to exuberant health, to *fullness* of existence ? Is there perhaps suffering in overfullness itself ? A seductive fortitude with the keenest of glances, which *yearns* for the terrible, as for the enemy, the worthy enemy, with whom it may try its strength ? from whom it is willing to learn what " fear " is ? What means *tragic* myth to the Greeks of the best, strongest, bravest era ? And the prodigious phenomenon of the Dionysian ? And that which was born thereof, tragedy ? And again : that of which tragedy died, the Socratism of morality, the dialectics, contentedness and cheerfulness of the theoretical man ?— indeed ? might not this very Socratism be a sign of decline, of weariness, of disease, of anarchically disintegrating instincts ? And the " Hellenic cheerfulness " of the later Hellenism merely a glowing sunset ? The Epicurean will *counter* to pessimism merely as a precaution of the sufferer ? And science itself, our science— ay, viewed as a symptom of life, what really signifies all science ? Whither, worse still, *whence*—all science ? Well ? Is scientificality perhaps only fear and evasion of pessimism ? A subtle defence against—*truth ?* Morally speaking, something like falsehood and cowardice ? And, unmorally speaking, an artifice ? O Socrates, Socrates, was this perhaps *thy* secret ?

Oh, mysterious ironist, was this perhaps thine—
irony ? . . .

What I then laid hands on, something terrible
and dangerous, a problem with horns, not necessarily a bull itself, but at all events a *new* problem : I should say to-day it was the *problem of
science* itself—science conceived for the first
time as problematic, as questionable. . . .

What if the Greeks in the very wealth of their
youth had the will to be tragic and were pessimists ? What if it was madness itself, to use
a word of Plato's, which brought the *greatest*
blessings upon Hellas ? And what if, on the
other hand and conversely, at the very time
of their dissolution and weakness, the Greeks
became always more optimistic, more superficial,
more histrionic, also more ardent for logic and
the logicising of the world—consequently at the
same time more " cheerful " and more " scientific " ? Ay, despite all " modern ideas " and
prejudices of the democratic taste, may not the
triumph of *optimism*, the *common sense* that has
gained the upper hand, the practical and
theoretical *utilitarianism*, like democracy itself,
with which it is synchronous—be symptomatic
of declining vigour, of approaching age, of
physiological weariness ? And *not* at all—
pessimism ? Was Epicurus an optimist—because a *sufferer ?* . . . We see it is a whole
bundle of weighty questions which this book
has taken upon itself—let us not fail to add its

weightiest question ! Viewed through the optics
of *life*, what is the meaning of—morality ?

Already in the foreword to Richard Wagner,
art—and *not* morality—is set down as the
properly *metaphysical* activity of man ; in the
book itself the piquant proposition recurs time
and again, that the existence of the world is
justified only as an æsthetic phenomenon. Indeed, the entire book recognises only an artist-
thought and artist-afterthought behind all
occurrences—a " God," if you will, but certainly
only an altogether thoughtless and unmoral
artist-God, who, in construction as in destruction, in good and evil, desires to become conscious of his own equable joy and sovereign
glory; who, in creating worlds, frees himself from
the *anguish* of fullness and *overfullness*, from the
suffering of the contradictions concentrated
within him.

It may be noted that Nietzsche's antagonism
to Christianity is already perceptible in this his
first published volume. Going on to speak of the
moral tendency of his book, he says :

Perhaps the depth of this anti-moral tendency may be best estimated from the guarded
and hostile silence with which Christianity is
treated throughout this book—Christianity, as
being the most extravagant burlesque of the
moral theme to which mankind has hitherto
been obliged to listen. In fact, to the purely

æsthetic world-interpretation and justification taught in this book, there is no greater anti-thesis than the Christian dogma, which is *only* and will be only moral, and which, with its absolute standards, for instance, its truthfulness of God, relegates—that is, disowns, convicts, condemns—art, *all* art, to the realm of false-hood. Behind such a mode of thought and valuation, which, if at all genuine, must be hostile to art, I always experienced what was *hostile to life* itself : for all life rests on appear-ance, art, illusion, optics, necessity of perspec-tive and error. From the very first Christianity was, essentially and thoroughly, the nausea and surfeit of Life for Life, which only disguised, concealed, and decked itself out under the belief in " another " or " better " life. The hatred of the " world," the curse on the affec-tions, the fear of beauty and sensuality, another world, invented for the purpose of slandering this world the more, at bottom a longing for Nothingness, for the end, for rest, for the " Sabbath of Sabbaths "—all this, as also the unconditional will of Christianity to recognise *only* moral values, has always appeared to me as the most dangerous and ominous of all possible forms of a " will to perish " ; at the least, as a symptom of a most fatal disease, of profoundest weariness, despondency, exhaus-tion, impoverishment of life—for before the tribunal of morality (especially Christian, that is, unconditional morality) life *must* constantly and inevitably be the loser, because life *is* something essentially unmoral—indeed, oppressed with the weight of contempt and the everlasting No, life *must* finally be regarded as unworthy of desire, as in itself unworthy. Morality itself, what ?—may not morality be a "will to disown life," a secret instinct for annihilation, a principle of decay, of depreciation, of slander, a beginning of the end ? And, consequently, the danger of dangers ? . . . It was *against* morality, therefore, that my instinct, as an intercessory instinct for life, turned in this questionable book, inventing for itself a fundamental counter-dogma and counter-valuation of life, purely artistic, purely *anti-Christian*. What should I call it ? As a philologist and man of words I baptised it, not without some liberty—for who could be sure of the proper name of the Antichrist ?—with the name of a Greek god : I called it *Dionysian*.

Nietzsche proceeds to set forth in the book itself how all art " is bound up with the duplexity of the Apollonian and the Dionysian : in like manner as procreation is dependent upon the duality of the sexes, involving perpetual conflicts with only periodically intervening reconciliations."

It is in connection with Apollo and Dionysus,

the two art-deities of the Greeks, that we learn
that there existed in the Grecian world a wide
antithesis, in origin and aims, between the
art of the shaper, the Apollonian, and the non-
plastic art of music, that of Dionysus : both
these so heterogeneous tendencies run parallel
to each other, for the most part openly at vari-
ance, and continually inciting each other to
new and more powerful births, to perpetuate in
them the strife of this antithesis, which is but
seemingly bridged over by their mutual term,
" Art " ; till at last, by a metaphysical miracle
of the Hellenic will, they appear paired with
each other, and through this pairing eventually
generate the equally Dionysian and Apollonian
art-work of Attic tragedy.

Nietzsche compares the Apollonian state to
a kind of dream of beauty; the Dionysian to a
state of intoxication due to existence itself.
Further, " we might designate Apollo as the
glorious divine image of the *principium individuationis* [of Schopenhauer]." Schopenhauer has
described to us

the stupendous *awe* which seizes upon man,
when of a sudden he is at a loss to account for
the cognitive forms of a phenomenon, in that
the principle of reason, in some one of its manifestations, seems to admit of an exception. Add
to this awe the blissful ecstasy which rises from

the innermost depths of man, ay, of Nature, at this same collapse of the *principium individuationis*, and we shall gain an insight into the being of the Dionysian, which is brought within closest ken perhaps by the analogy of drunkenness. It is either under the influence of the narcotic draught, of which the hymns of all primitive men and peoples tell us, or by the powerful approach of spring penetrating all Nature with joy, that those Dionysian emotions awake, in the augmentation of which the subjective vanishes to complete self-forgetfulness. So also in the German Middle Ages singing and dancing crowds, ever increasing in number, were borne from place to place under this same Dionysian power.

Having given the reader some conception of what is meant by Dionysian and Apollonian, Nietzsche brings us into contact with the Greeks themselves. Greek art and civilisation, we learn, were originally Apollonian. Afterwards the Dionysian element appeared, overwhelmed the Apollonian, and finally combined with it. " And here the sublime and highly celebrated art-work of Attic tragedy and dramatic dithyramb presents itself to our view as the common goal of both these impulses, whose mysterious union, after many and long precursory struggles, found its glorious consummation in such a child—which is at once Antigone and Cassandra." Hesiod is the

extreme type of Apollonian " naïve " * artist,
Homer is less so ; but the first to unite both types
within himself was Archilochus, the lyric poet.
In the ancient world, of course, the lyrist was a
musician ; and music is a Dionysian element.
This very Dionysism, however, gives rise to the
Apollonian state ; for the Dionysian lyric poet is
not altogether subjective. " As Dionysian artist
he has in the first place become altogether one
with the Primordial Unity, its pain and tradition,
and he produces a copy of this Primordial Unity
as music, granting that music has been correctly
termed a repetition and a recasting of the world ;
but now, under the Apollonian dream-inspiration,
this music again becomes visible to him as in a
symbolic dream-picture."

Nietzsche's wealth of learning is displayed
through several sections of the work to lead us
up to the origin of Greek tragedy and to show us
that it sprang from the tragic satyr-chorus of the
Bacchic festivals. Examining this chorus, we
find that the Greeks regarded the satyr as the
type of primitive man—the expression of their
desire for freedom, for a return to nature. " With
this chorus the deep-minded Hellene, who is so
singularly qualified for the most delicate and
severe suffering, consoles himself : he who has
glanced with piercing eye into the very heart of

---

* Naïve, naïveté: a noun and adjective applied by
Schiller to represent the harmony, the unity, of man with
Nature; applied in particular to the Apollonian Greek.

the terribly destructive processes of so-called universal history, as also into the cruelty of Nature, and is in danger of longing for a Buddhistic negation of the will. Art saves him, and through art life saves him—for herself." " The satyr, the fictitious natural being, is to the man of culture what Dionysian [i.e. Wagnerian] music is to civilisation. Concerning this latter, Richard Wagner says it is neutralised by music even as lamplight by daylight. In like manner, I believe, the Greek man of culture felt himself neutralised in the presence of the satyric chorus."

After this we come to discussions on Æschylus and Sophocles, to which commentators on the ancient Greek classics would do well to turn. Nietzsche throws new light on the *Prometheus*, and the opinions he puts forward, be it remembered, were held in high esteem by many of the greatest philologists of the last century. He shows us how all tragedy concerned itself at first with the god Dionysus, who was, at the beginning, not brought directly on the stage, but was afterwards objectised, the spectators being inspired by the chorus to see the god in the person of the masked actor.

We are then presented to Euripides, who brings everyday life on the stage. The gods disappear, to make way for the slaves. We see how Euripides was merely the mouthpiece of Socrates, who naturally comes in for severe handling. The drama ceases to be Dionysian, though it can hardly be said to become Apollonian, but rather naturalistic and inartistic. Socrates makes a critical pilgrimage through Athens, and is disgusted to find that the people live " only by instinct."

Only by instinct—with this phrase we touch upon the heart and core of the Socratic tendency. Socrates condemns therewith existing art as well as existing ethics ; wherever Socratism turns its searching eyes it beholds the lack of insight and the power of illusion ; and from this lack infers the inner perversity and objectionableness of existing conditions. From this point onwards Socrates believed that he was called upon to correct existence ; and, with an air of disregard and superiority, as the precursor of an altogether different culture, art, and morality, he enters single-handed into a world of which, if we reverently touched the hem, we should count it our greatest happiness. Here is the extraordinary hesitancy which always seizes on us with regard to Socrates, and again and again invites us to ascertain the sense and purpose of this most questionable phenomenon of antiquity. Who is it that ventures single-handed to disown the Greek character, which, as Homer, Pindar, and Æschylus, as Phidias, as Pericles, as Pythia, and Dionysus, as the deepest abyss and the highest height, is sure of our wondering admiration ? What demoniac power is it which would presume to spill this magic draught in the dust ? What demigod is it to whom the chorus of spirits of the noblest of mankind must call out : " Weh ! Weh ! Du hast sie zerstört, die schöne Welt, mit mächtiger Faust ; sie stürzt, sie zerfällt ! " (Woe, woe ! Thou hast it destroyed, the beautiful world ; with powerful fist, in ruin 'tis hurl'd !).*

A key to the character of Socrates is presented to us by the surprising phenomenon designated as the " daimonion " of Socrates. In special circumstances, when his gigantic intellect began to stagger, he got a serene support in the utterances of a divine voice which then spake to him. This voice, whenever it comes, always *dissuades*. In this totally abnormal nature instinctive wisdom only appears in order to hinder the progress of conscious perception here and there. While in all productive men it is instinct which is the creatively affirmative force, consciousness only comporting itself critically and dissuasively ; with Socrates it is instinct which becomes critic, it is consciousness which becomes creator—a perfect monstrosity *per defectum !* And we do indeed observe here a monstrous *defectus* of all mystical aptitude, so that Socrates might be designated as the specific *non-mystic*, in whom the logical nature is developed, through a

* *Faust* (Bayard Taylor's translation).

superfœtation, to the same excess as instinctive wisdom is developed in the mystic. On the other hand, however, the logical instinct which appeared in Socrates was absolutely prohibited from turning against itself; in its unchecked flow it manifests a native power such as we meet with, to our shocking surprise, only among the very greatest instinctive forces. He who has experienced even a breath of the divine naïveté and security of the Socratic course of life in the Platonic writings will also feel that the enormous driving-wheel of logical Socratism is in motion, as it were, *behind* Socrates, and that it must be viewed through Socrates as through a shadow. And that he himself had a boding of this relation is apparent from the dignified earnestness with which he everywhere, and even before his judges, insisted on his divine calling. To refute him here was really as impossible as to approve of his instinct-disintegrating influence. In view of this in-dissoluble conflict, when he had at last been brought before the forum of the Greek state, there was only one punishment demanded, namely exile; he might have been sped across the borders as something thoroughly enig-matical, irrubricable, and inexplicable, and so posterity would have been quite unjustified in charging the Athenians with a deed of ignominy. But that the sentence of death, and not mere exile, was pronounced upon him, seems to have been brought about by Socrates himself, with perfect knowledge of the circumstances, and without the natural fear of death : he met his death with the calmness with which, according to the description of Plato, he leaves the symposium at break of day, as the last of the revellers, to begin a new day ; while the sleepy companions remain behind on the benches and the floor, to dream of Socrates, the true eroticist. *The dying Socrates* became the new ideal of the Greek youths—an ideal they had never yet beheld—and, above all, the typical Hellenic youth, Plato, prostrated himself before this scene with all the fervent devotion of his visionary soul.

With Socrates, then, the slaves and their vices came to the front—utilitarianism, theories, reason, and so forth. And the evil effects of all this are still felt :

Our whole modern world is entangled in the meshes of Alexandrine culture, and recognises as its ideal the *theorist* equipped with the most potent means of knowledge, and labouring in the service of science, of whom the archetype and progenitor is Socrates. All our educational methods have originally this ideal in view ; every other form of existence must struggle onwards wearisomely beside it, as something tolerated, but not intended. In an almost alarming manner the cultured man was here

found for a long time only in the form of the
scholar : even our poetical arts have been
forced to evolve from learned imitations, and
in the main effect of the rhyme we still recognise the origin of our poetic form from artistic
experiments with a non-native and thoroughly
learned language. . . .

Now we must not hide from ourselves what
is concealed in the heart of this Socratic culture :
Opportunism, deeming itself absolute ! Well,
we must not be alarmed if the fruits of this
optimism ripen—if society, leavened to the
very lowest strata by this kind of culture,
gradually begins to tremble through wanton
agitations and desires, if the belief in the earthly
happiness of all, if the belief in the possibility
of such a general intellectual culture is gradually
transformed into the threatening demand for
such an Alexandrine earthly happiness, into
the conjuring of a Euripidean *deus ex machina.*
Let us mark this well : the Alexandrine culture
requires a slave class, to be able to exist perma-
nently : but, in its optimistic view of life, it
denies the necessity of such a class, and, consequently, when the effect of its beautifully
seductive and tranquillising utterances about
the " dignity of man " and the " dignity of
labour " is spent, it gradually drifts towards
a dreadful destination. There is nothing more
terrible than a barbaric slave class, who have
learned to regard their existence as an injustice,

and now prepare to take vengeance, not only for themselves, but for all generations. In the face of such threatening storms, who dares to appeal with confident spirit to our pale and exhausted religions, which even in their foundations have degenerated into scholastic religions? —so that myth, the necessary prerequisite of every religion, is already paralysed everywhere, and even in this domain, the optimistic spirit —which we have just designated as the annihilating germ of society—has attained the mastery.

It is hardly necessary for us to follow Nietzsche further—tracing with him the influence of Socrates on modern culture, and pointing out how it may be counteracted by German music ; and following his pregnant observations on the opera and modern music. One last quotation from this work will enable the reader to perceive what results Nietzsche expected from a resuscitation of Dionysian music, as put forth by Wagner:

Whoso not only comprehends the word Dionysian, but also grasps his *self* in this word, requires no refutation of Plato or of Christianity or of Schopenhauer—he *smells* the *putrefaction*.

My friends, ye who believe in Dionysian music, ye know also what tragedy means to us. There we have tragic myth, born anew from music—and in this latest birth ye can hope for everything and forget what is most afflicting.

What is most afflicting to all of us, however, is—the prolonged degradation in which the German genius has lives estranged from house and home in the service of malignant dwarfs. Ye understand my allusion—as ye will also, in conclusion, understand my hopes.

Music and tragic myth are equally the expression of the Dionysian capacity of a people, and are inseparable from each other. Both originate in an ultra-Apollonian sphere of art ; both transfigure a region in the delightful accords of which all dissonance, just like the terrible picture of the world, dies charmingly away ; both play with the sting of displeasure, trusting to their most potent magic ; both justify thereby the existence even of the " worst world." Here the Dionysian, as compared with the Apollonian, exhibits itself as the eternal and original artistic force, which in general calls into existence the entire world of phenomena : in the midst of which a new transfiguring appearance becomes necessary, in order to keep alive the animated world of individuation. If we could conceive an incarnation of dissonance —and what is man but that ?—then, to be able to live this dissonance, would require a glorious illusion which would spread a veil of beauty over its peculiar nature. This is the true function of Apollo as deity of art : in whose name we comprise all the countless manifestations of the fair realm of illusion, which each moment render life in general worth living, and make one impatient for the experience of the next moment.

At the same time, just as much of this basis of all existence—the Dionysian substratum of the world—is allowed to enter into the consciousness of human beings as can be surmounted again by the Apollonian transfiguring power, so that these two art-impulses are constrained to develop their powers in strictly mutual proportion, according to the law of eternal justice. When the Dionysian powers rise with such vehemence as we experience at present, there can be no doubt that, veiled in a cloud, Apollo has already descended to us; whose grandest beautifying influences a coming generation will perhaps behold.

That this effect is necessary, however, each one would most surely perceive by intuition, if once he found himself carried back—even in a dream—into an Old-Hellenic existence. In walking under high Ionic colonnades, looking upwards to a horizon defined by clear and noble lines, with reflections of his transfigured form by his side in shining marble, and around him solemnly marching or quietly moving men, with harmonisingly sounding voices and rhythmical pantomime, would he not in the presence of this perpetual influx of beauty have to raise his hand to Apollo and exclaim : " Blessed race of Hellenes ! How great Dionysus must be among you, when the Delian god deems such charms necessary to cure you of your dithrymbic madness !" To one in this frame of mind, however, an aged Athenian, looking up to him with the sublime eye of Æschylus, might answer : "Say also this, thou curious stranger : what sufferings this people must have undergone, in order to be able to become thus beautiful ! But now follow me to a tragic play, and sacrifice with me in the temple of both the deities !"

CHAPTER IV

MINOR PHILOLOGICO - PHILOSOPHICAL WORKS—
THE FUTURE OF OUR EDUCATIONAL INSTITU-
TIONS.

IT has been stated (p. 19) that *The Birth of
Tragedy* was but a portion, complete in
itself, of a great work on Greece which Nietzsche
had planned and partly written. The remaining
portions of this work were not published until
after his death. They consist of : *The Greek
State*, part of the preface, *The Greek Woman*, a
fragment, *On Music and Speech*, and *Homer's
Poetical Contest*—fragments from two to four
thousand words long. The first-named is interesting for its criticisms on Plato's perfect, ideal state,
as well as for its comments on Socialism and
Liberalism. To show how consistent Nietzsche
really was in his main principles, we need quote
only one sentence from it : " We must then come
to understand the cruel truth that *slavery is an
essential foundation for the existence of a culture.*" *
The Greek Woman contains many a shrewd
saying. " Woman is to the State what sleep is to
mankind. In her lies the curative power, restor-

* *Werke*, I, 211.

ing what has been used up ; the consolatory
tranquillity, which prescribes the bounds of
everything immoderate and extravagant ; the
eternal standards, by which everything immoderate and extravagant can be regulated.
The next generation slumbers in her. Woman is
more nearly related to Nature than man is ; and
she remains consistent in all essentials. . . . Only
think what sons these Greek women bore, and
what women they must have been to bear them !
True, the Hellenic woman, when a mother, had
to live in seclusion, because the political system
of the country, with its high aims, rendered this
necessary. She had to vegetate in a narrow
corner, like a plant, as the symbol of the Epicurean
wisdom : λάθε βιώσας." These tender words
hardly bear out the assertions of those critics
who say that Nietzsche despised women, that he
was a woman-hater, and all the rest of it. It is
rather unfortunate for such critics that these
fragmentary notes should have been preserved.*

Passing over the *Music and Speech* and the
Homer's Poetical Contest as being rather technical,

* Nietzsche's contempt for the feminist movement is
evidently shared by the *Saturday Review*. A recent incident
in suffragist propaganda drew the following from the editors
of that sedate journal : " The Greeks had an adjective com-
pounded of dog and shameless, which they applied to a
woman who had outrun the ordinary scale of opprobrious
language. English people use the equivalent, perhaps it is
a translation, but one cannot use it in print. We will be
bound though that it has come into many people's minds
when they read the accounts of the doings of certain suffragist women at Clovelly Court, where Mr. Asquith and other

we come to the lectures *On the Future of our Educational Institutions*. These have already been referred to (pp. 13–14) where a brief summary of their substance is given, so that it is only necessary to quote a few paragraphs here that Nietzsche's views may be presented to the reader in his own words. The dialogue is supposed to take place between a man of culture and a young student to whom he is endeavouring to point out the right way to attain culture.

" People should not have points of view, but thoughts. . . ."

" At present you are behaving as if you had not even heard the cardinal principle of all culture, which I went to such pains to inculcate upon you during our former intimacy. Tell me —what was that principle ? "

" I remember," replied the scolded pupil, " you used to say no one would strive to attain to culture if he knew how incredibly small the number of really cultured people actually is, and can ever be. And even this number of really cultured people would not be possible if a pro-

guests were staying. It is the last form of insolence when a party of female rowdies under the guise of politics insult the guests in a private house, and turn the house itself into a bill-sticking station for their vulgar posters. Fit to vote ! They are not fit to live with Swift's Yahoos."—*Saturday Review*, 5th June, 1909.

Splendid ! Nietzsche himself could not have done better. And when a dignified journal half a century old finds it necessary to make use of language like this, the virulence of a mere German philosopher may surely be excused.

digious multitude, from reasons opposed to their nature and only led on by an alluring illusion, did not devote themselves to education. It were therefore a mistake publicly to reveal the ridiculous disproportion between the number of really cultured people and the enormous magnitude of the educational apparatus. Here lies the whole secret of culture—namely, that an innumerable host of men struggle to achieve it and work hard to that end, ostensibly in their own interests, whereas at bottom only in order that it may be possible for the few to attain it."

" That is the principle," said the philosopher; " and yet you could so far forget yourself as to believe that you are one of the few? This thought has occurred to you, I can see. That, however, is the result of the worthless character of modern education. The rights of genius are being democratised in order that people may be relieved of the labour of acquiring culture, and their need of it. Every one wants if possible to recline in the shade of the tree planted by the genius, and to escape the dreadful necessity of working for him, so that his procreation may be made possible."

" In all cultivated circles people are in the habit of whispering to one another words something after this style: that it is a general fact that, owing to the present frantic exploitation of the scholar in the service of his science, his *education* becomes every day more accidental and more uncertain. For the study of science has been extended to such interminable lengths that he who, though not exceptionally gifted, yet possesses fair abilities, will need to devote himself exclusively to one branch and ignore all others if he ever wish to achieve anything in his work. Should he then elevate himself above the herd by means of his speciality, he still remains one of them in regard to all else—that is to say, in regard to the most important things in life. Thus, a specialist in science gets to resemble nothing so much as a factory workman who spends his whole life in turning one particular screw or handle on a certain instrument or machine, at which occupation he acquires the most consummate skill. In Germany, where we know how to drape such painful facts with the glorious garments of fancy, this narrow specialisation on the part of our learned men is even admired, and their ever greater deviation from the path of true culture is regarded as a moral phenomenon. ' Fidelity in small things,' 'dogged-faithfulness,' become expressions of highest eulogy, and the lack of culture outside the speciality is flaunted abroad as a sign of noble sufficiency."

" In all matters of a general and serious

nature, and, above all, in regard to the highest philosophical problems, we have now reached a point at which the scientific man, as such, is no longer allowed to speak. On the other hand, that adhesive and tenacious stratum which has now filled up the interstices between the sciences —Journalism—believes it has a mission to fulfil here, and this it does, according to its own particular lights—that is to say, as its name implies, after the fashion of a day labourer. It is precisely in Journalism that the two tendencies combine and become one. The expansion and diminution of education here join hands. The newspaper actually steps into the place of culture, and he who, even as a scholar, wishes to voice any claim for education, must avail himself of this viscous stratum of communication which cements the seams between all forms of life, all classes, all arts, and all sciences, and which is as firm and reliable as news paper is, as a rule. In the newspaper the peculiar educational aims of the present culminate, just as the journalist, the servant of the moment, has stepped into the place of the genius, of the leader for all time, of the deliverer from the tyranny of the moment."

" In order that I may not shock you with general propositions, let us first try to recall one of those public school experiences which we have all had, and from which we have all suffered. Under severe examination what, as a matter of fact, is the present system of teaching German in public schools ?

" I shall first of all tell you what it should be. Everybody speaks and writes German as thoroughly badly as it is possible to do in an age of newspaper German : that is why the growing youth who happens to be both noble and gifted has to be taken by force and put under the glass shade of good taste and of severe linguistic discipline. If this is not possible, I would prefer that in future Latin be spoken ; for I am ashamed of a language so bungled and vitiated.

" What would be the duty of a higher educational institution in this respect, if not this : namely, with authority and dignified severity to put youths, neglected, as far as their own language is concerned, on the right path, and to cry to them : ' Take your own language seriously ! He who does not regard this matter as a sacred duty does not possess even the germ of a higher culture. From your attitude in this matter, from your treatment of your mother tongue, we can judge how highly or how lowly you esteem art, and to what extent you are related to it. If you notice no physical loathing in yourselves when you meet with certain words and tricks of speech in our journalistic jargon, cease from striving after culture ; for here in your immediate vicinity, at every moment of your life, while you are either speaking or writing, you have a touchstone for testing how difficult, how stupendous, the task of the cultured man is, and how very improbable it must be that many of you will ever attain to culture.' "

Of course, these remarks apply to this country : for " German " read " English." Our own public schools are great offenders as regards the teaching of English. Probably the best writers of our own language come from London University, Trinity College, Dublin, and Edinburgh University, while the most miserable stylists hail from Oxford as a rule.* Again, consider the following, which likewise applies to England :

" Instead of that purely practical method of instruction by which the teacher accustoms his pupils to severe self-discipline in their own language, we everywhere find the rudiments of a historico-scholastic method of teaching the mother-tongue : that is to say : people deal with it as if it were a dead language and as if the present and future were under no obligations to it whatsoever. The historical method has become so universal in our time, that even the living body of the language is sacrificed for the sake of anatomical study. But this is precisely

* The Oxford *King's English* may help to remedy this defect.

where culture begins—namely, in understanding how to treat the quick as something vital, and it is here too that the mission of the cultured teacher begins : in suppressing the urgent claims of 'historical interests' wherever it is above all necessary to *do* properly and not merely to *know* properly. Our mother-tongue, however, is a domain in which the pupil must learn how to *do* properly, and to this practical end, alone, the teaching of German is essential in our scholastic establishments. The historical method may certainly be a considerably easier and more comfortable one for the teacher ; it also seems to be compatible with a much lower grade of ability and, in general, with a much smaller display of energy and will on his part. But we shall find that this observation holds good in every department of pedagogic life : the simpler and more comfortable method always masquerades in the disguise of grand pretensions and stately titles ; the really practical side, the *doing*, which should belong to culture, and which, at bottom, is the more difficult side, meets only with disfavour and contempt."

We now come to a point which is applicable to English and American schools of every grade. Those of us who have had the misfortune to be primed for the examinations of this or that body will surely remember the extraordinary and senseless manner in which English composition is

taught in nine schools out of ten. The subjects
set are such as should properly be dealt with only
by men of considerable insight, travel, and experience of the world. Complicated historical questions are often given—questions that necessitate
keen psychological penetration which cannot be
expected from the average boy in his teens. The
forced growth of juvenile thoughts, and the harm
occasioned thereby, is emphatically brought
home to us by Nietzsche, who would himself, but
for his own prolonged studies after school hours,
have been a victim of this evil system.

" The last department in which the German
teacher in a public school is at all active, which
is often regarded as his sphere of highest activity,
and is here and there even considered as the
pinnacle of public school education, is the so-
called German composition. Owing to the very
fact that in this department it is always the most
gifted pupils who display the greatest eagerness,
it ought to have been made clear how dangerously stimulating, precisely here, the task of the
teacher must be. German composition makes an
appeal to the individual, and the more strongly
a pupil is conscious of his various qualities, the
more personally will he do his German composition. This ' personal doing ' is urged on with yet
an additional fillip in some public schools by the
choice of the subject, the strongest proof of which
is, in my opinion, that even in the lower classes

the non-pedagogic subject is set, by means of which the pupil is led to give a description of his life and of his development. Now one has only to read the titles of the compositions set in a large number of public schools to be convinced that probably the large majority of pupils have to suffer their whole lives, through no fault of their own, owing to this premature demand for personal work—for the unripe procreation of thoughts. And how often are not the whole of a man's subsequent literary performances but a sad result of this pedagogic original sin against the intellect !

" Let us only think what takes place at such an age in the production of such work. It is the first individual creation ; the still undeveloped powers tend for the first time to crystallise ; the staggering sensation produced by the demand for self-reliance imparts a seductive charm to these early performances, which is not only quite new, but which never returns. All the doing of nature is hauled out of its depths ; all vanities—no longer constrained by mighty barriers—are allowed for the first time to assume a literary form : the young man, from that time forward, feels as if he had reached his consummation as a being not only able, but actually invited, to speak and to converse. The subject he selects obliges him either to express his judgment upon certain poetical works, to class historical persons to-

gether in a description of character, to discuss
serious ethical problems quite independently,
or even to turn the searchlight inwards, to
throw its rays upon his own development, and
to make a critical report of himself : in short,
a whole world of reflection is spread out before
the astonished young man who, until then, had
been almost unconscious, and is delivered up
to him to be judged.

" Now let us try to picture the teacher's
usual attitude towards these first highly influential examples of original composition.
What does he hold the most reprehensible
in this class of work ? What does he call his
pupil's attention to ? To all excess in form
or thought—that is to say, to all that which,
at their age, is essentially characteristic and
individual. Their really independent traits
which, in response to this very premature
excitation, can manifest themselves only in
awkwardness, crudeness, and grotesque features
—in short, their individuality is reproved and
rejected by the teacher in favour of an unoriginal
decent average. On the other hand, uniform
mediocrity gets peevish praise ; for, as a rule,
it is just the class of work likely to bore the
teacher thoroughly."

" None but the very fewest are aware that,
among many thousands, perhaps only *one* is

justified in describing himself as literary, and that all others who at their own risk try to be so deserve to be met with Homeric laughter by all competent men as a reward for every sentence they have ever had printed—for it is truly a spectacle meet for the gods to see a literary Hephaistos limping forward who would pretend to help us to something. To educate men to earnest and inexorable habits and views, in this respect, should be the highest aim of all mental training, whereas the general *laisser aller* of the ' free personality' can be nothing else than the hall-mark of barbarism. From what I have said, however, it must be clear that, at least, in the teaching of German, no thought is given to culture ; something quite different is in view—namely, the production of the afore-mentioned ' free personality.' And so long as German public schools prepare the road for outrageous and irresponsible scribbling, so long as they do not regard the immediate and practical discipline of speaking and writing as their most holy duty, so long as they treat the mother tongue as if it were only a necessary evil or a dead body, I shall not regard these institutions as belonging to real culture.''

" Everybody should himself be aware of the difficulties of the language : he should have learnt them from experience : after

long seeking and struggling he must reach the
path our great poets trod in order to be able
to realise how lightly and beautifully they
trod it, and how stiffly and swaggeringly the
others follow at their heels.

" Only by means of such discipline can the
young man acquire that physical loathing for
the beloved and much - admired ' elegance '
of style of our newspaper manufacturers and
novelists, and for the ' ornate style ' of our
literary men ; by it alone is he irrevocably
elevated at a stroke above a whole host of
absurd questions and scruples, such, for instance, as whether Gutzkow and Auerbach
are really poets, for his disgust at both will be
so great that he will be unable to read them
any longer, and thus the problem will be solved
for him. Let no one imagine that it is an easy
matter to develop this feeling to the extent
necessary in order to have this physical loathing;
but let no one hope to reach sound æsthetic
judgments along any other road than the thorny
one of language, and by this I do not mean
philological research, but self-discipline in one's
mother-tongue."

As Nietzsche rightly adds, not a suspicion
of the relationship between the classics themselves and classical education seems to have
pierced the antique walls of the public schools.
How are pupils introduced to the masterpieces

of Greece and Rome ? Not by preliminary training in their mother-tongue, so that they might appreciate the noble languages of the ancient worlds ; not by fostering their judgment and æsthetic taste, but by burying them under a heap of irrelevant detail, which should be reserved—if brought to their notice at all—until a much later period. They are, however, presented at once with the mysteries of variant readings, to take an instance : they make their way helplessly through long-winded and often unnecessarily complex courses of grammar ; and thus, by the time they have mastered the mythological, geographical, biographical, historical, and philological notes bearing on a particular passage, they find they have learnt perhaps six lines of Homer or Vergil—of whom they are now heartily sick. " Learnt," we may say, but not from a cultural standpoint : merely from a scholastic standpoint ; they are sufficiently crammed to enable them to answer some stupid examination questions touching the pay of certain squads of Cæsar's troops, or the number of ships in the famous Homeric catalogue. However senseless such questions may be, their correct answering brings credit on the school. Many English teachers * have protested against this system ; but the first steps towards improvement must apparently be taken

* *Vide* especially Dr. Henry Sweet's *Practical Study of Languages.*

by the examining bodies. In the meantime we need not be surprised if thousands of young men pass through our public schools and universities with hatred instead of admiration for the classics of Greece and Rome.

Philologists themselves begin their studies with too little reverence for the literatures of these mighty nations. " All of them," says Nietzsche, " with the most widely different aims in view, dig and burrow in Greek soil with a restlessness and blundering awkwardness that must surely be painful to a true friend of antiquity."

Consciously or unconsciously, large numbers of them [Philologists] have concluded that it is hopeless and useless for them to come into direct contact with classical antiquity, hence they are inclined to look upon this study as barren, superseded, out-of-date. This herd has turned with much greater zest to the science of language: here in this wide expanse of virgin soil, where even the most mediocre gifts can be turned to account, and where a kind of insipidity and dullness is even looked upon as decided talent, with the novelty and uncertainty of methods, and the constant danger of making fantastic mistakes—here, where dull regimental routine and discipline are desiderata—here the newcomer is no longer frightened by the majestic and warning voice that rises from the ruins of antiquity : here every one is welcomed with open arms, including even him who never arrived at any uncommon impression or noteworthy thought after a perusal of Sophocles and Aristophanes, with the result that they end in an etymological tangle, or are seduced into collecting the fragments of out-of-the-way dialects—and their time is spent in associating and dissociating, collecting and scattering, and running hither and thither consulting books. And such a usefully employed philologist would now fain be a teacher! He now undertakes to teach the youth of the public schools something about the ancient writers, although he himself has read them without any particular impression, much less with insight! What a dilemma! Antiquity has said nothing to him, consequently he has nothing to say about antiquity. A sudden thought strikes him : why is he a skilled philologist at all! Why did these authors write Latin and Greek! And with a light heart he immediately begins to etymologise with Homer, calling Lithuanian or Ecclesiastical Slavonic, or, above all, the sacred Sanskrit, to his aid, as if Greek lessons were merely the excuse for a general introduction into the study of languages, and as if Homer were lacking in only one respect, namely, not being written in pre-Indogermanic. Whoever is acquainted with our present public schools well knows what a wide gulf separates

their teachers from classicism, and how, from
a feeling of this want, comparative philology
and the allied professions have increased their
numbers to such an unheard-of degree."

"I may be wrong," said the philosopher,
"but I suspect that, owing to the way in which
Latin and Greek are now taught in schools, the
accurate grasp of these languages, the ability
to speak and write them with ease, is lost,
and that is something in which my own generation distinguished itself—a generation, indeed,
whose few survivors have by this time grown
old; whilst, on the other hand, the present
teachers seem to impress their pupils with the
genetic and historical importance of the subject to such an extent that, at best, their
scholars ultimately turn into little Sanskritists,
etymological spitfires, or reckless conjecturers;
but not one of them can read his Plato or
Tacitus with pleasure, as we old folk can. The
public schools may still be seats of learning:
not, however, of *the* learning which, as it were,
is only the natural and involuntary auxiliary
of a culture that is directed towards the noblest
ends; but rather of that culture which might
be compared to the hypertrophical swelling of
an unhealthy body."

"Be careful to remember that there are two
things you must not confuse. A man must

learn a great deal that he may live and take
part in the struggle for existence ; but every
thing that he as an individual learns and does
with this end in view has nothing whatever to
do with culture. This latter only takes its
beginning in a sphere that lies far above the
world of necessity, indigence, and struggle for
existence.

" True culture would scorn to contaminate
itself with the needy and covetous individual ;
it well knows how to give the slip to the man
who would fain employ it as a means of attaining to egoistic ends ; and if anyone cherishes
the belief that he has firmly secured it as a
means of livelihood, and that he can procure
the necessaries of life by its sedulous cultivation, then it suddenly steals away with noise-
less steps and an air of derisive mockery.

" I will thus ask you not to confound this
culture, this sensitive, fastidious, ethereal goddess, with that useful maid-of-all-work which
is also called ' culture,' but which is only the
intellectual servant and counsellor of one's
practical necessities, wants, and means of
livelihood. Every kind of training, however,
which holds out the prospect of breadwinning
as its end and aim, is not a training for culture
as we understand the word ; but merely a
collection of precepts and directions to show
how, in the struggle for existence, a man may
preserve and protect his own person. It may

be freely admitted that for the great majority of men such a course of instruction is of the highest importance ; and the more arduous the struggle is the more intensely must the young man strain every nerve to utilise his strength to the best advantage.

" But—let no one think for a moment that the schools which urge him on to this struggle, and prepare him for it, are in any way seriously to be considered as establishments of culture. They are institutions which teach one how to take part in the battle of life ; whether they promise to turn out civil servants, or merchants, or officers, or wholesale dealers, or farmers, or physicians, or men with a technical training. The regulations and standards prevailing at such institutions differ from those in a true educational institution ; and what in the latter is permitted, and even freely held out as often as possible, ought to be considered as a criminal offence in the former."

From this it will be apparent that only a few select individuals are destined for culture in the first place, and that the remaining large number will form the great mass of the people, the public, the crew summed up in the type we know so well as " the man in the street." Unfortunately for culture, this vast herd has now attained to power in most European countries, and it is only among more civilised races (e.g. the Mahommedans, Hindoos, Chinese, and Japanese) that great leaders and despots are still respected. The different aims of a cultural institution for the minority and a cultural institution for the majority are touched upon by Nietzsche in the following paragraphs :

" You are now at the parting of the ways, and you now know where each path leads. If you take the one, your age will receive you with open arms, you will not find it wanting in honours and decorations : you will form one of an enormous rank and file ; and there will be as many people like-minded standing behind you as in front of you. And when the leader gives the word it will be re-echoed from rank to rank. For here your first duty is this : to fight in rank and file ; and your second : to annihilate all those who refuse to form part of the rank and file. On the other path you will have but few fellow-travellers : it is more arduous, winding, and precipitous ; and those who take the first path will mock you, for your progress is more wearisome, and they will try to lure you over into their own ranks. When the two paths happen to cross, however, you will be roughly handled and thrust aside, or else shunned and isolated.

" Now take these two parties, so different from each other in every respect, and tell me what meaning an educational establishment would have for them. That enormous horde, crowding onwards on the first path towards its goal, would take the term to mean an institution by which each of its members would become duly qualified to take his place in the rank and file, and would be purged of everything which would tend to make him strive after higher and more remote aims. I don't deny, of course, that they can find pompous words in which to describe their aims : for example, they speak of ' the universal development of free personality upon a firm social national, and human basis,' or they announce as their goal : ' The founding of the peaceful sovereignty of the people upon reason, education, and justice.'

" An educational establishment for the other and smaller company, however, would be something vastly different. They would employ it to prevent themselves from being separated from one another and overwhelmed by the first huge crowd, to prevent their few select spirits from losing sight of their splendid and noble task through premature weariness, or from being turned aside from the true path, corrupted, or subverted. These select spirits must complete their work : that is the *raison d'être* of their common institution—a work, indeed, which, as it were, must be free from subjective traces, and must further rise above the transient events of future times as the pure reflection of the eternal and immutable essence of things. And all those who occupy places in that institution must co-operate in the endeavour to engender men of genius by this purification from subjectiveness and the creation of the works of genius."

The last of these lectures is a sweeping indictment of the entire educational system of modern Germany ; but when reading it we are shamefully conscious that the arguments apply equally to England. A huge state machine which represses individual tendencies ; which leaves blundering university students in their early twenties wondering what they are to do to " make their way in the world " ; which is guided by the age instead of guiding the age ; and which knowingly or unknowingly repudiates culture in every form : can we not still find evidence enough in our country to justify Nietzsche's invectives ? Take the present state of art in England, as represented by Burlington House. Consider the present state of the British theatre—if we can call a theatre British where nine plays out of ten are imported from America. Above all, consider the present state of English literature, a subject which, indeed, it is rather painful to touch on. Think of the little honour paid to Meredith and Swinburne while they were alive, and all the clumsy criticisms passed upon them and their works when they died. True,

as Arnold wrote, we may not know much about
the word Philistinism in England ; but, then,
they never spoke of solecisms at Soli. To
know in what a state our neglect of culture has
left us we have only to note the unconscious
humour of newspaper criticisms on new plays,
poems, and pictures. Think of the shocked
Puritanism which, in London as well as in the
provinces, objected to Salome dancers and living
statuary. Think of the sleek Christians who
object to bands in the parks on Sundays—a
natural consequence, of course, of undeveloped
intelligence following the Christian antagonism
to art in every form. Other instances could be
cited by the dozen ; but we have no doubt that
the cultured Continental reader who has paid
a visit to this country has already given way to
the Homeric ἄσβεστος γέλος.

To conclude his lectures, Nietzsche endeavoured
to convey to his audience what really happens
when a genius is at length able to place himself
at the head of his natural followers, and when the
followers themselves have at length found the
leader they have been consciously or unconsciously
seeking.

" When leader and followers have at last
met, wounded and sore, there is an impassioned
feeling of rapture, like the echo of an ever-
sounding lyre, a feeling which I can let you divine
only by means of a simile.

" Have you ever, at a musical rehearsal, looked at the strange, shrivelled-up, good-natured species of men who usually form the German orchestra ? What changes and fluctuations we see in that capricious goddess ' form ' ! What noses and ears, what clumsy, *danse macabre* movements ! Just imagine for a moment that you were deaf, and had never dreamed of the existence of sound or music, and that you were looking upon the orchestra as a company of actors, and trying to enjoy their performance as a drama and nothing more. Undisturbed by the idealising effect of the sound, you could never see enough of the stern, medieval, wood-cutting movement of this comical spectacle, this harmonious parody on the *homo sapiens*.

" Now, on the other hand, assume that your musical sense has returned, and that your ears are opened. Look at the honest conductor at the head of the orchestra performing his duties in a dull, spiritless fashion : you no longer think of the comical aspect of the whole scene, you listen—but it seems to you that the spirit of tediousness spreads out from the honest conductor over all his companions. Now you see only torpidity and flabbiness, you hear only the trivial, the rhythmically inaccurate, and the melodiously trite. You see the orchestra only as an indifferent, ill-humoured, and even wearisome crowd of players.

" But set a genius—a real genius—in the

midst of this crowd ; and you instantly perceive something almost incredible. It is as if
this genius, in his lightning transmigration,
had entered into these mechanical, lifeless
bodies, and as if only one demoniacal eye gleamed
forth out of them all. Now look and listen—
you can never listen enough ! When you
again observe the orchestra, now loftily storm-
ing, now fervently wailing, when you notice
the quick tightening of every muscle and the
rhythmical necessity of every gesture, then
you too will feel what a pre-established harmony
there is between leader and followers, and how
in the hierarchy of spirits everything impels us
towards the establishment of a like organisation.
You can divine from my simile what I would
understand by a true educational institution,
and why I am very far from recognising one
in the present type of university."

CHAPTER V

THE RELATIONSHIP OF SCHOPENHAUER'S PHILO-
SOPHY TO A GERMAN CULTURE—PHILOSOPHY
IN THE TRAGIC AGE OF GREECE—ON TRUTH
AND LYING IN AN AMORAL SENSE—THOUGHTS
OUT OF SEASON. *

THE *Relationship of Schopenhauer's Philosophy to a German Culture* is a fragment
composed in the autumn and winter of 1872. It
is remarkable only as containing the germs of a
few thoughts afterwards expanded and dealt with
more fully in *Schopenhauer as Educator.* The
Philosophy in the Tragic Age of Greece was
sketched out in 1873 and then laid aside. Mrs.
Foerster-Nietzsche tells us † that her brother
did not care to retouch his earlier works, more
especially when, as in the case of the present
fragment, his knowledge of the subject had considerably increased when he again took up the MS.
in 1879 to prepare it for the press. It did not,
however, appear during his lifetime. Of the
three essays, the *Philosophy in the Tragic Age of
Greece* is undoubtedly the most important. Al-

* With the exception of the last-named, all these were
issued posthumously.
† *Werke*, I, 530.

though only some thirty thousand words long, it gives an illuminating history of early Greek philosophy. (Nietzsche's original plan is indicated by a title he had in mind : *The Ante-Platonic Philosophy, with the Interpretation of Select Fragments*.) The object of the essay is indicated in the words which conclude his first preface, written in 1874 : " My task is to bring *that* to light which we must always love and honour, and which no later or more extensive knowledge will ever be able to take away from us : the great man." To find other works of equally deep learning, breadth of imagination, and felicity of style, we must turn to Dr. Gilbert Murray. The *Truth and Lying* was highly prized by Nietzsche himself, and he intended to expand it later into an essay uniform with those forming the *Thoughts out of Season ;* but his constant travelling and ill-health never gave him time to do so. The essay thus remains a fragment—one, however, with unmistakable Nietzschian touches.

We now come to the *Thoughts out of Season*. Four of these (*David Strauss, History, Schopenhauer, Wagner*) were published between 1873 and 1876 ; a fifth which, in order of composition, comes between the *Schopenhauer* and the *Wagner*, appeared posthumously.

" My four *Thoughts out of Season* are, above all things, bellicose," writes Nietzsche in the *Ecce Homo.** " They show that I was no John-o'-

* p. 69.

Dreams ; that it was a pleasure to me to draw my sword—perhaps also that my wrist was dangerously supple." He goes on to refer to the " culture " of the time, which he despised so much : " Without sense, without substance, without aim : nothing but a mere ' open mind,' " and it is this culture especially which he hits hard in the *David Strauss*. The second *Thought* shows the evils of the system of teaching history *à la* Hegel. The *Schopenhauer* and the *Wagner* point out the way to a higher culture. As he himself remarks, however, the thoughts he credits † to Schopenhauer and Wagner were actually his own (*v.* p. 17). Bearing in mind this brief outline of the four *Thoughts*, the reader will be able to follow the excerpts given below.

Of all the evil results due to the last contest with France, the most deplorable, perhaps, is that widespread and even universal error of public opinion and of all those who think publicly, that German culture was also victorious in the struggle, and that it should be now, therefore, decked with garlands, as a fit recognition of such extraordinary events and successes. This error is in the highest degree pernicious : not because it is an error—for there are illusions which are both salutary and blessed—but be cause it threatens to convert our victory into a signal defeat. A defeat ? I should say,

† *Ecce Homo,* p 70.

rather, into the uprooting of the German Mind for the benefit of the "German Empire" (*David Strauss*, sec. 1).

German culture did not even help towards the success of our arms. Severe military discipline, natural bravery and sustaining power, the superior generalship, unity and obedience in the rank and file—in short, factors which have nothing to do with culture, were instrumental in making us conquer an opponent in whom the most essential of these factors was absent (sec. 1).

Provided that it were possible to direct that calm and tenacious bravery which the German opposed to the pathetic and spontaneous fury of the Frenchman, against the inward enemy, against the highly suspicious, and, at all events, unnative "cultivation" which, owing to a dangerous misunderstanding, is called culture in Germany, then all hope of a really genuine German "culture"—the reverse of that "cultivation"—would not be entirely lost. For the Germans have never known any lack of clear-sighted and heroic leaders, though these, often enough, probably, have lacked Germans. But whether it is possible to turn German bravery into a new direction seems to me to become ever more and more doubtful; for I realise how fully convinced every one is that such a struggle and such bravery are no longer requisite; on the contrary, that most things are regulated as

satisfactorily as they can possibly be—or, at all
events, that everything of moment has long ago
been discovered and accomplished : in a word,
that the best seed of culture is already sown
everywhere, and is now either shooting up its
fresh green blades, or, here and there, even
bursting forth into luxuriant blossom.   In this
sphere not only happiness but ecstasy reigns
supreme.   I am conscious of this ecstasy and
happiness in the ineffable, truculent assurance
of German journalists and manufacturers of
novels, tragedies, poems, and histories (for it
must be clear that these people belong to one
category), who seem to have conspired to improve the leisure and ruminative hours—that is
to say, the " intellectual lapses "—of the modern
man, by bewildering him with their printed
paper.   Since the war, all is gladness, dignity,
and self-consciousness in this merry throng.
After the startling successes of German culture,
it regards itself, not only as approved and sanctioned, but almost as sanctified.   It therefore
speaks with gravity, affects to apostrophise the
German People, and issues complete works,
after the manner of the classics ; nor does it
shrink from proclaiming in those journals which
are open to it some few of its adherents as new
German classical writers and model authors.
It might be supposed that the dangers of such
an *abuse of success* would be recognised by the
more thoughtful and enlightened among culti-

vated Germans; or, at least, that these would feel how painful is the comedy that is being enacted around them : for what in truth could more readily inspire pity than the sight of a cripple strutting like a cock before a mirror, and exchanging complacent glances with his reflection ! But the " scholar " caste willingly allows things to remain as they are, and are too much concerned with their own affairs to busy themselves with the care of the German mind. Moreover, the units of this caste are too thoroughly convinced that their own scholarship is the ripest and most perfect fruit of the age—in fact, of all ages—to see any necessity for a care of German culture in general ; since, in so far as they and the legion of their brethren are concerned, preoccupations of this order have everywhere been, so to speak, surpassed. The more conscientious observer, more particularly if he be a foreigner, cannot help noticing withal that no great disparity exists between that which the German regards as his culture and that other triumphant culture of the new German classics, save in respect of the quantum of knowledge. Everywhere, where knowledge and not ability, where information and not art, hold the first rank—everywhere, therefore, where life bears testimony to the kind of culture extant, there is now only one specific German culture—and this is the culture that is supposed to have conquered France ? The contention appears to be

altogether too preposterous. It was solely to
the more extensive knowledge of the German
officers, to the superior training of their soldiers,
and to their more scientific military strategy,
that all impartial judges, and even the French
nation, in the end, ascribed the victory. To
speak of German scholarship and culture as
having conquered, therefore, can only be the
outcome of a misapprehension, probably result-
ing from the circumstance that every precise
notion of culture has now vanished from Germany (sec. 1).

Culture is, before all things, the unity of
artistic style, in every expression of the life of a
people. Abundant knowledge and learning,
however, are not essential to it, nor are they the
sign of its existence ; and, at a pinch, they
might coexist much more harmoniously with the
very opposite of culture—with barbarity : that
is to say, with a complete lack of style, or with a
riotous jumble of all styles (sec. 1).

The belief seems to be rife that we are in
possession of a genuine culture, and the enormous incongruity of this triumphant satisfaction in the face of the inferiority which should
be patent to all, seems only to be noticed by the
few and select. For all those who think with
the public mind have blindfolded their eyes
and closed their ears. The incongruity is not
even acknowledged to exist. How is this
possible ? What power is sufficiently influential

to deny this existence ? What species of men must have attained to supremacy in Germany that feelings which are so strong and simple should be denied or prevented from obtaining expression ? This power, this species of men, I will name—they are *the Philistines of Culture*.

As every one knows, the word " Philistine " is borrowed from the vernacular of student-life, and, in its widest and most popular sense, it signifies the reverse of a son of the Muses, of an artist, and of the genuine man of culture. The Philistine of culture, however, the study of whose type and the hearing of whose confessions (when he makes them) have now become tiresome duties, distinguishes himself from the general notion of the order " Philistine " by means of a superstition : he fancies that he is himself a son of the Muses and a man of culture. This incomprehensible error clearly shows that he does not even know the difference between a Philistine and his opposite. We must not be surprised, therefore, if we find him, for the most part, solemnly protesting that he is no Philistine. Owing to this lack of self-knowledge, he is convinced that his " culture " is the consummate manifestation of real German culture ; and, since he everywhere meets with scholars of his own type, since all public institutions, whether schools, universities, or academies, are so organised as to be in complete harmony with

his education and needs, wherever he goes he
bears with him the triumphant feeling that he
is the worthy champion of prevailing German
culture, and he frames his pretensions and
claims accordingly (sec. 2).

While professing to hate every form of
fanaticism and intolerance, what they [the
Culture-Philistines] really hated, at bottom,
was the dominating genius and the tyranny of
the real claims of culture. They therefore concentrated and utilised all their forces in those
quarters where a fresh and vigorous movement
was to be expected, and then paralysed, stupe-
fied, and tore it to shreds. In this way, a
philosophy which veiled the Philistine confessions of its founder beneath neat twists and
flourishes of language proceeded further to discover a formula for the canonisation of the
commonplace. It expatiated upon the rational-
ism of all reality, and thus ingratiated itself
with the Culture-Philistine, who also loves neat
twists and flourishes, and who, above all, considers himself real, and regards his reality as
the standard of reason for the world. From this
time forward he began to allow every one, and
even himself, to reflect, to investigate, to
æstheticise, and, more particularly, to make
poetry, music, and even pictures—not to mention systems of philosophy; provided, of course,
that everything were done according to the old
pattern, and that no assault were made upon the

" reasonable " and the " real "—that is to say, upon the Philistine (sec. 2).

Concerning Culture-Philistinism, David Strauss makes a double confession, by word and by deed ; that is to say, by the word of the confessor, and the act of the writer. His book entitled, *The Old Faith and the New*, is, first in regard to its contents, and secondly in regard to its being a book and a literary production, an un-interrupted confession ; while, in the very fact that he allows himself to write confessions at all about faith, there already lies a confession. Presumably, every one seems to have the right to compile an autobiography after his fortieth year ; for the humblest amongst us may have experienced things, and may have seen them at such close quarters, that the recording of them may prove of use and value to the thinker. But to write a confession of one's faith cannot but be regarded as a thousand times more pretentious, since it takes for granted that the writer attaches worth, not only to the experiences and investiga-tions of his life, but also to his beliefs. Now, what the nice thinker will require to know, above all else, is the kind of faith which happens to be compatible with natures of the Straussian order, and what it is they have " half dreamily con-jured up " concerning matters of which those alone have the right to speak who are acquainted with them at first hand. Whoever would have desired to possess the confessions, say, of a

Ranke or a Mommsen ?   And these men were scholars and historians of a very different stamp from David Strauss. If, however, they had ever ventured to interest us in their faith instead of in their scientific investigations, we should have felt that they were overstepping their limits in a most irritating fashion. Yet Strauss does this when he discusses his faith. Nobody wants to know anything about it, save, perhaps, a few bigoted opponents of the Straussian doctrines, who, suspecting as they do, a substratum of Satanic principles beneath these doctrines, hope that he may compromise his learned utterances by revealing the nature of these principles. These clumsy creatures may, perhaps, have found what they sought in his last book ; but we, who had no occasion to suspect a Satanic substratum, discovered nothing of the sort, and would have felt rather pleased than not had we been able to discern even a dash of the diabolical in any part of the volume. But surely no evil spirit could speak as Strauss speaks of his new faith. In fact, spirit in general seems to be altogether foreign to the book — more particularly the spirit of genius (s. 4)

Strauss strongly resented the action of one of his opponents who happened to refer to his reverence for Lessing . . . the fact that Strauss fosters these feelings towards Lessing has always excited my suspicion ; I find the same

warmth for Lessing raised almost to heat in
Gervinus—yea, on the whole, no great German
writer is so popular among little German writers
as Lessing is ; but for all that they deserve no
thanks for their predilection ; for what is it in
sooth that they praise in Lessing ? At one
moment it is his catholicity—the fact that he
was critic and poet, archæologist and philosopher,
dramatist and theologian. Anon, " it is the
unity in him of the writer and the man, of the
head and the heart." The last quality, as a rule,
is just as characteristic of the great writer as of
the little one ; as a rule, a narrow head agrees
only too fatally with a narrow heart. And as
to the catholicity, this is no distinction, more
especially when, as in Lessing's case, it was a
dire necessity. What astonishes one in regard
to Lessing-enthusiasts is rather that they have
no conception of the devouring necessity which
drove him on through life and to this catholicity ;
no feeling for the fact that such a man is too
prone to consume himself rapidly, like a flame ;
nor any indignation at the thought that the
vulgar narrowness and pusillanimity of his
whole environment, especially of his learned
contemporaries, so saddened, tormented, and
stifled the tender and ardent creature that he
was, that the very universality for which he is
praised should give rise to feelings of the deepest
compassion. " Have pity on the exceptional
man ! " Goethe cries to us ; " for it was his lot to

live in such a wretched age that his life was one long polemical effort." How can ye, my worthy Philistines, think of Lessing without shame ? He who was ruined precisely on account of your stupidity, while struggling with your ludicrous fetishes and idols, with the defects of your theatres, scholars, and theologists, without once daring to attempt that daring flight for which he had been born. And what are your feelings when ye think of Winckelmenn, who, in order to turn his eyes from your grotesque puerilities, went begging to the Jesuits for help, and whose ignominious conversion dishonours not him, but you ? Dare ye mention Schiller's name without blushing ? Look at his portrait. See the flashing eyes that glance contemptuously over your heads, the deadly red cheek—do these things mean nothing to you ? In him ye had such a magnificent and divine toy that ye shattered it. Suppose, for a moment, it had been possible to deprive this harassed and hunted life of Goethe's friendship, ye would then have been responsible for its still earlier end. Ye have had no finger in any one of the life-works of your great geniuses, and yet ye would make a dogma to the effect that no one is to be helped in the future. But for every one of them, ye were " the resistance of the obtuse world," which Goethe called by its name in his epilogue to *The Bell* ; for all of them ye were the grumbling imbeciles, or the envious bigots, or the malicious egoists : in spite of you each of them created his works, against you each directed his attacks, and thanks to you each prematurely sank, while his work was still unfinished, broken and bewildered by the stress of the battle (sec. 4).

A corpse is a pleasant thought for a worm, and a worm is a dreadful thought for every living creature. Worms fancy their kingdom of heaven in a fat body ; professors of philosophy seek theirs in rummaging among Schopenhauer's entrails (sec. 6).

Nietzsche afterwards proceeds to comment on the religious formulæ and criticisms put forth in Strauss's book, a matter which would not be very interesting to the English reader unless several sections of the book were quoted in full. I therefore pass over these to quote some remarks which are as applicable to England and America to-day as they were to Germany in 1873.

The notion which the Culture-Philistine has of a classic and standard author speaks eloquently for his pseudo-culture—he who only shows his strength by opposing a really artistic and severe style, and who, thanks to the persistence of the opposition, finally arrives at a certain uniformity of expression, which again almost appears to possess unity of genuine style. In view, therefore, of the right which is granted to every one to experiment with the language, how is it possible at all for individual authors to discover a generally agreeable tone ? What is so generally interesting in them ? In the first place, a negative quality—the total lack of offensiveness : but *every really productive thing is offensive.* The greater part of a German's daily reading matter is undoubtedly sought either in the pages of newspapers, periodicals, or reviews. The language of these journals gradually stamps itself on his brain, by means of its steady drip, drip, drip of similar phrases and similar words. And, since he generally devotes to reading those hours of the day during which his exhausted brain is in any case not inclined to offer resistance, his ear for his native tongue so slowly but surely accustoms itself to this everyday German that it ultimately cannot endure its absence without pain. But the manufacturers of these newspapers are, by virtue of their trade, most thoroughly inured to the effluvia of this journalistic jargon ; they have literally lost all taste, and their palate is rather gratified than not by the most corrupt and arbitrary innovations. Hence the *tutti unisono* with which, despite the general lethargy and sickliness, every fresh solecism is greeted ; it is with such impudent corruptions of the language that her hirelings are avenged against her for the incredible boredom she imposes ever more and more upon them. I remember having read " an appeal to the German nation," by Berthold Auerbach, in which every sentence was un-German, distorted,

and false, and which, as a whole, resembled a
soulless mosaic of words cemented together with
international syntax. As to the disgracefully
slipshod German with which Edward Devrient
solemnised the death of Mendelssohn, I do not
even wish to do more than refer to it. A grammatical error—and this is the most extraordinary
feature of the case—does not therefore seem an
offence in any sense to our Philistine, but a most
delightful restorative in the barren wilderness of
everyday German. He still, however, considers all *really* productive things to be offensive.
The wholly bombastic, distorted, and threadbare
syntax of the modern standard author—yea,
even his ludicrous neologisms—are not only
tolerated, but placed to his credit as the spicy
element in his works. But woe to the stylist
with character, who seeks as earnestly and persistently to avoid the trite phrases of everyday
parlance, as the " yester-night monster blooms
of modern ink-flingers," as Schopenhauer says !
When platitudes, hackneyed, feeble, and vulgar
phrases are the rule, and the bad and the corrupt
become refreshing exceptions, then all that is
strong, distinguished, and beautiful perforce
acquires an evil odour. From which it follows
that, in Germany, the well-known experience
which befell the normally built traveller in the
land of hunchbacks is constantly being repeated.
It will be remembered that he was so shamefully insulted there, owing to his quaint figure

and lack of dorsal convexity, that a priest had at last to harangue the people in his behalf as follows : " My brethren, rather pity this poor stranger, and present thank-offerings unto the gods, that ye are blessed with such attractive gibbosities."

If any one attempted to compose a positive grammar out of the international German style of to-day, and wished to trace the unwritten and unspoken laws followed by every one, he would get the most extraordinary notions of style and rhetoric. He would meet with laws which are probably nothing more than reminiscences of bygone schooldays, vestiges of impositions for Latin prose, and results perhaps of choice readings from French novelists, over whose incredible crudeness every decently educated Frenchman would have the right to laugh.   But no conscientious native of Germany seems to have given a thought to these extraordinary notions under the yoke of which almost every German lives and writes.

The reader should have little difficulty in calling to mind well-known English and American authors to whom these remarks apply. Nietzsche concludes his essay by quoting some specimens of Strauss's style and analysing them.

The Use and Abuse of History is an outcry against Hegelism as represented in the study of history in German colleges and universities.

" With Nietzsche the historical sense becomes a 'malady from which men suffer,' the world-process an illusion, evolutionary theories a subtle excuse for inactivity. History is for the few not the many, for the man not the youth, for the great not the small—who are broken and bewildered by it. It is the lesson of remembrance, and few are strong enough to bear that lesson. History has no meaning except as the servant of light and action : and most of us can only act if we forget. . . . Turning from history to the historian [Nietzsche] condemns the 'noisy little fellows' who measure the motives of the great men of the past by their own, and use the past to justify their present." *

" I hate everything that merely instructs me without increasing or directly quickening my activity." These words of Goethe, like a sincere *ceterum censeo*, may well stand at the head of my thoughts on the worth and worthlessness of history. I will show in them why instruction that does not " quicken," knowledge that slackens the reins of activity, why, in fact, history, in Goethe's phrase, must be serious, " hated " as a costly and superfluous luxury of the understanding : for we are still in want of the necessaries of life, and the superfluous is an enemy to the necessary. We do

* Mr. Adrian Collins in his Introduction to the English translation of *Thoughts out of Season*, Vol. II.

need history, but quite differently from the jaded idlers in the garden of knowledge, however grandly they may look down on our rude and unpicturesque requirements. In other words, we need it for life and action, or to excuse a selfish life and a cowardly or base action. We would serve history only in so far as it serves life ; but to value its study beyond a certain point mutilates and degrades life : and this is a fact that certain marked symptoms of our time make it as necessary as it may be painful to bring to the test of experience. . . . These thoughts are " out of season " because I am trying to represent something of which the age is rightly proud—its historical culture —as a fault and a defect in our time, believing, as I do, that we are all suffering from a malignant historical fever, and should at least recognise the fact (*History*, Preface).

The beast lives *unhistorically ;* for it " goes into " the present, like a number, without leaving any curious remainder. It cannot dissimulate, it conceals nothing ; at every moment it seems what it actually is, and thus can be nothing that is not honest. But man is always resisting the great and continually increasing weight of the past ; it presses him down and bows his shoulders ; he travels with a dark invisible burden that he can plausibly disown, and is only too glad to disown in converse with his fellows—in order to excite their envy. And so it hurts him, like the thought of a lost Paradise, to see a herd grazing, or, nearer still, a child, that has nothing yet of the past to disown, and plays in a happy blindness between the walls of the past and the future (sec. 1).

If happiness and the chase for new happiness keep alive in any sense the will to live, no philosophy has perhaps more truth than the cynic's : for the beast's happiness, like that of the perfect cynic, is the visible proof of the truth of cynicism. The smallest pleasure, if it be only continuous and make one happy, is incomparably a greater happiness than the more intense pleasure that comes as an episode, a wild freak, a mad interval between ennui, desire, and privation. But in the smallest and greatest happiness there is always one thing that makes it happiness : the power of forgetting, or, in more learned phrase, the capacity of feeling " unhistorically " throughout its duration. One who cannot leave himself behind on the threshold of the moment, and forget the past, who cannot stand on a single point, like a goddess of victory, without fear or giddiness, will never know what happiness is ; and, worse still, will never do anything to make others happy (sec. 1).

History, so far as it serves life, serves an unhistorical power, and will thus never become a pure science like mathematics. The question how far life needs such a service is one of the most serious questions affecting the well-being of a man, a people, and a culture. For by excess of history life becomes maimed and degenerate, and is followed by the degeneration of history as well.

The fact that life does need the service of history must be as clearly grasped as that an excess of history hurts it; this will be proved later. History is necessary to the living man in three ways: in relation to his action and struggle, his conservatism and reverence, his suffering and his desire for deliverance. These three relations answer to the three kinds of history—so far as they can be distinguished— the monumental, the antiquarian, and the critical.

History is above all necessary to the man of action and power who fights a great fight and needs examples, teachers, and comforters; he cannot find them among his contemporaries. It was necessary in this sense to Schiller; for our time is so evil, Goethe says, that the poet meets no nature that will profit him, among living men. Polybius is thinking of the active man when he calls political history the true preparation for governing a State; it is the great teacher, that shows us how to bear steadfastly the reverses of fortune, by reminding us what others have suffered. Whoever has learned to recognise this meaning in history must hate to see curious tourists and laborious beetle-hunters climbing up the great pyramids of antiquity. He does not wish to meet the idler who is rushing through the picture-galleries of the past for a new distraction or sensation, where he himself is looking for example and encouragement (secs. 1 and 2).

Secondly, history is necessary to the man of conservative and reverent nature, who looks back to the origins of his existence with love and trust ; through it he gives thanks for life. He is careful to preserve what survives from ancient days, and will reproduce the conditions of his own upbringing for those who come after him ; thus he does life a service. The possession of his ancestors' furniture changes its meaning in his soul : for his soul is rather possessed by it. All that is small and limited, mouldy and obsolete, gains a worth and inviolability of its own from the conservative and reverend soul of the antiquary migrating into it, and building a secret nest there. The history of his town becomes the history of himself ; he looks on the walls, the turreted gate, the town council, the fair, as an illustrated diary of his youth, and sees himself in it all—his strength, industry, desire, reasons, faults, and follies (sec. 3).

The greatest value of this antiquarian spirit of reverence lies in the simple emotions of

pleasure and content that it lends to the drab,
rough, even painful circumstances of a nation's
or individual's life : Niebuhr confesses that
he could live happily on a moor among free
peasants with a history, and would never
feel the want of art (sec. 3).

Here we see clearly how necessary a third
way of looking at the past is to man, beside
the other two. This is the " critical " way ;
which is also in the service of life. Man must
have the strength to break up the past ; and
apply it, too, in order to live. He must bring
the past to the bar of judgment, interrogate
it remorselessly, and finally condemn it. Every
past is worth condemning : this is the rule in
mortal affairs, which always contain a large
measure of human power and human weakness.
It is not justice that sits in judgment here ;
nor mercy that proclaims the verdict ; but
only life, the dim, driving force that insatiably
desires—itself. Its sentence is always un-
merciful, always unjust, as it never flows from
a pure fountain of knowledge : though it
would generally turn out the same, if Justice
herself delivered it. " For everything that
is born is *worthy* of being destroyed : better
were it then that nothing should be born."
It requires great strength to be able to live
and forget how far life and justice are one.
Luther himself once said that the world only
arose by an oversight of God : if He had ever

dreamed of heavy ordnance, He would never have created it (sec. 3).

This is how history can serve life. Every man and nation needs a certain knowledge of the past, whether it be through monumental, antiquarian, or critical history, according to his objects, powers, and necessities. The need is not that of the mere thinkers who only look on at life, or the few who desire knowledge and can only be satisfied with knowledge; but it has always a reference to the end of life, and is under its absolute rule and direction. This is the natural relation of an age, a culture, and a people to history; hunger is its source, necessity its norm, the inner plastic power assigns its limits. The knowledge of the past is only desired for the service of the future and the present, not to weaken the present or undermine a living future. All this is as simple as truth itself, and quite convincing to any one who is not in the toils of " historical deduction " (sec. 4).

Let me give a picture of the spiritual events in the soul of the modern man. Historical knowledge streams upon him from sources that are inexhaustible, strange incoherencies come together, memory opens all its gates, and yet is never open wide enough, nature busies herself to receive all the foreign guests, to honour them and put them in their places. But they are at war with each other : violent measures seem necessary, in order to escape destruction one's self. It becomes second nature to grow gradually accustomed to this irregular and stormy home-life, though this second nature is unquestionably weaker, more restless, more radically unsound than the first. The modern man carries inside him an enormous heap of indigestible knowledge-stones that occasionally rattle together in his body, as the fairy tale has it. And the rattle reveals the most striking characteristics of these modern men, the opposition of something inside them to which nothing external corresponds ; and the reverse. The ancient nations knew nothing of this. Knowledge, taken in excess without hunger, even contrary to desire, has no more the effect of transforming the external life ; and remains hidden in a chaotic inner world that the modern man has a curious pride in calling his " real personality." He has the substance, he says, and only wants the form ; but this is quite an unreal opposition in a living thing. Our modern culture is for that reason not a living one, because it cannot be understood without that opposition. In other words, it is not a real culture, but a kind of knowledge about culture, a complex of various thoughts and feelings about it, from which no decision as to its direction can come. . . . The " inner life " is now the only thing that matters to education, and all who see it hope that the education may not fail by being too indigestible. Imagine a Greek meeting it ; he would observe that for modern men " education " and " historical education " seem to mean the same thing, with the difference that the one phrase is longer. And if he spoke of his own theory, that a man can be very well educated without any history at all, people would shake their heads and think they had not heard aright. The Greeks, the famous people of a past still near to us, had the " unhistorical sense " strongly developed in the period of their greatest power. If a typical child of his age were transported to that world by some enchantment, he would probably find the Greeks very " uneducated." And that discovery would betray the closely guarded secret of modern culture to the laughter of the world. For we moderns have nothing of our own. We only become worth notice by filling ourselves to overflowing with foreign customs, arts, philosophies, religions, and sciences : we are wandering encyclopædias, as an ancient Greek who had strayed into our time would probably tell us. But the only value of an encyclopædia lies in the inside, in the contents, not in what is written outside, in the binding or the wrapper. And so the whole of modern culture is essentially internal : the bookbinder prints something like this on the cover : " Manual of Internal Culture for External Barbarians " (sec. 4).

An excess of history seems to be an enemy to the life of a time, and dangerous in five ways. Firstly, the contrast of inner and outer is emphasised, and personality weakened. Secondly, the time comes to imagine that it possesses the rarest of virtues, justice, to a higher degree than any other time. Thirdly, the instincts of a nation are thwarted, the maturity of the individual arrested no less than that of the whole. Fourthly, we get the belief in the old age of mankind, the belief, at all times harmful, that we are late survivals, mere Epigoni. Lastly, an age reaches a dangerous condition of irony with regard to itself, and a still more dangerous state of cynicism, when a cunning egoistic theory of action is matured that maims and at last destroys the vital strength (sec. 5).

Great learning and great shallowness go together very well under one hat (sec. 6).

If you live yourselves back into the history of great men, you will find in it the high command to come to maturity and leave that blighting system of cultivation offered by your time : which sees its own profit in not allowing you to become ripe, that it may use and dominate you whilst you are yet unripe. And if you want biographies, do not look for those with the legend, *Mr. So-and-so and His Times*, but for one whose title-page might be inscribed, *A Fighter Against His Time*. Feast your souls on Plutarch, and dare to believe in yourselves when you believe in his heroes.*

What the Florentines did under the influence of Savonarola's exhortations, when they made the famous holocaust of pictures, manuscripts, masks, and mirrors, Christianity would like to do with every culture that allured to further effort, and bore that *memento vivere* on its standard. . . . The *memento mori*, spoken to humanity as well as the individual, was a sting that never ceased to pain, the crown of medieval knowledge and consciousness. The opposite message of a later time, *memento vivere*, is spoken rather timidly, without the full power of the lungs ; and there is something almost dishonest about it (sec. 8).

I believe there has been no dangerous turning-point in the progress of German culture in this century that has not been made more dangerous by the enormous and still living influence of this Hegelian philosophy. The belief that one is a late-comer in the world is, anyhow, harmful and degrading : but it must appear frightful and devastating when it raises our late-comer to godhead, by a neat turn of the wheel, as the true meaning and object of all past creation, and his conscious misery is set

---

* It may be recollected that a curious set of fanatics, contemptuously dubbed "the heathens" by the Cromwellian party, had a similar object in view during the time of the Commonwealth.

up as the perfection of the world's history. Such a point of view has accustomed the Germans to talk of a " world-process," and justify their own time as its necessary result (sec. 8).

The man who has once learnt to crook the knee and bow the head before the power of history, nods " yes " at last, like a Chinese doll, to every power, whether it be a government or a public opinion or a numerical majority ; and his limbs move correctly as the power pulls the string. If each success have come by a " rational necessity," and every event show the logic or the " idea " then—down on your knees quickly, and let every step in the ladder of success have its reverence ! There are no more living mythologies, you say ? Religions are at their last gasp ? Look at the religion of the power of history, and the priests of the mythology of Ideas, with their scarred knees ! Do not all the virtues follow in the train of this new faith ? (sec. 8)

Hegel once said, "When the spirit makes a fresh start, we philosophers are at hand." Our time did make a fresh start—into irony, and lo ! Edward von Hartmann was at hand, with his famous philosophy of the Unconscious —or, more plainly, the philosophy of unconscious irony. We have seldom read a more jovial production, a greater philosophical joke, than Hartmann's book. Any one whom it does not fully enlighten about " becoming," who is not swept and garnished throughout by it, is ready to become a monument of the past himself. The beginning and end of the world-process, from the first throb of consciousness to its final leap into nothingness, with the task of our generation settled for it—all drawn from that clever fount of inspiration, the Unconscious, and glittering in Apocalyptic light, imitating an honest seriousness to the life, as if it were a serious philosophy and not a huge joke— such a system shows its creator to be one of the first philosophical parodists of all time. Let us then sacrifice on his altar, and offer the inventor of the true universal medicine a lock of hair, in Schleiermacher's phrase. For what medicine would be more salutary to combat the excess of historical culture than Hartmann's parody of the world's history ?

If we wished to express in the fewest words what Hartmann really has to tell us from his mephitic tripod of unconscious irony, it would be something like this : our time could only remain as it is, if men should become thoroughly sick of this existence. And I fervently believe he is right. The frightful petrifaction of the time, the restless rattle of the ghostly bones, held naïvely up to us by David Strauss as the most beautiful fact of all—is justified by Hartmann not only from the past, *ex causis efficienti-*

bus, but also from the future, *ex causa finali* (sec. 9).

There are perhaps a hundred men now who know what poetry is : perhaps in another century there will be a hundred more who have learned in the meantime what culture is, and that the Germans have had as yet no culture, however proudly they may talk about it. The general satisfaction of the Germans at their culture will seem as foolish and incredible to such men as the once lauded classicism of Gottsched, or the reputation of Ramler as the German Pindar, seemed to us. They will perhaps think this " culture " to be merely a kind of knowledge about culture, and a false and superficial knowledge at that. False and superficial, because the Germans endured the contradiction between life and knowledge, and did not see what was characteristic in the culture of really educated peoples, that it can only rise and bloom from life. But by the Germans it is worn like a paper flower, or spread over like the icing on a cake ; and so must remain a useless lie for ever.

The education of youth in Germany starts from this false and unfruitful idea of culture. Its aim, when faced squarely, is not to form the liberally educated man, but the professor, the man of science, who wants to be able to make use of his science as soon as possible, and stands on one side in order to see life clearly.

The result, even from a ruthlessly practical point of view, is the historically and æsthetically trained Philistine.

Nietzsche's attitude towards Schopenhauer has already been referred to (p. 21). Nietzsche clearly explains· in the *Ecce Homo* that " not Schopenhauer as Educator is in question, but his opposite, Nietzsche as Educator." He read his own thoughts into Schopenhauer, and thus made him his ideal for a time. The reader will thus bear in mind that any praise given to Schopenhauer in this essay is intended for Nietzsche's ideal Schopenhauer—i.e. Nietzsche himself or Zarathustra—and not the real Schopenhauer, from whom Nietzsche afterwards turned away in disgust.

When the traveller, who had seen many countries and nations and continents, was asked what common attribute he had found existing among men, he answered, " They have a tendency to sloth." Many may think that the fuller truth would have been, " They are all timid." They hide themselves behind " manners " and " opinions." At bottom every man knows well enough that he is a unique being, only once on this earth ; and by no extraordinary chance will such a marvellously picturesque piece of diversity in unity as he is, ever be put together a second time. He knows this, but hides it like an evil conscience ;

and why ? From fear of his neighbour, who looks for the latest conventionalities in him, and is wrapped up in them himself. But what is it that forces the man to fear his neighbour, to think and act with his herd, and not seek his own joy ? Shyness, perhaps, in a few rare cases, but in the majority it is idleness, the " taking things easily," in a word the " tendency to sloth," of which the traveller spoke. He was right ; men are more slothful than timid, and their greatest fear is of the burdens that an uncompromising honesty and nakedness of speech and action would lay on them. It is only the artists who hate this lazy wandering in borrowed manners and ill-fitting opinions, and discover the secret of the evil conscience, the truth that each human being is a unique marvel. The man who will not belong to the general mass has only to stop " taking himself easily " ; to follow his conscience, which cries out to him, " Be thyself ! all that thou docst and thinkest and desirest, is not—thyself ! " (sec. 1).

There is no more desolate or Ishmaelitish creature in nature than the man who has broken away from his true genius, and does nothing but peer aimlessly about him. There is no reason to attack such a man at all, for he is a mere husk without a kernel, a painted cloth, tattered and sagging, a scarecrow ghost, that can rouse no fear and certainly no pity (sec. 1).

In order to describe properly what an event my first look into Schopenhauer's writings was for me, I must dwell for a minute on an idea that recurred more constantly in my youth, and touched me more nearly than any other. I wandered then as I pleased in a world of wishes, and thought that destiny would relieve me of the dreadful and wearisome duty of educating myself : some philosopher would come at the right moment to do it for me—some true philosopher, who could be obeyed without further question, as he would be trusted more than one's self. Then I said within me : " What would be the principles, on which he might teach thee ? " And I pondered in my mind what he would say to the two maxims of education that hold the field in our time. The first demands that the teacher should find out at once the strong point in his pupil, and then direct all his skill and will, all his moisture and all his sunshine, to bring the fruit of that single virtue to maturity. The second requires him to raise to a higher power all the qualities that already exist, cherish them, and bring them into a harmonious relation (sec. 2).

In the meantime I could not find my philosopher, however I tried ; I saw how badly we moderns compare with the Greeks and Romans, even in the serious study of educational problems. You can go through all Germany, and especially all the universities, with this need in your heart, and will not find what you seek ; many humbler wishes than that are still unfulfilled there. For example, if a German seriously wish to make himself an orator, or to enter a " school for authors," he will find neither master nor school : no one yet seems to have thought that speaking and writing are arts which cannot be learnt without the most careful method and untiring application. But, to their shame, nothing shows more clearly the insolent self-satisfaction of our people than the lack of demand for educators ; it comes partly from meanness, partly from want of thought. Anything will do as a so-called " family tutor," even among our most eminent and cultured people : and what a menagerie of crazy heads and mouldy devices go to make up the belauded Gymnasium ! (sec. 2).

Schopenhauer never poses : he writes for himself, and no one likes to be deceived—least of all a philosopher who has set this up as a law : " deceive nobody, not even thyself," neither with the " white lies " of social intercourse, which writers almost unconsciously imitate, still less with the more conscious deceits of the platform, and the artificial methods of rhetoric. Schopenhauer's speeches are to himself alone ; or if you like to imagine an auditor, let it be a son whom the father is instructing. It is a rough, honest, good-humoured talk to one who " hears and loves."

Such writers are rare. His strength and sanity surround us at the first sound of his voice : it is like entering the heights of the forest, where we breathe deep and are well again. We feel a bracing air everywhere, a certain candour and naturalness of his own, that belongs to men who are at home with themselves, and masters of a very rich home indeed : he is quite different from the writers who are surprised at themselves if they have said something intelligent, and whose pronouncements for that reason have something nervous and unnatural about them. We are just as little reminded in Schopenhauer of the professor with his stiff joints worse for want of exercise, his narrow chest and scraggy figure, his slinking or strutting gait. And again his rough and rather grim soul leads us not so much to miss as to despise the suppleness and courtly grace of the excellent Frenchmen ; and no one will find in him the gilded imitations of pseudo-gallicism that our German writers prize so highly. His style in places reminds me a little of Goethe, but is not likewise on any German model. For he knows how to be profound with simplicity, striking without rhetoric; and severely logical without pedantry : and of what German could he have learnt that ? He also keeps free from the hair-splitting, jerky, and (with all respect) rather un-German manner of Lessing : no small merit in him, for Lessing is the most tempting of all models for German prose style. The highest praise I can give his manner of presentation is to apply his own praise to himself : " A philosopher must be very honest to avail himself of no aid from poetry or rhetoric " (sec. 2).

I know only a single author whom I can rank with Schopenhauer, or even above him, in the matter of honesty ; and that is Montaigne. The joy of living on this earth is increased by the existence of such a man. The effect on myself, at any rate, since my first acquaintance with that strong and masterful spirit, has been that I can say of him as he of Plutarch : " As soon as I open him, I seem to grow a pair of wings." If I had the task of making myself at home on the earth, I would choose him as my companion.

Schopenhauer had a second characteristic in common with Montaigne, besides honesty : a joy that really makes others joyful. " Aliis laetus, sibi sapiens." There are two very different kinds of joyfulness. The true thinker always communicates joy and life, whether he is showing his serious or comic side, his human insight or his godlike forbearance : without surly looks or trembling hands or watery eyes, but simply and truly, with fearlessness and strength, a little cavalierly, perhaps, and sternly, but always as a conqueror : and it is this that brings the deepest and intensest joy, to see

the conquering god with all the monsters that
he has fought. But the joyfulness one finds
here and there in the mediocre writers and
limited thinkers makes some of us miserable ;
I felt this, for example, with the " joyfulness "
of David Strauss. We are generally ashamed
of such a quality in our contemporaries, because they show the nakedness of our time, and
of the men in it, to posterity. Such *fils de joie*
do not see the sufferings and the monsters, that
they pretend, as philosophers, to see and fight ;
and so their joy deceives us, and we hate it ;
it tempts to the false belief that they have
gained the victory. At bottom there is only
joy where there is victory : and this applies
to true philosophy as much as to any work of
art (sec. 2).

The first danger in whose shadow Schopenhauer lived was—isolation. The second is
called—doubting of the truth. To this every
thinker is liable who sets out from the philosophy
of Kant, provided that he be strong and sincere
in his sorrows and his desires, and not a mere
tinkling thought-box or calculating machine.
We all know the shameful state of things im-
plied by this last reservation, and I believe it
is only a very few men that Kant has so vitally
affected as to change the current of their blood
(sec. 3).

Schopenhauer knew that one must guess the
painter in order to understand the picture.

But now the whole learned fraternity is engaged in understanding the colours and canvas, and not the picture : and only he who has kept the universal panorama of life and being firmly before his eyes, will use the individual sciences without harm to himself ; for, without this general view as a norm, they are threads that lead nowhere and only confuse still more the maze of our existence.   Here we see, as I said, the greatness of Schopenhauer, that he follows up every idea, as Hamlet follows the ghost, without allowing himself to turn aside for a learned digression, or to be drawn away by the scholastic abstractions of a rabid dialectic (sec. 3).

In this way must Schopenhauer's philosophy always be interpreted ; as an individualist philosophy, starting from the single man, in his own nature, to gain an insight into his personal miseries, and needs, and limitations, and find out the remedies that will console them: namely, the sacrifice of the ego, and its submission to the nobler ends, especially those of justice and mercy. He teaches us to distinguish between the true and the apparent furtherance of man's happiness : how neither the attainment of riches, nor honour, nor learning, can raise the individual man from his deep despair at his unworthiness ; and how the quest for these good things can only have meaning through a universal end that transcends and explains them—the gaining of power to aid our physical nature by them, and, as far as may be, correct its folly and awkwardness. For one's self only, in the first instance : and finally through one's self for all. It is a task that leads to scepticism : for there is so much to be made better yet, in one and all !

Applying this to Schopenhauer himself, we come to the third and most intimate danger in which he lived, and which lay deep in the marrow of his being. Every one is apt to discover a limitation in himself, in his gifts of intellect as well as his moral will, that fills him with yearning and melancholy ; and as he strives after holiness through a consciousness of sin, so, as an intellectual being, he has a deep longing after the " genius " in himself. This is the root of all true culture ; and if we say this means the aspiration of man to be " born again " as saint and genius, I know that no one need be a Buddhist to understand the myth. We feel a strong loathing when we find talent without such aspiration, in the circle of the learned, or among the so-called educated ; for we see that such men, with all their cleverness, are no aid, but a hindrance to the beginnings of culture. There is a rigidity in them, parallel to the cold arrogance of conventional virtue, which also remains at the opposite pole to true holiness. Schopenhauer's nature contained an extraordinarily dangerous dualism. Few thinkers have felt as he did the complete and unmistakable certainty of genius within them; and his genius made him the highest of all promises—that there could be no deeper furrow than that which he was ploughing in the ground of the modern world. He knew one-half of his being to be fulfilled according to its strength, with no other need; and he followed with greatness and dignity his vocation of consolidating his victory. In the other half there was a gnawing aspiration, which we can understand, when we hear that he turned away with a sad look from the picture of Rancé, the founder of the Trappists, with the words: " That is a matter of grace." For genius ever more yearns after holiness as it sees farther and more clearly from its watch-tower than any other man, deep into the reconciliation of Thought and Being, the kingdom of peace and the denial of the will, and up to that other shore, of which the Indians speak. The wonder is that Schopenhauer's nature should have been so inconceivably stable and unshakable that it could neither be destroyed nor petrified by this yearning. Every one will understand this after the measure of his own character and greatness: none of us will understand it in the fullness of its meaning.

The more one considers these three dangers, the more extraordinary will appear his vigour in opposing them and his safety after the battle.

True, he gained many scars and open wounds : and a cast of mind that may seem somewhat too bitter and pugnacious. But his single ideal transcends the highest humanity in him. Schopenhauer stands as a pattern to men, in spite of all those scars and scratches. We may even say that what was imperfect and " all too human " in him, brings us nearer to him as a man, for we see a sufferer and a kinsman to suffering, not merely a dweller on the unattainable heights of genius.

These three constitutional dangers that threatened Schopenhauer, threaten us all. Each one of us bears a creative solitude within himself, and his consciousness of it forms an exotic aura of strangeness round him. Most men cannot endure it, because they are slothful, as I said, and because their solitude hangs round them a chain of troubles and burdens. No doubt, for the man with this heavy chain, life loses almost everything that one desires from it in youth—joy, safety, honour : his fellow-men pay him his due of—isolation ! The wilderness and the cave are about him, wherever he may live. He must look to it that he be not enslaved and oppressed, and become melancholy thereby. And let him surround himself with the pictures of good and brave fighters such as Schopenhauer.

The second danger, too, is not rare. Here and there we find one dowered by nature with a keen vision; his thoughts dance gladly in the witches' Sabbath of dialectic; and if he uncautiously give his talent the rein, it is easy to lose all humanity and live a ghostly life in the realm of " pure reason " : or through the constant search for the " pros and cons " of things, he may go astray from the truth, and live without courage or confidence, in doubt, denial, and discontent, and the slender hope that waits on disillusion : " No dog could live long thus ! "

The third danger is a moral or intellectual hardening : man breaks the bond that united him to his ideal : he ceases to be fruitful and reproduce himself in this or that province, and becomes an enemy or a parasite of culture. The solitude of his being has become an indivisible, unrelated atom, an icy stone. And one can perish of this solitude as well as of the fear of it, of one's self as well as one's self-sacrifice, of both aspiration and petrifaction : and to live is ever to be in danger (sec. 3).

I sometimes amuse myself with the idea that men may soon grow tired of books and their authors, and the savant of to-morrow come to leave directions in his will that his body be burned in the midst of his books, including, of course, his own writings. And in the gradual clearing of the forests, might not our libraries be very reasonably used for straw and brushwood ? Most books are born from the smoke and vapour of the brain : and to vapour and smoke they may well return. For having no fire within themselves, they shall be visited with fire (sec. 4).

We are feeling the consequences of the doctrine, preached lately from the housetops, that the state is the highest end of man and there is no higher duty than to serve it : I regard this not as a relapse into paganism, but into stupidity. A man who thinks state-service to be his highest duty very possibly knows no higher one ; yet there are both men and duties in a region beyond —and one of these duties, that seems to me at least of higher value than state-service, is to destroy stupidity in all its forms—and this particular stupidity among them. And I have to do with a class of men whose teleological conceptions extend further than the well-being of a state, I mean with philosophers—and only with them in their relation to the world of culture, which is again almost independent of the " good of the state." Of the many links that make up the twisted chain of humanity, some are of gold and others of pewter (sec. 4).

The waters of religion are ebbing, and leaving swamps or stagnant pools : the nations are drawing away in enmity again, and long to tear each other in pieces. The sciences, blindly driving along, on a *laisser faire* system, without a common standard, are splitting up, and losing hold of every firm principle. The educated classes are being swept along in the contemptible struggle for wealth. Never was the world more worldly, never poorer in goodness and love. Men of learning are no longer beacons or sanctuaries in the midst of this turmoil of worldliness ; they themselves are daily becoming more restless, thoughtless, loveless. Everything bows before the coming barbarism, art and science included. The educated men have degenerated into the greatest foes of education, for they will deny the universal sickness and hinder the physician (sec. 4).

There are three images of Man fashioned by our modern time, which for a long while yet will urge mortal men to transfigure their own lives ; they are the men of Rousseau, Goethe, and Schopenhauer. The first has the greatest fire, and is most calculated to impress the people : the second is only for the few, for those contemplative natures " in the grand style " who are misunderstood by the crowd. The third demands the highest activity in those who will follow it : only such men will look on that image without harm, for it breaks the spirit of that merely contemplative man, and the rabble shudder at it. From the first has come forth a strength that led and still leads to fearful revolution : for in all socialistic upheavals it is ever Rousseau's man who is the Typhœus under the Etna. Oppressed and half crushed to death by the pride of caste and the pitilessness of wealth, spoilt by priests and bad education, a laughing-stock even to himself, man cries in his need on " holy mother Nature," and feels suddenly that she is as far from him as any god of the Epicureans. His prayers do not reach her ; so deeply sunk is he in the chaos of the unnatural. He contemptuously throws aside all that finery that seemed his truest humanity a little while ago—all his arts and sciences, all the refinements of his life—he beats with his fists against the walls, in whose shadow he has degenerated, and goes forth to seek the light and sun, the forest and the crag. And crying out, " Nature alone is good, the natural man alone is human," he despises himself and aspires beyond himself ; a state wherein the soul is ready for a fearful resolve, but calls the noble and the rare as well from their utter depths.

Goethe's man is no such threatening force ; in a certain sense he is a corrective and a sedative to those dangerous agitations of which Rousseau's man is a prey. Goethe himself in his youth followed the " gospel of kindly Nature " with all the ardour of his soul : his Faust was the highest and boldest picture of Rousseau's man, so far at any rate as his hunger for life, his discontent and yearning, his intercourse with the demons of the heart could be represented. But what comes from these congregated storm-clouds ? Not a single lightning-flash ! And here begins the new image of man —the man according to Goethe. One might have thought that Faust would have lived a continual life of suffering, as a revolutionary and a deliverer, as the negative force that proceeds from goodness, as the genius of ruin, alike religious and dæmonic, in opposition to his utterly undæmonic companion ; though, of course, he could not be free of this companion, and had at once to use and despise his evil and destructive scepticism—which is the tragic destiny of all revolutionary deliverers. One is wrong, however, to expect anything of the sort : Goethe's man here parts company with Rousseau's ; for he hates all violence, all sudden transition—that is, all action : and the universal deliverer becomes merely the universal traveller. All the riches of life and nature, all antiquity—arts, mythologies, and sciences—pass before his eager eyes, his deepest desires are aroused and satisfied ; Helen herself can hold him no more—and the moment must come for which his mocking companion is waiting. At a fair spot on the earth his flight comes to an end : his pinions drop, and Mephistopheles is at his side. When the German ceases to be Faust, there is no danger greater than that of becoming a Philistine and falling into the hands of the devil—heavenly powers alone can save him. Goethe's man is, as I said, the contemplative man in the grand style, who is only kept from dying of ennui by feeding on all the great and memorable things that have ever existed, and by living from desire to desire. He is not the active man ; and when he does take a place among active men, as things are, you may be sure that no good will come of it (think, for example, of the zeal with which Goethe wrote for the stage !) ; and, further, you may be sure that " things as they are " will suffer no change. Goethe's man is a conciliatory and conservative spirit, though in danger of degenerating into a Philistine, just as Rousseau's may easily become a Catiline. All his virtues would be the better by the addition of a little brute force and elemental passion. Goethe appears to have seen where the weakness and danger of his creation lay, as is clear from Jarno's word to Wilhelm Meister : " You are bitter and ill-tempered—which is quite an excellent thing : if you could only become really angry it would be still better."

To speak plainly, it is necessary to become really angry in order that things may be better. The picture of Schopenhauer's man can help us here. *Schopenhauer's man voluntarily takes upon himself the pain of telling the truth :* this pain serves to quench his individual will and make him ready for the complete transformation of his being, which it is the inner meaning of his life to realise (sec. 4).

A " highly civilised state " generally implies, at the present time, the task of setting free the spiritual forces of a generation just so far as they may be of use to the existing institutions—as a mountain stream is split up by embankments and channels, and its diminished power made to drive mill-wheels, its full strength being more dangerous than useful to the mills. And thus " setting-free " comes to mean rather " chaining up." Compare, for example, what the self-interest of the state has done for Christianity. Christianity is one of the purest manifestations of the impulse towards culture and the production of the saint : but being used in countless ways to turn the mills of state authorities, it gradually became sick at heart, hypocritical and degenerate, and in antagonism with its original aim. Its last phase, the German Reformation, would have been nothing but a sudden flickering of its dying flame, had it not taken new strength and light from the clash and conflagration of states (sec. 6).

To speak honestly, the savant is a complex of very various impulses and attractive forces—he is a base metal throughout.

Take first a strong and increasing desire for intellectual adventure, the attraction of the new and rare as against the old and tedious. Add to that a certain joy in nosing the trail of dialectic, and beating the cover where the old fox, Thought, lies hid ; the desire is not so much for truth as the chase of truth, and the chief pleasure is in surrounding and artistically killing it. Add thirdly a love of contradiction whereby the personality is able to assert itself against all others : the battle's the thing, and the personal victory its aim—truth only its pretext. The impulse to discover " particular truths " plays a great part in the professor, coming from his submission to definite ruling persons, classes, opinions, churches, governments, for he feels it a profit to himself to bring truth to their side.

The following characteristics of the savant are less common, but still found. First, downrightness and a feeling for simplicity, very valuable if more than a mere awkwardness and inability to deceive, deception requiring some mother-wit. (Actually, we may be on our guard against too obvious cleverness and resource, and doubt the man's sincerity.) Otherwise this downrightness is generally of little value, and rarely of any use to knowledge, as it follows tradition and speaks the truth only in " adiaphora " ; it being lazier to speak the truth here than ignore it. Everything new means something to be unlearnt, and your downright man will respect the ancient dogmas and accuse the new evangelist of failing in the *sensus recti*. There was a similar opposition, with probability and custom on its side, to the theory of Copernicus. The professor's frequent hatred of philosophy is principally a hatred of the long trains of reasoning and artificiality of the proofs. Ultimately the savants of every age have a fixed limit ; beyond which ingenuity is not allowed, and everything suspected as a conspirator against honesty.

Secondly, a clear vision of near objects, combined with great short-sightedness for the distant and universal. The professor's range is generally very small, and his eye must be kept close to the object. To pass from a point already considered to another, he has to move his whole optical apparatus. He cuts a picture into small sections, like a man using an opera-glass in a theatre, and sees now a head, now a bit of dress, but nothing as a whole. The single sections are never combined for him, he only infers their connection, and consequently has no strong general impression. He judges a literary work, for example, by certain paragraphs or sentences or errors, as he can do nothing more ; he will be driven to see in an oil painting nothing but a mass of daubs.

Thirdly, a sober conventionality in his likes and dislikes. Thus he especially delights in history because he can put his own motives into the actions of the past. A mole is most comfortable in a mole-hill. He is on his guard against all ingenious and extravagant hypotheses ; but digs up industriously all the commonplace motives of the past, because he feels in sympathy with them. He is generally quite incapable of understanding and valuing the rare or the uncommon, the great or the real.

Fourthly, a lack of feeling, which makes him

capable of vivisection. He knows nothing of the
suffering that brings knowledge, and does not
fear to tread where other men shudder. He is
cold and may easily appear cruel. He is thought
courageous, but he is not—any more than the
mule who does not feel giddiness.

Fifthly, diffidence, or a low estimate of himself. Though he lives in a miserable alley of the
world, he has no sense of sacrifice or surrender ;
he appears often to know in his inmost heart
that he is not a flying, but a crawling creature.
And this makes him seem even pathetic.

Sixthly, loyalty to his teachers and leaders.
From his heart he wishes to help them, and
knows he can do it best with the truth. He has
a grateful disposition, for he has only gained
admittance through them to the high hall of
science ; he would never have entered by his
own road. Any man to-day who can throw
open a new province where his lesser disciples
can work to some purpose is famous at once, so
great is the crowd that presses after him. These
grateful pupils are certainly a misfortune to
their teacher, as they all imitate him ; his
faults are exaggerated in their small persons, his
virtues correspondingly diminished.

Seventhly, he will follow the usual road of all
the professors, where a feeling for truth springs
from a lack of ideas, and the wheel once started
goes on. Such natures become compilers, commentators, makers of indices and herbaria ;

they rummage about one special department because they have never thought there are others. Their industry has something of the monstrous stupidity of gravitation ; and so they can often bring their labours to an end.

Eighthly, a dread of ennui. While the true thinker desires nothing more than leisure, the professor fears it, not knowing how it is to be used. Books are his comfort ; he listens to everybody's different thoughts and keeps himself amused all day. He especially chooses books with a personal relation to himself, that make him feel some emotion of like or dislike ; books that have to do with himself or his position, his political, æsthetic, or even grammatical doctrines ; if he have mastered even one branch of knowledge, the means to flap away the flies of ennui will not fail him.

Ninthly, the motive of the bread-winner, the " cry of the empty stomach," in fact. Truth is used as a direct means of preferment when she can be attained ; or as a way to the good graces of the fountains of honour—and bread. Only, however, in the sense of the " particular truth " : there is a gulf between the profitable truths that may serve and the unprofitable truths to which only those few people devote themselves whose motto is not *ingenii largitor venter*.

Tenthly, a reverence for their fellow professors and a fear of their displeasure—a higher and rarer motive than the last, though not uncommon.

All the members of their guild are jealously on guard, that the truth which means so much bread and honour and position may really be baptised in the name of its discoverer. The one pays the other reverence for the truth he has found, in order to exact the toll again if he should find one himself. The Untruth, the Error, is loudly exploded, that the workers may not be too many ; here and there the real truth will be exploded to let a few bold and stiff-necked errors be on show for a time ; there is never a lack of " moral idiosyncrasies "—formerly called rascalities.

Eleventhly, the " savant for vanity," now rather rare. He will get a department for himself somehow, and investigate curiosities, especially if they demand unusual expenditure, travel, research, or communication with all parts of the world. He is quite satisfied with the honour of being regarded as a curiosity himself, and never dreams of earning a living by his erudite studies.

Twelfthly, the " savant for amusement." He loves to look for knots in knowledge and to untie them ; not too energetically, however, lest he lose the spirit of the game. Thus he does not penetrate the depths, though he often observes something that the microscopic eyes of the bread-and-butter scientist never see.

If I speak, lastly, of the " impulse towards justice " as a further motive of the savant, I may be answered that this noble impulse, being metaphysical in its nature, is too indistinguishable from the rest, and really incomprehensible to mortal mind ; and so I leave the thirteenth heading with the pious wish that the impulse may be less rare in the professor than it seems. For a spark in his soul from the fire of justice is sufficient to irradiate and purify it, so that he can rest no more and is driven for ever from the cold or lukewarm condition in which most of his fellows do their daily work.

All these elements, or a part of them, must be regarded as fused and pounded together, to form the Servant of Truth. For the sake of an absolutely inhuman thing—mere purposeless and therefore motiveless knowledge—a mass of very human little motives has been chemically combined, and as the result we have the professor—so transfigured in the light of that pure unearthly object that the mixing and pounding which went to form him are all forgotten ! It is very curious (sec. 6).

An artist, and especially a philosopher, seems often to have been dropped by chance into his age, as a wandering hermit or straggler cut off from the main body. Think how utterly great Schopenhauer is, and what a small and absurd effect he has had ! An honest man can feel no greater shame at the present time than at the thought of the casual treatment Schopenhauer has received and the evil powers that have up to

now killed his effect among men. First there
was the want of readers—to the eternal shame
of our cultivated age ; then the inadequacy of
his first public adherents, as soon as he had any ;
further, I think, the crassness of the modern man
towards books, which he will no longer take
seriously. As the outcome of many attempts to
adapt Schopenhauer to this enervated age, the
new danger has gradually arisen of regarding
him as an odd kind of pungent herb, of taking
him in grains, as a sort of metaphysical pepper.
In this way he has gradually become famous,
and I should think more have heard his name
than Hegel's ; and, for all that, he is still a
solitary being, who has failed of his effect
(sec. 7).

The "freedom" that the state bestows
on certain men for the sake of philosophy is,
properly speaking, no freedom at all, but an
office that maintains its holder. The "encouragement of philosophy" means that there
are to-day a number of men whom the state
enables to make their living out of philosophy ;
whereas the old sages of Greece were not paid
by the state, but at best were presented, as
Zeno was, with a golden crown and a monument in the Ceramicus. I cannot say generally
whether truth is served by showing the way to
live by her, since everything depends on the
character of the individual who shows the way.
I can imagine a degree of pride in a man saying

to his fellow-men, "Take care of me, as I have something better to do—namely, to take care of you." We should not be angry at such a heightened mode of expression in Plato and Schopenhauer ; and so they might properly have been university philosophers—as Plato, for example, was a court philosopher for a while without lowering the dignity of philosophy. But in Kant we have the usual submissive professor, without any nobility in his relations with the state ; and thus he could not justify the university philosophy when it was once assailed. If there be natures like Schopenhauer's and Plato's, which can justify it, I fear they will never have the chance, as the state would never venture to give such men these positions, for the simple reason that every state fears them, and will only favour philosophers it does not fear. The state obviously has a special fear of philosophy and will try to attract more philosophers, to create the impression that it has philosophy on its side—because it has those men on its side who have the title without the power. But if there should come one who really proposes to cut everything to the quick, the state included, with the knife of truth, the state, that affirms its own existence above all, is justified in banishing him as an enemy, just as it bans a religion that exalts itself to be its judge. The man who consents to be a state philosopher, must also consent to be regarded as renouncing the search for truth in all its secret retreats. At any rate, so long as he enjoys his position, he must recognise something higher than truth—the state. And not only the state, but everything required by it for existence—a definite form of religion, a social system, a standing army; a *noli me tangere* is written above all these things. Can a university philosopher ever keep clearly before him the whole round of these duties and limitations ? I do not know. The man who has done so and remains a state official is a false friend to truth ; if he has not—I think he is no friend to truth either (sec. 8).

But granting that this herd of bad philosophers is ridiculous—and who will deny it ?—how far are they also harmful ? They are harmful just because they make philosophy ridiculous. As long as this imitation thinking continues to be recognised by the state, the lasting effects of a true philosophy will be destroyed, or at any rate circumscribed ; nothing does this so well as the curse of ridicule that the representatives of the great cause have drawn on them, for it attacks that cause itself. And so I think it will encourage culture to deprive philosophy of its political and academic standing, and relieve state and university of the task, impossible for them, of deciding between true and false philosophy. Let the philosophers run wild, forbid them any thoughts of office or civic position, hold them out no more bribes—nay, rather persecute them and treat them ill—you will see a wonderful result. They will flee in terror, and seek a roof where they can, these poor phantasms ; one will become a parson, another a schoolmaster, another will creep into an editorship, another write school-books for young ladies' colleges, the wisest of them will plough the fields, the vainest go to court. Everything will be left suddenly empty, the birds flown : for it is easy to get rid of bad philosophers—one has only to cease paying them. And that is a better plan than the open patronage of any philosophy, whatever it be, for state reasons. The state has never any concern with truth, but only with the truth useful to it, or rather, with anything that is useful to it, be it truth, half-truth, or error (sec. 8).

It is clear why our university philosophers are not dangerous ; for their thoughts bloom as peacefully in the shade of tradition "as ever tree bore its apples." They do not frighten ; they carry away no gates of Gaza ; and to all their little contemplations one can make the answer of Diogenes when a certain philosopher was praised : " What great result has he to show, who has so long practised philosophy and yet has *hurt* nobody ? " Yes, the university philosophy should have on its monument, " It has hurt nobody." But this is rather the praise one gives to an old woman than to a goddess of truth ; and it is not surprising that those who know the goddess only as an old woman are the less men for that, and are naturally neglected by men of real power (sec. 8).

In order that the reader may better understand in what relationship Nietzsche stands to Schopenhauer and Wagner, the matter may be more minutely explained than has hitherto been done. From the very first, as we can see from Nietzsche's autobiography, posthumous works, and prefaces, he never gave himself up entirely to the pessimist or the musician. In *Truth and Lying* especially he condemns Schopenhauer's " pessimistic wisdom " which sacrifices to science humanity itself. On Wagner, too, he passes judgments which show that his enthusiasm is tempered by severe criticism. He finds, for example, that, in the *Walküre*, marvellous beauties are balanced by serious defects.

" Nietzsche's doubts," says Lichtenberger, " grew stronger and stronger at the time when he was working at *Richard Wagner at Bayreuth ;* we find in his fragments a number of ideas which were later developed into *The Case of Wagner*. He notes what is *extravagant* in Wagner's character and gifts, and finds that Bach and Beethoven show us ' a purer nature ' ;

he lets fall severe judgments upon Wagner's political life, on his relations with the revolutionaries and with the King of Bavaria, on his anti-Semitism ; he has significant doubts as to Wagner's value, not as an 'integral' artist, but as a specialist, i.e. as musician, poet, dramatist, and even thinker ; he discerns in him certain 'reactionary elements' : sympathy for the Middle Ages and for Christianity, Buddhistic tendencies, love of the marvellous, German patriotism ; he is sceptical as to the real influence Wagner can exercise in Germany. In short, Nietzsche, whilst affirming that he is grateful to Wagner's music 'for the purest happiness I have ever enjoyed,' shows plainly that he is a heretic in the matter of Wagnerism at the very time when, in public, he covered Wagner with laurels. How can this apparent duplicity be explained ?

"Nietzsche himself gives us the key to his conduct : 'At first we believe in a philosopher,' he remarks, in regard to his relations with Schopenhauer. 'Then we say : if he errs in his manner of proving his statements, these statements are true nevertheless. Finally, we conclude : his statements themselves are of indifferent value ; but this man's *nature* is worth a hundred systems. As a teacher he may be wrong a thousand times ; but his personality itself is always right : and it is that we should pay attention to. There is in a philosopher something that will never be in a philosophy : the cause of many philosophies : genius.' This aphorism, paradoxical in appearance, well explains the evolution of Nietzsche's feelings in regard to Wagner and Schopenhauer. He began by becoming enamoured with their works, then his love and respect were directed to the personalities of the authors : he loved them as men and as geniuses independently of their works, and, as a consequence, took particular care to avoid doing anything likely to interrupt the friendship he felt for them ; in particular he refrained from publicly criticising those passages in their works which did not please him. Finally, the moment came when he perceived that the differences which separated him from his masters weic too great for him to be silent without exhibiting a want of sincerity towards himself ; and, with his heart broken, he obeyed the imperious exigencies of his conscience as a thinker : he turned his criticism against his educators. He then saw that he had regarded them in a mistaken light. What he had sought for in them was not to understand them as they really were, but to understand himself by coming into touch with them. And this manner of acting had yielded a result paradoxical in appearance, but in reality perfectly logical : instead of his making himself like Schopenhauer or Wagner, he had transformed them on the contrary to his own likeness."

Let us see, then, how Nietzsche writes about Wagner just before the Bayreuth festivals.

For an event to be great, two things must be united—the lofty sentiment of those who accomplish it, and the lofty sentiment of those who witness it. No event is great in itself, even though it be the disappearance of whole constellations, the destruction of several nations, the establishment of vast empires, or the prosecution of wars at the cost of enormous forces : over things of this sort the breath of history blows as if they were flocks of wool. But it often happens, too, that a man of might strikes a blow which falls without effect upon a stubborn stone ; a short, sharp report is heard, and all is over. History is able to record little or nothing of such abortive efforts. Hence the anxiety which every one must feel who, observing the approach of an event, wonders whether those about to witness it will be worthy of it (sec. 1).

They who hold by gradual development as a kind of moral law must be somewhat shocked at the sight of one who, in the course of a single lifetime, succeeds in producing something absolutely new. Being dawdlers themselves, and insisting upon slowness as a principle, they are very naturally vexed by one who strides rapidly ahead, and they wonder how on earth he does it. No omens, no periods of transition, and no concessions preceded the enterprise at Bayreuth; no one except Wagner knew either the goal or the long road that was to lead to it. In the realm of art it signifies, so to speak, the first circumnavigation of the world, and by this voyage there was discovered not only a new art, but Art itself (sec. 1).

Some readers may think that the following paragraph is partly applicable to Nietzsche himself:

The dramatic element in Wagner's development cannot be ignored, from the time when his ruling passion became self-conscious and took possession of his whole being. From that time forward there is an end to all groping, straying, and sprouting of offshoots, and over his most tortuous deviations and excursions, over the eccentric disposition of his plans, a single law and will are seen to rule, in which we have the explanation of his actions, however strange this explanation may sometimes appear (sec. 2).

Lofty aspirations, which continually meet with failure, ultimately turn to evil. The inadequacy of means for obtaining success may, in certain circumstances, be the result of an inexorable fate, and not necessarily of a lack of strength; but he who under such circumstances cannot abandon his aspirations, despite the inadequacy of the means, will only become embittered, and consequently irritable and intolerant. He may possibly seek the cause of his failure in other people ; he may even, in a fit of passion, hold the whole world guilty ; or he may turn defiantly down secret byways and secluded lanes, or resort to violence. In this way, noble natures, on their road to the most high, may turn savage. Even among those who seek but their own personal moral purity, among monks and anchorites, men are to be found who, undermined and devoured by failure, have become barbarous and hopelessly morbid. There was a spirit full of love and calm belief, full of goodness and infinite tenderness, hostile to all violence and self-deterioration, and abhorring the sight of a soul in bondage. And it was this spirit which manifested itself to Wagner. It hovered over him as a consoling angel, it covered him with its wings, and showed him the true path. At this stage we bring the other side of Wagner's nature into view : but how shall we describe this other side ?

In the Niebelungen Ring, where Brunhilda is awakened by Siegfried, I perceive the most moral music I ever heard. Here Wagner attains to such a level of sacred feeling that our mind unconsciously wanders to the glistening ice and snow peaks of the Alps, to find a likeness there ; —so pure, isolated, inaccessible, chaste, and bathed in love-beams does Nature herself here display herself, that clouds and tempests—yea, and even the sublime itself—seem to lie beneath her. Now, looking down from this height upon

Tannhäuser and *The Flying Dutchman*, we begin
to perceive how the man in Wagner was evolved :
how restlessly and darkly he began ; how tempes-
tuously he strove to gratify his desires, to acquire
power and to taste those rapturous delights
from which he often fled in disgust ; how he
wished to throw off a yoke, to forget, to be
negative, and to renounce everything. The
whole torrent plunged, now into this valley,
now into that, and flooded the most secluded
chinks and crannies. In the night of these semi-
subterranean conclusions a star appeared and
glowed high above him with melancholy vehem,
ence ; as soon as he recognised it he named it
Fidelity—unselfish fidelity. Why did this star
seem to him the brightest and purest of all ?
What secret meaning had the word " fidelity "
to his whole being ? For he has graven its image
and problems upon all his thoughts and compositions. His works contain almost a complete
series of the rarest and most beautiful examples
of fidelity : that of brother to sister, of friend to
friend, of servant to master ; of Elizabeth to
Tannhäuser, of Senta to the Dutchman, of Elsa
to Lohengrin, of Isolde, Kurvenal, and Marke to
Tristan, of Brunhilda to the most secret vows of
Wodin—and many others. It is Wagner's most
personal and most individual experience, which
he reveres like a religious mystery, and which
he calls Fidelity ; he never wearies of breathing
it into hundreds of different characters, and

of endowing it with the sublimest that in him lies, so overflowing is his gratitude. It is, in short, the recognition of the fact that the two sides of his nature remained faithful to each other, that out of free and unselfish love, the creative, ingenuous, and brilliant side kept loyally abreast of the dark, the intractable, and the tyrannical side (sec. 2).

In the path of every true artist, whose lot is cast in these modern days, despair and danger are strewn. He has many means whereby he can attain to honour and might ; peace and plenty persistently offer themselves to him, but only in that form recognised by the modern man, which to the straightforward artist is no better than choke damp. In this temptation, and in the act of resisting it, lie the dangers that threaten him—dangers arising from his disgust at the means modernity offers him of acquiring pleasure and esteem, and from the indignation provoked by the selfish ease of modern society. Imagine Wagner's filling an official position, as for instance that of bandmaster at public and court theatres, both of which positions he has held : think how he, a serious artist, must have struggled in order to enforce seriousness in those very places which, to meet the demands of modern conventions, are designed with almost systematic frivolity to appeal only to the frivolous. Think how he must have partially succeeded, though only to fail on the whole.

How constantly disgust must have been at his
heels despite his repeated attempts to flee it,
how he failed to find the haven to which he
might have repaired, and how he had ever to
return to the Bohemians and outlaws of our
society, as one of them. If he himself broke
loose from any post or position, he rarely found
a better one in its stead, while more than once
distress was all that his unrest brought him.
Thus Wagner changed his associates, his dwelling-
place, and his country, and when we come to
comprehend the nature of the circles into which
he gravitated we can hardly realise how he was
able to tolerate them for any length of time.
The greater half of his past seems to be shrouded
in heavy mist ; for a long time he appears to
have had no general hopes, but only hopes for
the morrow, and thus, although he reposed no
faith in the future, he was not driven to despair.
He must have felt like a nocturnal traveller,
broken with fatigue, exasperated from want of
sleep, and tramping wearily along beneath a
heavy burden, who, far from fearing the sudden
approach of death, rather longs for it as something exquisitely charming. His burden, the
road and the night—all would disappear ! The
thought was a temptation to him. Again and
again, buoyed up by his temporary hopes, he
plunged anew into the turmoil of life, and left
all his apparatus behind him. But his method
of doing this, his lack of moderation in the

doing, betrayed what a feeble hold his hopes had upon him ; how they were only stimulants to which he had recourse in an extremity. The conflict between his aspirations and his partial or total inability to realise them tormented him like a thorn in the flesh. Infuriated by constant privations, his imagination lapsed into the dissipated, whenever the state of want was momentarily relieved. Life grew ever more and more complicated for him ; but the means and artifices that he discovered in his art as a drama- tist became ever more resourceful and daring. Albeit, these were little more than palpable dramatic makeshifts and expedients, which deceived, and were invented, only for the moment. In a flash such means occurred to his mind and were used up. Examined closely and without prepossession, Wagner's life, to recall one of Schopenhauer's expressions, might be said to consist largely of comedy, not to men- tion burlesque. And what the artist's feelings must have been, conscious as he was, during whole periods of his life, of this undignified element in it—he who more than any one else, perhaps, breathed freely only in sublime and more than sublime spheres—the thinker alone can form any idea (sec. 3).

Nothing distinguishes a man more from the general pattern of his age than the use he makes of history and philosophy. According to present views, the former seems to have been allotted the

duty of giving modern man breathing-time, in
the midst of his panting and strenuous hurry
towards his goal, so that he may, for a space,
imagine he has slipped his leash. What Montaigne was as an individual amid the turmoil of
the Reformation—that is to say, a creature inwardly coming to peace with himself, serenely
secluded in himself and taking breath, as his best
reader, Shakespeare, understood him—that is
what history is to the modern spirit to-day. The
fact that the Germans, for a whole century, have
devoted themselves more particularly to the
study of history only tends to prove that they
are the stemming, retarding, and becalming
force in the activity of modern society—a circumstance which some, of course, will place to their
credit. On the whole, however, it is a dangerous
symptom when the mind of a nation turns with
preference to the study of the past. It is a sign
of flagging strength, of decline, of degeneration ;
it denotes that its people are perilously near to
falling victims to the first fever that may happen
to be rife—the political fever among others
(sec. 3).

Were history not always a disguised Christian
theodicy, were it written with more justice and
fervent feeling, it would be the very last thing
on earth to be made to serve the purpose it now
serves, namely, that of an opiate against everything subversive and novel. And philosophy is
in the same plight : all that the majority

demand of it is that it may teach them to understand approximate facts—very approximate
facts—in order that they may then become
adapted to them. And even its noblest expo-
nents press its soporific and comforting powers
so strongly to the fore, that all lovers of sleep
and loafing must think that their aim and the
aim of philosophy are one. For my part, the
most important question philosophy has to
decide seems to be, how far things have acquired an unalterable stamp and form, and, once
this question has been answered, I think it the
duty of philosophy unhesitatingly and courage-
ously to proceed with the task of *improving that
part of the world which has been recognised as still
susceptible to change*. But genuine philosophers
do, as a matter of fact, teach this doctrine themselves, inasmuch as they work at endeavouring
to alter the very changeable views of men, and
do not keep their opinions to themselves.
Genuine disciples of genuine philosophers also
teach this doctrine ; for, like Wagner, they
understand the art of deriving a more decisive
and inflexible will from their master's teaching,
rather than an opiate or a sleeping draught.
Wagner is most philosophical where he is most
powerfully active and heroic. It was as a philosopher that he went, not only through the fire
of various philosophical systems without fear,
but also through the vapours of science and
scholarship, while remaining ever true to his

highest self. And it was this highest self which exacted *from his versatile spirit works as complete as his were*, which bade him suffer and learn, that he might accomplish such works (sec. 3).

The history of the development of culture since the time of the Greeks is short enough, when we take into consideration the actual ground it covers, and ignore the periods during which man stood still, went backwards, hesitated or strayed. The Hellenising of the world —and to make this possible, the Orientalising of Hellenism—that double mission of Alexander the Great, still remains the most important event : the old question whether a foreign civilisation may be transplanted is still the problem that the peoples of modern times are vainly endeavouring to solve. The rhythmic play of those two factors against each other is the force that has determined the course of history heretofore. Thus Christianity appears, for instance, as a product of oriental antiquity, which was thought out and pursued to its ultimate conclusions by men, with almost intemperate thoroughness. As its influence began to decay, the power of Hellenic culture was revived, and we are now experiencing phenomena so strange that they would hang in the air as unsolved problems, if it were not possible, by spanning an enormous gulf of time, to show their relation to analogous phenomena in

Hellenic culture. Thus, between Kant and the Eleatics, Schopenhauer and Empedocles, Æschylus and Wagner, there is so much relationship, so many things in common, that one is vividly impressed by the very relative nature of all notions of time. It would even seem as if a whole diversity of things were really all of a piece, and that time is only a cloud which makes it hard for our eyes to perceive the oneness of them (sec. 4).

The earth which, up to the present, has been more than adequately orientalised, begins to yearn once more for Hellenism. He who wishes to help her in this respect will certainly need to be gifted for speedy action and to have wings on his heels, in order to synthetise the multitudinous and still undiscovered facts of science and the many conflicting divisions of talent so as to reconnoitre and rule the whole enormous field. It is now necessary that a generation of *anti-Alexanders* should arise, endowed with the supreme strength necessary for gathering up, binding together, and joining the individual threads of the fabric, so as to prevent their being scattered to the four winds. The object is not to cut the Gordian knot of Greek culture after the manner adopted by Alexander, and then to leave its frayed ends fluttering in all directions ; it is rather *to bind it after it has been loosed*. That is our task to-day. In the person of Wagner, I recognise one of these anti-Alexanders : he rivets and locks together all that is isolated, weak, or in any way defective ; if I may be allowed to use a medical expression, *he has an astringent power.* And in this respect he is one of the greatest civilising forces of his age. He dominates art, religion, and folklore, yet he is the reverse of a polyhistor or of a mere collecting and classifying spirit ; for he constructs with the collected material, and breathes life into it, and is a *Simplifier of the Universe* (sec. 4).

It is quite impossible to reinstate the art of drama in its purest and highest form without effecting changes everywhere in the customs of the people, in the State, in education, and in social intercourse. When love and justice have become powerful in one department of life, namely, in art, they must, in accordance with the law of their inner being, spread their influence around them, and can no more return to the stiff stillness of their former pupal condition. In order even to realise how far the attitude of the arts towards life is a sign of their decline, and how far our theatres are a disgrace to those who build and visit them, everything must be learnt over again, and that which is usual and commonplace should be regarded as something unusual and complicated. An extraordinary lack of clear judgment, a badly-concealed lust of pleasure, of entertainment at any cost, learned scruples, assumed airs of importance, and trifling with the seriousness of art on the part of those who represent it ; brutality of appetite and money-grubbing on the part of the promoters ; the empty-mindedness and thoughtlessness of society, which only thinks of the people in so far as these serve or thwart its purpose, and which attends theatres and concerts without giving a thought to its duties— all these things constitute the stifling and deleterious atmosphere of our modern art conditions : when, however, people like our men of culture have grown accustomed to it, they imagine that it is a condition of our healthy existence, and would immediately feel unwell if, for any reason, they were compelled to dispense with it for a while. In point of fact, there is but one speedy way of convincing one's self of the vulgarity, weirdness, and confusion of our theatrical institutions, and that is to compare them to those which once flourished in ancient Greece (sec. 4).

Day and battle dawn together, the sacred shadows vanish, and Art is once more far away from us ; but the comfort she dispenses is with men from the earliest hour of day, and never leaves them. Wherever he turns, the individual realises only too clearly his own shortcomings, his insufficiency and his incompetence ; what courage would he have left were he not rendered impersonal by this consecration ! The greatest of all torments harassing him, the conflicting opinions and beliefs among men, the unreli-

ability of these beliefs and opinions, and the unequal character of men's abilities—all these
things make him hanker after art. We cannot
be happy so long as everything about us suffers
and causes suffering ; we cannot be moral so
long as the course of human events is determined
by violence, treachery, and injustice ; we cannot
even be wise, so long as the whole of mankind
does not compete for wisdom, and does not lead
the individual to the most sober and reasonable
form of life and knowledge. How, then, would
it be possible to endure this feeling of threefold
insufficiency if one were not able to recognise
something sublime and valuable in one's struggles, strivings, and defeats, if one did not learn
from tragedy how to delight in the rhythm of
the great passions, and in their victim ? Art is
certainly no teacher or educator of practical
conduct : the artist is never in this sense an
instructor or adviser ; the things after which a
tragic hero strives are not necessarily worth
striving after. As in a dream so in art, the
valuation of things only holds good while we are
under its spell. What we, for the time being,
regard as so worthy of effort, and what makes us
sympathise with the tragic hero when he prefers
death to renouncing the object of his desire, this
can seldom retain the same value and energy
when transferred to everyday life : that is why
art is the business of the man who is recreating
himself. The strife it reveals to us is a simplifica-

tion of life's struggle ; its problems are abbreviations of the infinitely complicated phenomena of man's actions and volitions. But from this very·fact—that it is the reflection, so to speak, of a simpler world, a more rapid solution of the riddle of life—art derives its greatness and indispensability. No one who suffers from life can do without this reflection, just as no one can exist without sleep. The more difficult the science of natural laws becomes, the more fervently we yearn for the image of this simplification, if only for an instant ; and the greater becomes the tension between each man's general knowledge of things and his moral and spiritual faculties. Art is with us *to prevent the bow from snapping* (sec. 4).

Wagner concentrated upon life, past and present, the light of an intelligence strong enough to embrace the most distant regions in its rays. That is why he was a simplifier of the universe ; for the simplification of the universe is only possible to him whose eye has been able to master the immensity and wildness of an apparent chaos, and to relate and unite those things which before had lain hopelessly asunder. Wagner did this by discovering a connection between two objects which seemed to exist apart from each other as if in separate spheres—that between music and life, and similarly between music and the drama. Not that he invented or was the first to create this relationship, for it must always have existed and been noticeable to all ; but, as is usually the case with a great problem, it is like a precious stone which thousands stumble over before one finally picks it up (sec. 5).

Nietzsche, following Wagner, then takes up the problem : why have such an art and music ever become so important features in the lives of modern men ? The appearance of a whole group of modern musicians, such as had never been equalled except in the time of the ancient Greeks, was something that seemed at first sight almost inexplicable. Wagner, however, stumbled on the answer to the question, and Nietzsche puts it into words for him.

He was the first to recognise an evil which is as widespread as civilisation itself among men ; language is everywhere diseased, and the burden of this terrible disease weighs heavily upon the whole of man's development. Inasmuch as language has retreated ever more and more from its pure province—the expression of strong feelings, which it was once able to convey in all their simplicity—and has always had to strain after the practically impossible achievement of communicating the reverse of feeling, that is to say, thought, its strength has become so exhausted by this excessive extension of its duties during the comparatively short period of modern civilisation, that it is no longer able to perform even that function which alone justifies its existence, to wit, the assisting of those who suffer, in communicating with each other concerning the sorrows of existence. Man can no longer make his misery known unto others by means of language ; hence he cannot really express himself any longer. And under these conditions, which are only vaguely felt at present, language has gradually become a force in itself which with spectral arms coerces and drives humanity where it least wants to go. As soon as they would fain understand one another and unite for a common cause, the craziness of general concepts, and even of the ring of modern words, lays hold of them. The result of this inability to communicate with one another is that every product of their co-operative action bears the stamp of discord, not only because it fails to meet their real needs, but because of the very emptiness of those all-powerful words and notions already mentioned. To the misery already at hand, man thus adds the curse of convention—that is to say, the agreement between words and actions without an agreement between words and feelings (sec. 5).

Let us regard this as *one* of Wagner's answers to the question, What does music mean in our time ? for he has a second. The relation between music and life is not merely that existing between one kind of language and another ; it is, besides, the relation between the perfect world

of sound and that of sight. Regarded merely as
a spectacle, and compared with other and earlier
manifestations of human life, the existence of
modern man is characterised by indescribable
indigence and exhaustion, despite the unspeak-
able garishness at which only the superficial
observer rejoices. If one examines a little more
closely the impression which this vehement and
kaleidoscopic play of colours makes upon one,
does not the whole seem to blaze with the
shimmer and sparkle of innumerable little stones
borrowed from former civilisations ? Is not
everything one sees merely a complex of in-
harmonious bombast, aped gesticulations, arro-
gant superficiality ?—a ragged suit of motley
for the naked and the shivering ? A seeming
dance of joy enjoined upon a sufferer ? Airs of
overbearing pride assumed by one who is sick
to the backbone ? And the whole moving with
such rapidity and confusion that it is disguised
and masked—sordid impotence, devouring dis-
sention, assiduous ennui, dishonest distress !
The appearance of present-day humanity is all
appearance, and nothing else : in what he now
represents man himself has become obscured
and concealed ; and the vestiges of the creative
faculty in art, which still cling to such countries
as France and Italy, are all concentrated upon
this one task of concealing. Wherever form is
still in demand in society, conversation, literary
style, or the relations between governments, men

have unconsciously grown to believe that it is adequately met by a kind of agreeable dissimulation, quite the reverse of genuine form conceived as a necessary relation between the proportions of a figure, having no concern whatever with the notions "agreeable" or "disagreeable," simply because it is necessary and not optional. But even where form is not openly exacted by civilised people, there is no greater evidence of this requisite relation of proportions ; a striving after the agreeable dissimulation, already referred to, is on the contrary noticeable, though it is never so successful even if it be more eager than in the first instance. How far this dissimulation is *agreeable* at times, and why it must please everybody to see how modern men at least endeavour to dissemble, every one is in a position to judge, according to the extent to which he himself may happen to be modern. "Only galley slaves know each other," says Tasso, "and if we *mistake* others, it is only out of courtesy, and with the hope that they, in their turn, should mistake us " (sec. 5).

I shall give only two instances showing how utterly the sentiment of our time has been perverted, and how completely unconscious the present age is of perversion. Formerly financiers were looked down upon with honest scorn, even though they were recognised as needful ; for it was generally admitted that every society must have its viscera. Now,

however, they are the ruling power in the soul
of modern humanity, for they constitute the
most covetous portion thereof. In former
times people were warned especially against
taking the day or the moment too seriously :
the *nil admirari* was recommended, and the
care of things eternal. Now there is but
one kind of seriousness left in the modern mind,
and it is limited to the news brought by the
newspaper and the telegraph. Improve each
shining hour, turn it to some account, and
judge it as quickly as possible ! One would
think modern men had but one virtue left—
presence of mind. Unfortunately, it much
more closely resembles the omnipresence of
disgusting and insatiable cupidity, and spying
inquisitiveness become universal. For the question is whether *mind is present at all to-day ;*
but we shall leave this problem for future
judges to solve ; they, at least, are bound to
pass modern men through a sieve. But this
age is vulgar, we can see now, and it is so because it reveres precisely what nobler ages
contemned (sec. 6).

How Nietzsche himself acted the part of a
" future judge " and passed modern men through
a sieve may be seen from his later works.

Wagner's actual life—that is to say, the
gradual evolution of the dithyrambic dramatist
in him—was at the same time an uninterrupted

struggle with himself, a struggle which never ceased until his evolution was complete. His fight with the opposing world was grim and ghastly, only because it was this same world—this alluring enemy—which he heard speaking out of his own heart, and because he nourished a violent demon in his breast—the demon of resistance. When the ruling idea of his life gained ascendancy over his mind—the idea that drama is, of all arts, the one that can exercise the greatest amount of influence over the world—it aroused the most active emotions in his whole being. It gave him no very clear or luminous decision, at first, as to what was to be done and desired in the future ; for the idea then appeared merely as a form of temptation—that is to say, as the expression of his gloomy, selfish, and insatiable will, eager for *power and glory*. Influence—the greatest amount of influence—how ? over whom? —these were henceforward the questions and problems which did not cease to engage his head and heart. He wished to conquer and triumph as no other artist had ever done before, and, if possible, to reach that height of tyrannical omnipotence at one stroke for which all his instincts secretly craved. With a jealous and cautious eye, he took stock of everything successful, and examined with special care all that upon which his influence might be brought to bear. With the magic sight of the dramatist, which scans souls as easily as the most familiar book, he scrutinised the nature of the spectator and the listener, and, although he was often perturbed by the discoveries he made, he very quickly found means wherewith he could enthral them. These means were ever within his reach : everything that moved him deeply he desired and could also produce ; at every stage in his career he understood just as much of his predecessors as he himself was able to create, and he never doubted that he would be able to do what they had done. In this respect his nature is perhaps more presumptuous even than Goethe's, despite the fact that the latter said of himself : " I always thought I had mastered everything ; and even had I been crowned king, I should have regarded the honour as thoroughly deserved " (sec. 8).

He who marvels at the rapid succession of the two operas, *Tristan* and the *Meistersingers*, has failed to understand one important side of the life and nature of all great Germans : he does not know the peculiar soil out of which that essentially German gaiety, which characterised Luther, Beethoven, and Wagner, can grow, the gaiety which other nations quite fail to understand, and which even seems to be missing in the Germans of to-day—that clear golden and thoroughly fermented mixture of simplicity, deeply discriminating love, ob-

servation, and roguishness, which Wagner
has dispensed, as the most precious of drinks,
to all those who have suffered deeply through
life, but who, nevertheless, return to it with
the smile of convalescents (sec. 8).

All those to whom the thought of Wagner's
development as a man may have caused pain
will find it both restful and healing to reflect
upon what he was as an artist, and to observe
how his ability and daring attained to such a
high degree of independence. If art mean
only the faculty of communicating to others
what one has one's self experienced, and if
every work of art confutes itself which does
not succeed in making itself understood, then
Wagner's greatness as an artist would certainly
lie in the almost demoniacal power of his nature
to communicate with others, to express itself
in all languages at once, and to make known
its most intimate and personal experience
with the greatest amount of distinctness possible.
His appearance in the history of art resembles
nothing so much as a volcanic eruption of the
united artistic faculties of Nature herself,
after mankind had grown to regard the practice
of a special art as a necessary rule. It is
therefore a somewhat moot point whether he
ought to be classified as a poet, a painter, or a
musician, even using each of these words in its
widest sense, or whether a new word ought not
to be invented in order to describe him (sec. 9).

In general it may be said of Wagner the
musician that he endowed everything in nature
which hitherto had no wish to speak with the
power of speech : he refuses to admit that
anything must be dumb, and, resorting to
the dawn, the forest, the mist, the cliffs, the
hills, the thrill of night, and the moonlight, he
observes a desire common to them all—they
too wish to sing their own melody. If the
philosopher says it is will that struggles for
existence in animate and inanimate nature,
the musician adds : And this will, wherever
it manifests itself, yearns for a melodious
existence (sec. 9).

Viewing him generally as an artist, and calling
to mind a more famous type, we see that Wagner
is not at all unlike Demosthenes : in him also
we have the terrible earnestness of purpose
and that strong prehensile mind which always
obtains a complete grasp of a thing ; in him,
too, we have the hand's quick clutch and the
grip as of iron. Like Demosthenes, he conceals his art or compels one to forget it by the
peremptory way he calls attention to the subject he treats ; and yet, like his great prede-
cessor, he is the last and greatest of a whole
line of artist-minds, and therefore has more
to conceal than his forerunners : his art acts
like nature, like nature recovered and restored.
Unlike all previous musicians, there is nothing
bombastic about him ; for the former did not

mind playing at times with their art, and making an exhibition of their virtuosity.   One associates Wagner's art neither with interest nor with diversion, nor with Wagner himself and art in general.   All one is conscious of is the great *necessity* of it all (sec. 9).

In Wagner the man of letters we see the struggle of a brave fighter, whose right hand has, as it were, been lopped off, and who has continued the contest with his left.   In his writings he is always the sufferer, because a temporary and insuperable destiny deprives him of his own and the correct way of conveying his thoughts—that is to say, in the form of apocalyptic and triumphant examples.   His writings contain nothing canonical or severe : the canons are to be found in his works as a whole.   Their literary side represents his at-tempts to understand the instinct which urged him to create his works and to get a glimpse of himself through them.   If he succeeded in transforming his instincts into terms of know-ledge, it was always with the hope that the reverse process might take place in the souls of his readers—it is with this intention that he wrote (sec. 10).

What the reader who is only imperfectly initiated will probably find most impressive is the general tone of authoritative dignity which is peculiar to Wagner, and which is very difficult to describe : it always strikes me as though Wagner were continually *addressing enemies ;* for the style of all these tracts more resembles that of the spoken than of the written language, hence they will seem much more intelligible if heard read aloud, in the presence of his enemies, with whom he cannot be on familiar terms, and towards whom he must therefore show some reserve and aloofness. The entrancing passion of his feelings however, constantly pierces this intentional disguise, and then the stilted and heavy periods, swollen with accessory words, vanish, and his pen dashes off sentences, and even whole pages, which belong to the best in German prose (sec. 10).

A magnificent panegyric on Wagner ends this delightful essay ; but even when writing the final words Nietzsche's thoughts were elsewhere. A new problem, as Lichtenberger rightly remarks, had appeared to him : he saw that the nineteenth century was a century of decadence, of men who were tired of living, tired of suffering, aspiring to peace ; calling out for Nirvana.

This new problem, which never ceased to occupy his mind until the end of his conscient life, was : What does this modern decadence consist of ? What are the symptoms which characterise it, the signs that reveal it ? What is the depth and breadth of the nihilistic evil ? How can it be cured ? As soon as the matter appeared to him in this light, his judgment on Wagner and Schopenhauer was modified from top to bottom. His former allies in the war against optimism became his enemies in the war against nihilism—all the more dangerous enemies because they exercised on him, and continued to exercise generally on his contemporaries, a very great fascination. He suddenly came to perceive that his passionate friendship for his two educators had been a grave danger for him. If he had not shaken off their influence in time, he would never have been quite himself, he would never have arrived at the full knowledge of his philosophy of the " Superman," the germs of which were already seen in the notion of Dionysian wisdom as he had outlined it in *The Birth of Tragedy*.

From yet another standpoint Nietzsche had been deceived in his cult of Wagner. Loving " beautiful form " as he did, admiring the great classic style in Greece and France, he might have allowed himself to be seduced and misled by the over-rich and overcharged style of the Wagnerian drama. He had been taken in by the wiles of a " comedian " of genius, a prodigious magician. He had looked upon Wagner as a primitive, spontaneous genius, of elementary power and unlimited gifts, instead of which he was an ultra-refined decadent, one of those late-comers who, in the twilight of

periods of high culture, can employ, with
marvellous art, all the resources accumulated
by former ages, and produce rare and curious,
skilful and complex works, of magnificent
and glittering colouring like that of an autumn
landscape or a sunset : works, however, which
are extraordinary rather than truly beautiful,
which lack true nobleness, and also that simple
perfection, triumphant, and sure of itself.*

Now Nietzsche found it impossible to convey
these thoughts to Wagner. His new point of
view had come almost as a shock to himself,
and he could not be expected to transfer all
the *nuances* of his ideas to the composer. Hence
Wagner came to look upon Nietzsche's apostasy
as treason pure and simple ; a mere whim—
envy, jealousy ; anything but the true motive.
While Nietzsche still entertained a high regard
for Wagner the man,† he could not refrain from
publicly disavowing any connection with Wagner's ideas. Hence the rupture at Bayreuth ;
and hence, too, those bitter pamphlets, *The
Case of Wagner* and *Nietzsche contra Wagner*.
" He was deceived in his admiration for Wagner,"
adds Lichtenberger, " he was right in altering
his mind, and it has long been a proverb that
only God and madmen never change." ‡   " The

* *La Philosophie de Friedrich Nietzsche*, p. 75.
† *Vide* his sister's *Leben*, Vol. I, *passim*.
‡ *La Philosophie de Friedrich Nietzsche*, p. 78.

s

greatest event in my life was a *recovery*," wrote Nietzsche long afterwards ; " Wagner was only one of my diseases."

We Philologists does not seem to have received Nietzsche's finishing touches. In its present form it resembles *Human, All-too-Human*, i.e. it consists of a number of more or less disjointed aphorisms, not, however, divided under separate chapter headings ; while its substance tends to show that it was to have formed part of Nietzsche's great work on Greece rather than one of the *Thoughts out of Season*. A few of the ideas in it are brought to our notice in Nietzsche's later works, and the following aphorisms will give the reader some conception of its general trend.

It is my aim to create bitter enmity between our present so-called " culture " and antiquity. Whoever feels inclined to serve the former must necessarily *hate* the latter (No. 119).

It is the business of the *free* man to live on his own account, and not for the sake of others. For this reason the Greeks looked down on handicrafts (No. 121).

It is generally thought that Philology is worn out—and I think it has not yet begun. The greatest events in the history of Philology were Goethe, Schopenhauer, and Wagner :

with their assistance we can look farther and wider than ever before. The fifth and sixth centuries still remain to be investigated and brought to light * (No. 123).

I recommend students to form their style after Grecian models rather than Latin, especially on Demosthenes : simplicity ! Let Leopardi stand as a proof of this, who is perhaps the greatest stylist of the century (No. 162).

Classical Education ? What do people see in it ? Something by the help of which they may be relieved from military service and get letters after their names ! (No. 163.)

The following aphorisms are quoted from this essay by Mrs. Foerster-Nietzsche, to show how her brother conceived of the superman even so far back as 1873 :

How can one praise and glorify a nation as a whole ? Even among the Greeks it was the individuals that counted (No. 197).

The Greeks are interesting and extremely important because they reared such a vast number of great individuals. How was this possible ? This question is one that ought to be studied (No. 200).

I am interested only in the relations of a people to the rearing of the individual man,

---

* This refers to the fifth and sixth centuries B.C., the ante-Platonic period of Greek philosophy in which Nietzsche was so much interested.

and among the Greeks the conditions were unusually favourable for the development of the individual ; not by any means owing to the goodness of the people, but because of the struggles of their evil instincts. *With the help of favourable measures great individuals might be reared who would be both different from and higher than those who heretofore have owed their existence to mere chance.* Here we may still be hopeful : in the rearing of exceptional men (No. 199).

And, lastly, let the reader note this :

Educate educators ! But the first educators must educate themselves ! *And it is for these that I write* (No. 287).

CHAPTER VI

"HUMAN"—"THE DAWN OF DAY"—"THE JOYFUL WISDOM"

BEYOND what has been said regarding *Human, All-too-Human*, on pp. 29 and 30, these books call for little comment. The second part, which was originally published in two volumes as *Mixed Opinions and Apophthegms* and *The Traveller and his Shadow*, is simply a continuation of the first; and the two books may be regarded as a prelude to the views on morality expounded more fully in *The Dawn of Day* and *The Joyful Wisdom*. The 1400 odd aphorisms forming the two parts cannot be adequately condensed into a summary; and the following excerpts are merely characteristic examples of Nietzsche's thoughts at this period. He tells us in one of his prefaces, however, that some of the opinions expressed in the *Human, All-too-Human*, date back very far beyond their period of composition—in many cases the germs of them were forming in his mind even before he wrote *The Birth of Tragedy* and the *Thoughts out of Season*.

LOVE AND JUSTICE.—Why do we over-estimate Love to the disadvantage of Justice, and say the most beautiful things about it, as if it were something on a very much higher plane than the latter ? Is it not visibly more stupid than Justice ? Certainly ; but precisely for that reason all the pleasanter : it is blind, and possesses an abundant cornucopia, out of which it distributes its gifts to all, even if they do not deserve them, even if they express no thanks for them. It is as impartial as the rain, which, according to the Bible and experience, makes not only the unjust, but also occasionally the just, wet through to the skin (I, 69).

THE LIMITS OF PHILANTHROPY.—A man who has declared that another is an idiot and a bad companion is angry when the latter eventually proves himself to be otherwise (I, 90).

THE SINLESSNESS OF MAN.—If it is understood how " sin came into the world," namely, through errors of reason by which men held one another—even the single individual held himself—to be much blacker and much worse than was actually the case, the whole sensation will be much lightened, and man and the world will appear in a blaze of innocence which it will do one good to contemplate. In the midst of Nature man is always the child *per se*. This child sometimes has a heavy and terrifying dream, but when it opens its eyes it always finds itself back again in Paradise (I, 124).

AUTHORS' PARADOXES.—The so-called paradoxes of an author to which a reader objects are often not in the author's book at all; but in the reader's head (I, 185).

THINKERS AS STYLISTS.—Most thinkers write badly, because they communicate not only their thoughts, but also the thinking of them (I, 188).

JUSTICE AGAINST THE COMING GOD.—When the entire history of culture unfolds itself to our gaze, as a comparison of evil and noble, of true and false ideas, and we feel almost seasick at the sight of these tumultuous waves, we then understand what comfort resides in the conception of a *coming God*. This Deity is unveiled ever more and more throughout the changes and fortunes of mankind, it is not all blind mechanism, a senseless and aimless confusion of forces. The deification of the process of being is a metaphysical outlook, seen as from a lighthouse overlooking the sea of history, in which an all-too-historical generation of scholars found their comfort. This must not arouse anger, however erroneous this view may be. Only those who, like Schopenhauer, deny development, also feel none of the misery of this historical wave, and therefore, because they know nothing of the coming God and the need of his protection, they should in justice withhold their scorn (I, 238).

A SIGN OF ESTRANGEMENT.—The surest sign of the estrangement of two persons is when they both say something ironical to each other and neither of them feels the irony (I, 331).

DIFFERENT SIGHS.—Some husbands have sighed over the elopement of their wives: the greater number, however, have sighed because nobody would elope with theirs (I, 388).

WAR.—Against war it may be said that it makes the victors stupid and the vanquished revengeful. In favour of war it may be said that it barbarises in both its above-named results and thereby renders more natural: it is the sleep, or the winter period, of culture; man emerges from it with greater strength for good and for evil (I, 444).

ENVY AND JEALOUSY.—Envy and Jealousy are the private parts of the human soul. The comparison may perhaps be carried further (I, 503).

TRUTH AS CIRCE.—Error has made animals into men; is Truth perhaps capable of turning man back again into an animal? (I, 519).

DEBAUCHERY.—The mother of debauchery is not joy; but the lack of joy (II, *Mixed Opinions*, 77).

THE CIRCLE MUST BE CLOSED.—Whoever has followed a philosophy or an art to the end of its career, and even beyond this end, will understand from his own inner knowledge why its surviving masters and prophets turn away from it disdainfully to follow a new path. The circle must indeed be closed—but the single individual, even if he be the greatest of all, sits firmly at a point of the periphery with an expression of obstinate doggedness, as if the circle were never to be closed (*ib.*, 125).

STANDING ON ONE'S HEAD.—When we turn truth upside down and stand it on its head, we do not see, as a rule, that our own head, too, is not situated where it ought to be (*ib.*, 208).

DISGUST FOR TRUTH.—It is in the nature of women to be disgusted with all truths (so far as they concern man, love, child, society, aim in life), and to try to revenge themselves on any one who opens their eyes (*ib.*, 286).

WHAT IS GENIUS ?—To aspire to a high aim, *and* the means thereto (*ib.*, 378).

EQUITY.—Equity is a development of justice arising among those who do not offend against equality in the community : it applies to cases where there is no law already laid down, or where that subtle sense of balance comes into play, taking the past and future into its consideration, and having for motto : " Do as you would be done by." *Aequum* simply means " *It conforms to our equality :* equity smooths down our little differences to an apparent equality, and would have us pardon many things which we *need not*" (II, *Traveller*, 32).

THE PERSECUTOR OF GOD.—St. Paul thought out the notion, and Calvin developed it: from time immemorial an incalculable number of men have been adjudged to eternal damnation ; and this beautiful, universal plan has been elaborated in this way so that the glory of God might be manifested in it: heaven and hell and man must exist, then—to satisfy God's vanity ! What a cruel and insatiable vanity must have arisen in the soul of the first man, or the second, who imagined that ! So Paul merely remained Saul—*the persecutor of God* (*ib.*, 85).

DRAMATIC SINGERS.—" Why does that beggar sing ? "—" Probably he doesn't know how to groan."—" He does well : but as for our dramatic singers, who groan because they don't know how to sing : do they also do well ? " (*ib.*, 162).

END AND GOAL.—Every end is not a goal. The end of melody is not its goal : nevertheless, if melody has not attained its end, it has not attained its goal. A symbol (*ib.*, 204).

THE WISDOM OF THE GREEKS.—Since the Greek will to conquer and master was an invincible trait of their nature, older and more original than their pride of and joy in equality, the Greek state sanctioned gymnastic and musical contests between equals, thus marking out an arena where this instinct could discharge itself without endangering the political order. When these contests degenerated, the Greek state was given up to civil wars and general disintegration (*ib.*, 226).

PREMISSES OF AN AGE OF MACHINERY.—The Press, machinery, railways, the telegraph, are premisses, from which no one has yet dared to draw the conclusion that will follow in a thousand years (*ib.*, 278).

FATE AND THE STOMACH.—A slice of bread and butter more or less in the stomach of a jockey may decide the success of races and bets, and hence the happiness or unhappiness of thousands of people. So long as the fate of peoples depends on diplomatists, the stomachs of diplomatists will always be a subject of patriotic anxiety. *Quousque tandem.* . . . (*ib.*, 291).

MAN!—What is the vanity of the vainest man compared with the vanity of the humblest man who, in Nature and in the world, considers himself as " man " ! (*ib.*, 304).

" With this book," writes Nietzsche, in the *Ecce Homo*,* referring to *The Dawn of Day*, " begins my campaign against current morality . . . that a reader should close the book with a rather timid chariness concerning everything that has hitherto been worshipped and honoured as ' morality ' is

* p. 83.

not in contradiction to the fact that no negative phrase is to be found in the work ; no sudden attack, no malignity."

Mrs. Foerster-Nietzsche tells us in her introduction to this volume * that her brother, during its preparation, devoted a great deal of time and attention to the study of political questions, particularly Socialism. " In this book," she writes, " he [Nietzsche] expressed as favourable an opinion as possible on such subjects, which did not, however, hinder him from adhering to his earlier formula, that the worth of a nation—yea, of all mankind—is seen in its highest specimens of men. Despite his personal good-will, therefore, my brother had perforce to be an enemy of social democracy, and especially of its leaders, not only on account of the ignobleness of their sentiments and aims, which were in opposition to everything mighty, beautiful, and cultured ; but also because, as he threw in their teeth, they made the masses discontented and unhappy : they aroused their eagerness for conditions, and consoled them with hopes, which were neither desirable nor attainable." Says Peter Gast † : " Nietzsche saw in democracy a clear sign of degeneration and, above all, of want of noble feelings and of conspicuous and directing master minds ; and it was his opinion that the design of correcting and improving the human race by

* *Werke*, Vol. V, xviii.
† *Ibid.*, xx.

beginning with men of the third and fourth order (instead of at the top), or of leading to a higher level by the emancipation of woman, was the most baleful aberration of judgment it was possible to conceive."

While the 575 aphorisms comprising *The Dawn of Day* can scarcely be called interdependent, it is hoped that the following selection may show the trend of Nietzsche's thoughts at this time.*

In this book we find some one who works in the bowels of the earth, tunnelling, digging, undermining. You can see him, always provided that you have eyes for such deep work—how he makes his way slowly, cautiously, gently but surely, without showing signs of the weariness which usually accompanies a long privation of light and air. You might even call him happy, despite his work in these deep regions. . . . No one comes to help him in his task : he must face everything quite alone : danger, bad luck, wickedness, foul weather. He goes his *own* way and, as is only right, meets with bitterness and occasional irritation because he does so : for instance, the knowledge that not even his friends can guess who he is and whither he is going, and that they ask themselves now and then : " Well ? Is he really moving at all ? Has he still a path before him ? " At that time

* The book appeared in 1881, the preface being added in 1886.

I had undertaken something which could not have been done by everybody : I went down into the deepest depths ; I tunnelled to the very bottom ; I started to investigate and unearth the old *faith* which for thousands of years we philosophers used to build on as the safest of all foundations—which we built on again and again although every previous structure fell in : I began to undermine our *faith* in *morals* (Preface, 1 and 2).

Morality has been from time immemorial well qualified in every branch of the art of persuading : even in our own time there is no orator who would not have recourse to it (just hearken to our anarchists, for instance : how morally they speak when they would fain convince ! Even in the end they call themselves " the good and the just.") (Preface, 3.)

We two—I and my book—are friends of the *lento*. I have not been a philologist in vain—perhaps I am still one : a teacher of slow reading, in other words. I even come to write slowly. At present it is not only my habit, but even my fantasy—a perverse fantasy, maybe—to write nothing but what will drive to despair every one who is " in a hurry." For Philology is that venerable art which exacts from its followers one thing above all—to step to one side, to leave themselves spare moments, to grow silent, to become slow—the leisurely art of the goldsmith applied to language : an art which

has to carry out slow, fine work, and attains
nothing if not *lento*. For this very reason
Philology is now more desirable than ever before ; for this very reason it is the highest
attraction and incitement in an age of " work " :
that is to say, of haste, of unseemly and immoderate hurry-skurry, which is intent upon
" getting things done " at once, even every
book, whether old or new. It itself, perhaps,
will not " get things done " so hurriedly : it
teaches how to read *well :* i.e. slowly, profoundly, attentively, prudently, with inner
thoughts, the mental doors ajar, with delicate
fingers and eyes. . . . My patient friends, this
book appeals only to perfect readers and
Philologists : *learn* to read me well ! (Preface, 5).

THE NEW EDUCATION OF MANKIND.—Help,
all ye who are well disposed and willing to
assist, lend your aid in the endeavour to do away
with that conception of punishment which has
swept over the whole world ! No weed more
harmful than this ! It is not only to the consequences of our actions that this conception has
been applied—and how horrible and senseless
it is to confuse cause and effect with cause and
punishment !—but worse has followed : the
pure accidentality of events has been robbed of
its innocence by this execrable manner of inter-
preting the conception of punishment. Yea,
they have even pushed their folly to such ex-

tremes that they would have us look upon existence itself as a punishment—from which it would appear that the education of mankind has hitherto been confided to fantastic gaolers and hangmen (No. 13).

The means of becoming a medicine-man among the Indians, a saint among Christians of the Middle Ages, an Angekok among Greenlanders, a Pagee among Brazilians, are the same in essence : senseless fasting, continual abstention from sexual intercourse, isolation in a wilderness, ascending a mountain or a pillar, or "sitting on an aged willow that looks out upon a lake," and thinking of absolutely nothing but what may give rise to ecstasy or mental derangements. Who would dare to glance at the desert of the bitterest and most superfluous agonies of spirit, in which probably the most productive men of all ages have pined away ? (No. 14).

THE BROKEN-HEARTED ONES.—Christianity has the instinct of a hunter for finding out all those who may by hook or by crook be driven to despair—only a very small number of men can be treated in this way. Pascal made an attempt to find out whether it was not possible, with the help of the very subtlest knowledge, to lead everybody into despair : he failed, to his second despair (No. 64).

NEITHER EUROPEAN NOR NOBLE.—There is something oriental and feminine in Christianity, and this is shown in the thought, " Whom the Lord loveth, He chasteneth " ; for women in the Orient consider castigations and the strict seclusion of their person from the world as a sign of their husbands' love, and complain if these signs of love cease (No. 75).

THE PHILOLOGY OF CHRISTIANITY.—How little Christianity cultivates the sense of honesty and fair dealing can be inferred from the character of the writings of its learned men. They set out their conjectures as if they were dogmas, and are but seldom at a disadvantage in regard to the interpretation of a text of scripture. Their continual cry is : " I am right, for it is written " —and then follows an explanation so shameless and capricious that a philologist, when he hears it, must stand stock still between anger and laughter, asking himself again and again : Is it possible ? Is it honest ? Is it even decent ? (No. 84).

A MALCONTENT.—He is one of the old " warriors " : angry with civilisation because he believes that its object is to make all good things—honour, rewards, fair women—accessible even to cowards (No. 154).

DIGNITY AND TIMIDITY.—Ceremonies, official robes and court dresses, grave countenances, solemn aspects, the slow pace, involved speech—everything, in short, known as dignity—are all pretences adopted by those who are timid at heart : they wish to make themselves feared (themselves or the things they represent). Original and fearlessly-minded men, who naturally inspire others with awe, have no need of dignity and ceremonies : they bring into repute — or, better, into ill - repute — honesty and straightforward words and deeds, as characteristics of self-confident arrogance (No. 220).

Who, then, is ever alone ! The faint-hearted wretch does not know what loneliness is : an enemy of mankind is always prowling in his tracks. Oh, for the man who could give us the history of that noble feeling of loneliness ! (No. 249).

THE TRANSFORMED BEING.—Now he becomes virtuous ; but only for the sake of hurting others by being so. Don't pay so much attention to him (No. 275).

PERNICIOUS.—A young man can be most surely corrupted when he is taught to value the like-minded more highly than the differently-minded (No. 297).

WEAK SECTS.—Those sects which feel that they will always remain weak hunt up a few intelligent individual adherents, wishing to make up in quality what they lack in quantity. This gives rise to no little danger for intelligent minds (No. 316).

WOMEN-HATERS.—" Woman is the enemy." The man who speaks to men in this way reveals an uncontrollable lust, which hates not only itself but also its means (No. 346).

COURAGE AND POLITICAL PARTIES.—The poor sheep say to their shepherd : " Lead the way, and we shall never lack courage to follow you." The poor shepherd, however, thinks : " Only follow me always, and I shall never lack the courage to lead " (No. 419).

CASTING ONE'S SKIN.—The snake that cannot cast its skin perishes. So, too, with those minds which are prevented from changing their views : they cease to be minds (No. 573).

Never forget : the higher we soar the smaller we appear to those who cannot fly (No. 574).

The fruits of Nietzsche's study of political questions are found in a series of notes jotted down while he was preparing the *Dawn*, and published posthumously by Mrs. Foerster-Nietzsche. They cover many pages, and contain a bitter indictment of Socialistic doctrines. The following is his long introductory form of objection :

FIRSTLY. As onlookers we deceive ourselves in regard to the sufferings and privations of the lower classes, for we involuntarily set up our own feelings as a standard, as if we ourselves, with our own brains, which are so excitable and capable of suffering, were in the place of such people. As a matter of fact, sufferings and privations increase with the increase of the culture of the individual : the lower orders are the most stupid ; to " better their lot " means simply to render them more capable of suffering.*

SECONDLY. If our eyes are not set upon the well-being of the individual, but upon the aims of mankind, it is very questionable whether, under the systematic state of things demanded by Socialism, great men *can* actually arise similar to those we have had from the un-systematic societies of the past. Probably the great man and the great work grow up only in the freedom of the wilderness. Mankind has no aims other than the production of great men and great works.†

THIRDLY. Since a great deal of hard, dirty work has to be done, some men must be brought up to undertake such work, so far as it cannot be done by machinery. If the need, and the improvement, of higher education is felt among the working classes, they can no longer carry out their coarse duties without disproportionate suffering. A workman developed by education aims at having some leisure time to himself— he does not want his work to be made lighter, but he wishes to be relieved from it altogether ; he would like to turn it over to some one else.

---

* No one valued or respected mediocrity more than Nietzsche—*in its proper place.* " Let mediocrity alone ! " he says in *The Will to Power* (Aph. 893), " a hatred of mediocrity is unworthy of a true philosopher."

† " Civilisation is always the work of the few, if not of one man." Dr. Oscar Levy in *The Revival of Aristocracy*, Ch. VII.

It might be that these wishes could be gratified by huge importations of barbaric tribes from Asia or Africa, so that the civilised world could be continually occupied in making the un-civilised world serviceable to it, and in this way non-culture would come to be recognised as a necessary qualification for the lower kinds of labour. In European countries, indeed, the culture of workman and employer is so closely identified that the further pretensions of ex-hausting mechanical labour raise a feeling of indignation.

FOURTHLY. If we fully understand how the sense of justice and equality has arisen, we must contradict the Socialists when they make equality one of their own principles. In the state of Nature the saying does not apply : " What is right for one is just for another " ; force alone decides. It is only when these advocates of the new state of society form up in line of battle before the defenders of the old order and find their opponents weaker or stronger, as the case may be, that an agreement can be reached, and the equity *must be based upon* this agreement. There are no " rights of man."

FIFTHLY. When a low-grade workman says to his employer, " You don't deserve your happi-ness," he is quite right ; but the inference he draws from this statement is false : no one deserves his happiness ; no one his unhappiness.

SIXTHLY. Happiness will not be increased on earth by merely changing the form of our institutions ; but only by getting rid of gloomy, feeble, speculative, bilious temperaments. Anything merely exterior does little or no good in this direction. And as Socialists mostly possess the loathsome kind of temperaments I have referred to above, they would inevitably diminish happiness on earth in any circumstances, even if it fell to their lot to establish a new order of society.

SEVENTHLY. It is only within the limits of tradition, fixed customs, and moderation, that ease and comfort can be found on earth : the Socialists, however, are allied to those forces which tend towards the breaking-up of tradition, fixed customs, and moderation ; and they have as yet shown no signs of new creative elements.

EIGHTHLY. The best thing that follows in the train of Socialism is the agitation and excitement which it gives rise to in all classes : it *nourishes* mankind, and brings into the lowest ranks of society a species of practico-philosophical speech. To this extent it is a source of spiritual strength.

The *Joyful Wisdom* was written at a time when Nietzsche was beginning to recover from his stomach trouble and various minor illness, hence perhaps the exuberance, unusual even for Nietzsche, of some of its pages. As usual, the work consists of a series of aphorisms, numbering nearly four hundred, together with a few pieces of poetry. Like most of Nietzsche's works, it does not lend itself readily to being put before the reader in an abridged form ; for there is no continuous connection between the various aphorisms. Those that follow are merely specimens of the shorter ones, sufficiently interesting in themselves, and giving as clear a perception of the work as can be conveyed in a summary.

ANCIENT PRIDE.—We cannot feel the ancient shade of distinction, because we can form no conception of the slave of antiquity. Between his own superiority and the lowest inferiority of the slave, a Greek of noble birth felt so many intermediate stages, and such a sense of distance, that he could scarcely see the slave clearly : even Plato did not see him in his entirety. It is different with us, accustomed as we are to the *doctrine* of the equality of mankind, if not indeed to this very equality itself. An individual whose time and energy are at the disposal of some one else, and who never has any leisure hours for himself—our eyes would see nothing contemptible in all this ; for there is but too much of this slavish disposition in every one of us, according to our social duties and place in society, both of which are entirely different from those of the ancients. The Greek philosopher went through life with the secret feeling that he had far more slaves than people thought—i.e. that every one was a slave who was not a philosopher. His pride increased when he reflected that even the mighty ones of the earth could be numbered among his slaves. Even this pride itself is something strange and impossible to us : even when using the word "slave" as a simile we cannot conceive all it represents (No. 18).

WHAT MEANS LIFE ?—To live : that means, to thrust away from us everything that wants to die ; to live : that means, to be cruel and inexorable towards everything that grows old and weak within ourselves (and not only within ourselves). To live, then, means : that we should have no pity for those who are dying, wretched or old ? To be murderers all the time ? And yet old Moses said : "Thou shalt not kill !" (No. 26).

They took a youth to a wise man and said : "Look ; here is a young fellow who is being ruined by women." The wise man shook his head, and smiled. "It is the men," he answered, "who ruin and corrupt the women ; and everything in which women are found wanting should be expiated and rectified by men— for man has made for himself an image of woman, and woman forms herself after that image." "You show yourself too well disposed towards women," said a man in the crowd ;

" you don't know them ! " The wise man answered : " The characteristic of man is will; that of woman is willingness. Such is the law of the sexes ; a hard law for women, truly ! All human beings are innocent of their existence ; but women are doubly innocent : how much sweetness and gentleness could we not show towards them ! " " Sweetness ! Gentleness ! " cried another of the crowd. " Women must be brought up better than that ! " " Nay, but men must be brought up better," said the wise man, and beckoned to the young man to follow him. But the latter did not (No. 68).

. . . In a word, we can never be sufficiently indulgent where women are concerned (No. 71, *ad fin*).

NEW BATTLES.—For whole centuries after Buddha's death they exhibited his shade in a cave—a huge, gruesome shade. God is dead : but, after the manner of men, there will probably be caves for thousands of years where his shade will be on view. And we—well, we must overcome his shade also ! (No. 108).

GOD'S NEEDS.—" God himself cannot subsist without wise men," said Luther, and justly ; but : " Still less can God subsist without madmen "—honest Luther didn't say that ! (No. 129).

TOO ORIENTAL.—What ? A God who loves men, *provided that* they believe in him, and who overwhelms with menaces and frowns those who put no faith in this love ! What ! A love with saving clauses and reservations is put forward as the sentiment of an omnipotent deity ! A love which has not even mastered the feeling of honour and enraged vengeance ! How oriental is all this ! " If I do love you, what does it matter to you ? "—this is an adequate criticism of all Christianity (No. 141).

Our thoughts are the shadows of our feelings : always more obscure, more empty, and more simple than they (No. 179).

A LAUGHING MATTER.—Look ! Look ! He is running *away* from men—but they are running after him, because he is running *in front of* them—so great is their herd-instinct ! (No. 195).

LIBERALITY.—Liberality in rich men is only a kind of shyness (No. 199).

THE ROAD TO HAPPINESS.—A wise man asked a fool where the way to happiness lay. The latter immediately replied, as if some one had merely inquired the way to the next town : " Admire yourself, and live in the street." " Stop ! " cried the wise man, " you ask too much ; it is enough to admire one's self." The fool answered : " But how can one keep on admiring without continually despising ? " (No. 213).

FORBEARANCE.—Fathers and sons get on much better together than mothers and daughters (No. 221).

PRAISE IN THE CHOICE.—The artist chooses

his subjects : that is his way of praising them (No. 245).

BOOKS.—Of what use is a book which does not carry us far above all books ? (No. 248).

ORIGINALITY.—What is originality ? To *see* something which is as yet without a name, and which cannot yet be named, although it lies before all eyes. As men are now constituted, they cannot see things until they hear them named. Original men have generally been name-givers (No. 261).

WHAT WE DO.—What we do is never understood—it is merely praised or blamed (No. 264).

HIGH AIMS.—With a high aim in view one is superior even to justice itself, not only to one's actions and judges (No. 267).

FAITH IN ONE'S SELF.—Generally speaking, only a few men have faith in themselves ;—and of this small number two or three are born with this faith, like a useful blindness, as it were, or a partial clouding of their mind—(what a sight, if they could only *see into themselves* !). The others must begin to acquire this faith : everything good, firm, and great that they do is from the first an argument with the sceptic who dwells within them : their task to convince and persuade *him*, and for this something very like genius is necessary. They are the great self-*un*satisfied ones (No. 284).

HOW EACH SEX IS PREJUDICED IN REGARD TO LOVE.—In spite of every concession I am ready to make to monogamic prejudices, I will never admit that we can speak of *equal* rights in love for man or woman : such rights do not exist. The fact is, a man and a woman take different meanings out of the word " love," and it is one of the conditions of love in both sexes that the one does *not* suppose that the same feeling exists in the other. What a woman understands by " love " is clear enough : a complete surrendering (not merely devotion) of her body and soul, without restrictions or saving clauses—rather looking on a conditional surrender with shame and horror. In the absence of such conditions, her love is a true *faith :* a woman has no other faith. A man, when he loves a woman, exacts this love from her, and is thus far removed from the feminine conception of love : if, however, it is contended that there are men who do not exact this complete surrender on the part of the woman—well, such men are : not men ! A man who loves like a woman becomes thereby a slave : on the other hand, a woman who loves like a woman becomes a more *complete* woman. A woman's passion, with her complete abandonment of her own rights, takes it exactly for granted that a similar feeling, a similar will to renounce, does *not* exist in her partner : for, if both renounced themselves out of love for each other, what would be the consequences ?—I do not know—perhaps a mere vacuum.—A woman wishes to be taken,

accepted, as property ; she wishes to be merged
into the conception of "property," of "possession " : she therefore desires some one who
takes, who does not give and abandon himself ;
but who on the contrary wishes to enrich—and
must enrich—his "ego" by the addition of
power, happiness, belief, and as such a woman
gives herself up to him. The woman gives, the
man takes—and it is my opinion that this
natural contrast will never be superseded,
whether by social contracts or the desire to
establish justice and equality between the
sexes : however desirable one may think it to
get rid of the sight of everything hard, terrible,
enigmatic, and immoral in this antagonism.
For love, complete and great, in all its entirety,
is Nature, and as such is "immoral" for all
eternity. Hence *fidelity* is comprised in a
woman's love, out of the definition of which it
follows : in a man, love *may* sometimes include
fidelity, whether as gratitude or idiosyncrasy of
taste and the so-called "elective affinity" * ;
but it forms no part of the *nature* of his love—
and even then it plays such a minor rôle that we
may speak with more justice of a natural
antinomy between love and fidelity in man :
which love is a will to possess, and *not* a renouncing and abandonment : but this will to
possess always finishes by actually *possessing*.

* Referring to Goethe's novel, *Die Wahlverwandtschaften*,
translated under the title *The Elective Affinities*.

In fact, it is the subtle and jealous desire of man, who seldom and tardily admits this " posses- sion," which enables his love to endure—it is possible, indeed, that his love increases after the abandonment—the man is unwilling to admit that the woman has nothing more to " abandon " to him (No. 263).

WE HOMELESS ONES.—Among the Europeans of to-day, there is no want of those who may justly, in a distinctive and honourable sense, be called Homeless Ones, and it is at their feet particularly that I lay the treasure of my secret wisdom, my *gaya scienza*. For their fate is hard, their hope uncertain, it is quite a work of art to invent a consolation for them : but to what end ! We children of the future, how *could* we feel at home to-day ! For we are hostile to every ideal which would enable us to feel at home in this frail, dilapidated period of transition : and as regards its " realities," we do not believe they will last. The ice, which can still bear a weight, has become very thin ; a thawing wind blows : we ourselves, we homeless ones, aid in breaking the ice and other too thin " realities." We " conserve " nothing, we would return to no past epoch ; we are by no means " liberal " ; we do not labour for " progress " ; we have no need to stop our ears to the Sirens of the future chanting in the market-place. What they are singing : " Equal Rights ! " " Free Society ! " " No more masters or servants ! "—all this has no attraction

for us ! In fine, we do not think it at all desirable that the kingdom of justice and harmony
should be established on earth (for in every case
this would mean the reign of the most profound
mediocrity and Chinaism) ; we delight in all
those that, like ourselves, love danger, war, and
adventure, who will not agree to compromises
and adaptations, conciliations and reconciliations ; we reckon ourselves among the conquerors ; we reflect upon the necessity for a new
order of things and also of a new form of slavery
—since a new form of slavery is always necessary
for the strengthening and elevation of the type
man—am I not right ? It follows from all this
that we do not feel quite at home in an age
which boasts of being the most humane, gentle,
and just on which the sun has ever shone. It
is sad enough that these fine words contain the
suggestion that our inward and most secret
thoughts are ugly ! that we should see in them
only the expression—and the masquerade—of
profound weakness, fatigue, old age, diminishing
strength ! What do we care for the embellishment with which a sick man decks out his weakness ! . . . We are no humanitarians ; we
should never allow ourselves to speak of our
" love of humanity." . . . Humanity ! was
there ever a more disgusting old woman among
all disgusting old women ! . . . In a word—and
it shall be our word of honour—we are *Good
Europeans*, the heirs of Europe, rich and over-

loaded, but likewise rich in obligations, the heirs of millenniums of European thought : and as such we have outgrown Christianity, which we do not look on with a friendly eye—and that is precisely why we have outgrown it ; because our ancestors were out-and-out Christians of unequalled loyalty, who would have given up everything for their faith : life and property, rank and country. We—do the same. Why ? For our unbelief ? For every kind of unbelief ? Nay ; ye know that much better, my friends ! The hidden Yea in you is stronger than all the Nays and Perhapses of which Ye and your time are suffering, and when ye feel obliged to set sail, ye wanderers, ye also are forced to do so by—a *faith !* (No. 377).

CHAPTER VII

THE doctrine of the Eternal Recurrence is an important part of Nietzsche's teaching, although its essential feature is to be found in the far-off philosophers of ancient India, whence it gradually spread to Egypt and Greece. It is evident from Nietzsche's notes and his sister's testimony, however, that he thought it out himself in a somewhat altered form. If we love life, we must not only accept it gladly with all its joys and sorrows ; we must be prepared to accept it scores and hundreds of times. The earth was gradually formed out of a fortuitous concourse of atoms ; it will continue in its present shape for ages to come ; we shall enter the glacial period about which scientists have warned us ; a little while, and the planets will be shivered into infinite fragments ; and again, a little while, and the earth will be formed once more, man gradually being evolved from the lower animals as formerly.

When Nietzsche conceived this doctrine he was just recovering from his illnesses and beginning to write the *Joyful Wisdom*. His vitality was at its zenith, and he could cry exultantly in the first pages of the new book: " No ! Life has not disappointed me ! " But later on the horror of this teaching came to him. He was now formulating the doctrine of the superman in the *Zarathustra*, to which work the *Joyful Wisdom* may be considered as a kind of prelude. But why should the superman be aimed at—how could races be encouraged to rear him—if he were to endure for only a tiny space in the long span of time ? And then the tiring battle would begin all over again : the inclemency of nature would once more have to be overcome; once more an amorphous, asexual body would develop into a lower primate and the lower primate into civilised man ; once again Homer would sing the Trojan war, and once again, centuries after his death, Philistines and bookworms would split his works into fragments ; once again Nietzsche himself would be re-born and would fight the same dreadful battle with the Philistines of Europe, tormented by Christianity and the passing phases of other evanescent religions.

Nietzsche's mind was thus divided between the doctrine of the eternal—i.e. constantly recurring—life, and the thought of the weary, continual struggle. For while the ancient philosophers merely looked for the constant recurrence of the world, Nietzsche accepted the constant recurrence of the world together with every man, woman, and animal, and every event, that had appeared on it millions of years before. How far the stupendous weight of this thought influenced his madness cannot yet be definitely known ; but I have no doubt that it did influence the fourth part of *Zarathustra*. The strange, grotesque poetry has new meanings for those who see in it much more than is actually written there—the brain of the philosopher seems to be bowed down under the weight of a huge thought, from which, in every line, we see him struggling to free himself. But few school philosophers, comfortably established professors, and such men, have any notion of the weight of thoughts : can it be said, indeed, that such men have thoughts at all ? *Nuances* of opinion, perhaps, prejudices, certainly ; but —thoughts ? Use rather their own favourite expression—a much less noble term—" Contributions to the Study of——"

Nietzsche's thoughts, then, press heavily upon his mind ; and an analogy may be suggested. What he suffered mentally, other men have suffered physically under the ancient form of punishment by pressing to death, known somewhat naïvely as *peine forte et dure*. Nathaniel Hawes, lying in Newgate gaol under two hundredweight of iron chains, bolts, and bars, suffered even less physically than Nietzsche did mentally under the weight of the idea of the Eternal Recurrence as he conceived it.

This idea came to him, as he notes in the *Ecce Homo*, when he was " wandering through the woods beside the lake of Silvaplana at Sils-Maria." He was, he tells us, " six thousand feet above the level of the sea, and infinitely higher above his contemporaries and all human events." Then came the *Joyful Wisdom*, followed by the book we have now to consider, *Thus Spake Zarathustra*.

The more liberal side of Protestantism, particularly in Germany, as Lichtenberger has remarked,* does not try to restrain its followers from scientific investigations ; but it believes that all science can be reconciled with the Bible. Hence we find Nietzsche early in life fully determined to make the search for truth his great aim, not realising at the time, of course, that a more extended knowledge of the sciences must inevitably undermine his belief in Christianity. At Pforta, when he was fifteen years old, we find him drawing up a long list of special sciences which he wishes to make himself master of, adding at the end of the list : " And, above all, *Religion*, the firm basis of all knowledge." Very gradually, however, he saw that Christianity and science were irreconcilable. Shortly after his confirmation he says that " all Christianity rests on hypotheses ; the existence of

* *La Philosophie de Friedrich Nietzsche*, p. 17.

God, immortality, the authority of the Bible, inspiration, etc., will always be problems. I have tried to deny all this ; but after one destroys one must construct ! And even destroying seems easier than it really is." * And then he goes on to remark how the scientist is influenced during a great part of his life by the impressions of his childhood, his teachers, and his religious surroundings. When Nietzsche was about twenty-one years of age, he saw that truth did not lie in Christianity : and thus he abandoned the faith of his childhood and youth without a struggle. His ideals lay elsewhere : truth ; the elevation of the type man.

After this came his studies at Leipzig, his discovery of Schopenhauer, his increased knowledge of the difficulties of the task that lay before him, his endeavour to raise Philology to a higher status, and finally his resignation of his professorship and his campaign against almost everything held sacred by his contemporaries : a campaign, however, conducted on Nietzsche's part with a sincere desire to follow truth : " Truth at any cost, no matter how horrible and dreadful to look upon." Nietzsche's illnesses, together with his campaign of destruction, absorbed all his energies for several years, and it was only towards the end of his conscient life that he was able to put his early conception of the Superman into words, and to show the

* *Leben*, I, 314 foll.

world what substitute he had to offer for Christianity. For eternal life hereafter he substituted the Eternal Recurrence ; for God he substituted the Superman.

"Nietzsche is like a pitiless doctor of souls," writes Lichtenberger ; "the treatment he prescribes for his patients is rigorous and dangerous to follow, but strengthening. He has no consolation for those who come to him to tell of their sufferings ; he lets their wounds go on bleeding ; but he gradually hardens them to pain : he cures his patients radically—or else kills them." * He looked upon Europe as degenerate ; and, with a courage which calls for our highest admiration, he dared to attack all the causes which, in his opinion, contributed to that degeneracy. His constructive genius is shown, but only partly, in the *Joyful Wisdom*, but it is shown us almost in its entirety in the *Zarathustra* and *Beyond Good and Evil*. He cast the *Zarathustra* in the mould of poetic prose : he wished to wear a mask and hide his innermost thoughts from the vulgar rabble. "I will have railings round my thoughts," he says in section 54 of this work, "and even round my words, lest swine and enthusiasts break into my gardens." Words were symbols ; but as he pointed out in one of the *Thoughts out of Season*, they were like coins which had become debased by continuous passing from hand to

* *La Philosophie de Friedrich Nietzsche*, p. 182.

hand. His constructive maxims are put into
the mouth of Zarathustra (Zoroaster), as he
was the only prophet of antiquity who sincerely
sought truth ; but their poetical mould in-
tentionally renders them obscure. The extracts
from *Zarathustra* which follow cannot do more
than give glimpses of certain portions of the
work ; for in order to understand it thoroughly,
every line of it must be pondered over with more
than ordinary care. It is well to bear in mind
that Nietzsche was now firmly convinced that
the motive force in man was not Schopenhauer's
" Will to Live " ; but the higher and nobler
" Will to Power."

Again, we must remember that, intermingled
with Zarathustra's philosophy, there are scores
of allusions to Nietzsche's own past life : his
ideals, his friendships, his battles, his joys, his
sorrows, his disappointments—all are before
us in this book. Out of several commentaries
published on this work alone, that of Mr. Ludovici * is the best and most concise ; but this
modern Bible will necessarily be judged from
many different points of view. For example,
when the first part was issued, many readers
admired it for the elegance of its style ; for in
it Nietzsche shows his supreme command over
his own language. It is somewhat amusing to

* All the allusions are explained in this commentary,
which is affixed to the translation of *Zarathustra* in Dr.
Levy's English edition.

recall that, in connection with this first part, Nietzsche had some difficulty with his publisher. It was held back for three months, because five hundred thousand copies of a Sunday-school hymn-book had to be sent out first! What Nietzsche's thoughts were when this information was conveyed to him we unfortunately do not know. At the end of this period the work was held over for several weeks, because an anti-Semitic pamphlet was in the printer's hands. This was too much; and Nietzsche's next communication to his easy-going publisher caused the work to be issued without loss of time.

When Zarathustra was thirty years old he left his home and the lake of his home, and went into the mountains. There he enjoyed his spirit and his solitude, and for ten years did not weary of it. But at last his heart changed —and, rising one morning with the rosy dawn, he went before the sun, and spake thus unto it:

Thou great star! What would be thy happiness if thou hadst not those for whom thou shinest! . . . Lo! I am weary of my wisdom, like the bee that hath gathered too much honey; I need hands outstretched to take it. . . . Like thee must I go down, as men say, to whom I shall descend. Lo! this cup is again going to empty itself, and Zarathustra is again going to be a man (Prologue, 1).

Zarathustra went down the mountain alone,
no one meeting him. When he entered the
forest, however, there suddenly stood before
him an old man, who had left his holy cot to
seek roots. And thus spake the old man to
Zarathustra : "No stranger to me is this
wanderer : many years ago passed he by.
Zarathustra he was called ; but he hath
altered. . . ."

"And what doth the saint in the forest ? "
asked Zarathustra.

The saint answered : "I make hymns and
sing them ; and in making hymns I laugh
and weep and mumble : thus do I praise God.
With singing, weeping, laughing, and mumb-
ling do I praise the God who is my God. But
what dost thou bring us as a gift ? "

When Zarathustra had heard these words,
he bowed to the saint and said : "What should
I have to give thee ! Let me rather hurry
hence, lest I take aught away from thee ! "
And thus they parted from one another, the
old man and Zarathustra, laughing like school-
boys.

When Zarathustra was alone, however, he
said in his heart : "Could it be possible !
This old saint in the forest hath not yet heard
of it, that *God is dead !* " (Prologue, 2).

When Zarathustra arrived at the nearest
town which adjoineth the forest, he found
many people assembled in the market-place ;

for it had been announced that a rope-dancer would give a performance. And Zarathustra spake thus unto the people :

I teach you the Superman. Man is something to be surpassed. What have ye done to surpass man ?

All beings hitherto have created something beyond themselves : and ye want to be the ebb of that great tide, and would rather go back to the beast than surpass man ?

What is the ape to man ? A laughing-stock, a thing of shame. And just the same shall man be to the Superman : a laughing-stock, a thing of shame. Ye have made your way from worm to man, and much within you is still worm. Once were ye apes, and even yet man is more of an ape than many of the apes. . . .

Once blasphemy against God was the greatest blasphemy : but God died, and therewith also these blasphemers. To blaspheme the earth is now the dreadfullest sin, and to rate the heart of the unknowable higher than the meaning of the earth ! (Prologue, 3).

Man is a rope slung between animal and superman (Prologue, 4).

Three metamorphoses of the spirit do I designate to you : how the spirit becometh a camel, the camel a lion, and the lion at last a child. What is heavy ? so asketh the load-bearing spirit.; then kneeleth it down like the camel, and wanteth to be well laden. What is the heaviest thing, ye heroes? asketh the load-bearing spirit, that I may take it upon me and rejoice in my strength. . . .

But in the loneliest wilderness happeneth the second metamorphosis: here the spirit becometh a lion; freedom will it capture, and lordship in its own wilderness. Its last lord it here seeketh: hostile will it be to him, and to its last God; for victory will it struggle with the great dragon.

What is the great dragon which the spirit is no longer inclined to call Lord and God? "Thou Shalt" is the great dragon called. But the spirit of the lion saith, "I will." . . .

My brethren, wherefore is there need of the lion in the spirit? Why sufficeth not the beast of burden, which renounceth and is reverent? To create new values—that, even the lion cannot yet accomplish: but to create to itself freedom for new creating—that can the might of the lion do. To create itself freedom, and give a holy Nay even unto duty: for that, my brethren, there is need of the lion. . . . But tell me, my brethren, what can the child do, which even the lion could not do? Why hath the preying lion still to become a child?

Innocence is the child, and forgetfulness, a new beginning, a game, a self-rolling wheel, a first movement, a holy Yea.

Ay, for the game of creating, my brethren, there is needed a holy Yea unto life : its *own* will, willeth now the spirit, *his own* world winneth the world's outcast.

Three metamorphoses of the spirit have I designated to you : how the spirit became a camel, the camel a lion, and the lion at last a child.

Thus spake Zarathustra (chap. i).

The awakened one, the knowing one, saith : " Body am I entirely, and nothing more ; and soul is only the name of something in the body." The body is a big sagacity, a plurality with one sense, a war and a peace, a flock and a shepherd.

An instrument of thy body is also thy little sagacity, my brother, which thou callest " spirit " —a little instrument and plaything of thy big sagacity. " Ego," sayest thou, and art proud of that word. But the greater thing—in which thou art unwilling to believe—is thy body with its big sagacity ; it saith not " ego," but doth it.* . . . Behind thy thoughts and feelings, my brother, there is a mighty lord, an unknown sage—it is called Self ; it dwelleth in thy body, it is thy body.

There is more sagacity in thy body than in thy best wisdom. And who then knoweth why thy body requireth just thy best wisdom ?

* Compare *The Education of the Will*, by T. Sharper Knowlson, Ch. XI, also p. 88 foll.

Thy self laugheth at thine ego, and its proud prancings. " What are these prancings and flights of thought unto me ? " it saith to itself, " a byway to my purpose. I am the leading-string of the ego, and the prompter of its notions " (chap. iv).

I am a railing alongside the torrent : who-ever is able to grasp me may grasp me ! Your crutch, however, I am not (chap. vi).

Of all that is written, I love only what a person hath written with his blood. Write with blood, and thou wilt find that blood is spirit. . . . Once spirit was God, then it became man, and now it even becometh populace (chap. vii).

Your enemy shall ye seek ; your war shall ye wage, and for the sake of your thoughts ! And if your thoughts succumb, your upright-ness shall still shout triumph thereby !

Ye shall love peace as a means to new wars —and the short peace more than the long.

You I advise not to work, but to fight. You I advise not to peace, but to victory. Let your work be a fight, let your peace be a victory !

Ye say it is the good cause which halloweth even war ? I say unto you : it is the good war which halloweth every cause.

War and courage have done more things than charity. Not your sympathy, but your bravery, hath hitherto saved the victims.

Thus spake Zarathustra (chap. x).

Do I counsel you to slay your instincts ? I counsel you to innocence in your instincts.

Do I counsel you to chastity ? Chastity is a virtue with some, but with many almost a vice.

These are continent, to be sure : but doggish lust looketh enviously out of all that they do. . . .

To whom chastity is difficult, it is to be dissuaded : lest it become the road to hell— to filth and lust of soul (chap. xiii).

Everything in woman is a riddle, and everything in woman hath one solution : it is called pregnancy. Man is for woman a means : the purpose is always the child.

Two different things wanteth the true man : danger and diversion. Therefore wanteth he woman, as the most dangerous plaything.

Man shall be trained for war and woman for the recreation of the warrior : all else is folly. . . .

Thou goest to woman ? Don't forget thy whip ! (chap. xviii).

Careful, have I found all buyers, and all of them have astute eyes. But even the astutest of them buyeth his wife in a sack (chap. xx).

Die at the right time : so teacheth Zarathustra. . . .

Verily, too early died that Hebrew whom the preachers of slow death honour : and to many hath it proved a calamity that he died too early. As yet had he known only tears, and the melancholy of the Hebrews, together with the hatred of the good and the just—the Hebrew Jesus : then he was seized with the longing for death.

Had he but remained in the wilderness, and far from the good and the just ! Then, perhaps, would he have learned to live, and love the earth—and laughter also !

Believe it, my brethren ! He died too early ; he himself would have disavowed his doctrine had he attained to my age ! Noble enough was he to disavow ! (chap. xxi).

Tell me, my brother, what do we think bad, and worst of all ? Is it not *degeneration ?* —And we always suspect degeneration when the bestowing soul is lacking. Upward goeth our course from genera to super-genera. But a horror to us is the degenerating sense, which saith : " All for myself " (chap. xxii).

Dead are all Gods : now we will that Super-man live.—Thus spake Zarathustra (chap. xxii).

Lo, this is the tarantula's den ! Wouldst thou see the tarantula itself ? Here hangeth its web : touch this, so that it tremble.

There cometh the tarantula willingly : Welcome, tarantula ! * Black on thy back is thy triangle and symbol ; and I know also what is in thy soul.

Revenge is in thy soul : wherever thou

* i.e., the Socialist or Democrat.

bitest, there ariseth the black scab; with revenge, thy poison maketh the soul giddy!

Thus do I speak unto you in parable, ye who make the soul giddy, ye preachers of *equality!* Tarantulas are ye unto me, and secretly revengeful ones! . . .

In all their lamentations soundeth vengeance, in all their eulogies is maleficence; and being judge seemeth to them bliss. . . . And when they call themselves the good and the just, forget not, that for them to be Pharisees, nothing is lacking but—power! (chap. xxix).

Unspoken and unrealised hath my highest hope remained! And there have perished for me all the visions and consolations of my youth!

How did I ever bear it? How did I survive and surmount such wounds? How did my soul rise again out of those sepulchres?

Yea, something invulnerable, unburiable is with me, something that would rend rocks asunder: it is called my *Will*. Silently doth it proceed, and unchanged throughout the years (chap. xxxiii).

Wherever I found a living thing, there found I Will to Power; and even in the will of the servant found I the will to be master.

That to the stronger the weaker shall serve —thereto persuadeth he whose will would be master over a still weaker one. That delight alone he is unwilling to forgo.

And as the lesser surrendereth himself to the greater so that he may have delight and power over the least of all, so doth even the greatest surrender himself, and staketh—life, for the sake of power (chap. xxxiv).

For men are *not* equal : so speaketh justice. And what I will, *they* may not will !

Thus spake Zarathustra (chap. xxxviii).

The earth hath a skin ; and this skin hath diseases. One of these diseases, for example, is called man (chap. xl).

" Cripples " is Zarathustra's name for the specialists, those who develop one pet subject to the exclusion of all else.

It is the smallest thing unto me since I have been among man, to see one person lacking an eye, another an ear, and a third a leg, and that others have lost the tongue, or the nose, or the head.

I see, and have seen worse things, and divers things so hideous, that I should neither like to speak of all matters, nor even to keep silent about some of them : namely, men who lack everything, except that they have too much of one thing—men who are nothing more than a big eye, or a big mouth, or something else big,—reversed cripples, I call such men.

And when I came out of my solitude, and for the first time passed over this bridge, then I could not trust mine eyes, but looked again

and again, and said at last : " That is an ear !
An ear as big as a man ! " I looked still more
attentively—and actually there did move
under the ear something that was pitiably
small and poor and slim. And in truth this
immense ear was perched upon a small, slender
stalk—the stalk, however, was a man ! A
person putting a glass to his eyes, could even
recognise further a small envious countenance,
and also that a bloated soullet dangled at the
stalk. The people told me, however, that the
big ear was not only a man, but a great man,
a genius. But I never believed in the people
when they spake of great men—and I hold to
my belief that it was a reversed cripple, who
had too little of everything, and too much of
one thing (chap. xlii.).

Knowest thou not who is most needed by
all ? He who commandeth great things.

To execute great things is difficult : but the
more difficult task is to command great things
(chap. xliv).

Zarathustra laughed and said mockingly :
" Happiness runneth after me. That is because
I do not run after women. Happiness, how-
ever, is a woman " (chap. xlvii).

I pass through this people and keep mine
eyes open : they have become smaller, and
ever become smaller : *the reason thereof is
their doctrine of happiness and virtue*. For
they are moderate also in virtue—because

they want comfort. With comfort, however, moderate virtue only is compatible. . . .

Of man there is little here, therefore do their women masculinise themselves. For only he who is man enough will—*save the woman* in woman (chap. xlix).

With the old Deities hath it long since come to an end : and verily, a good joyful Deity-end had they !

They did not " begloom " themselves to death—that do people fabricate ! On the contrary, they—*laughed* themselves to death once on a time !

That took place when the ungodliest came from a God himself—the utterance : " There is but one God ! Thou shalt have no other Gods before me ! "

An old grim-beard of a God, a jealous one, forgot himself in such wise :—

And all the Gods then laughed, and shook upon their thrones, and exclaimed : " It is not just divinity that there are Gods, but no God ? "

He that hath an ear let him hear.

Thus spake Zarathustra (chap. liii).

By divers ways and windings did I arrive at my truth; not by one ladder did I mount to the height where mine eye roveth into my remoteness.

And unwillingly only did I ask my way— that was always counter to my taste ! Rather did I question and test the ways themselves.

A testing and questioning hath been all my travelling : and verily, one must also *learn* to answer such questioning ! That, however, is my taste :

—Neither a good nor a bad taste, but *my* taste, of which I have no longer either shame or secrecy.

" This—is now *my* way—where is yours ? " Thus did I answer those who asked me " the way." For *the* way—it doth not exist !

Thus spake Zarathustra (chap. lv).

When I came unto men, then found I them resting on an old infatuation : all of them thought they had long known what was good and what was bad for men.

An old wearisome business seemed to them all discourse about virtue ; and he who wished to sleep well spake of " good " and " bad " ere retiring to rest.

This somnolence did I disturb when I taught that *no one yet knoweth* what is good and bad —unless it be the creating one ! (chap. lvi, sec. 2).

Behold, here is a new table ; but where are my brethren who will carry it with me to the valley and into hearts of flesh ?

Thus demandeth my great love to the remotest ones : *be not considerate of thy neighbour !* Man is something that must be surpassed. . . .

Surpass thyself even in thy neighbour : and a right which thou canst seize upon, shalt thou not allow to be given thee !

He who cannot command himself shall obey. And many a one *can* command himself, but still sorely lacketh self-obedience ! (chap. lvi, sec. 4).

Oh, my brethren, he who is a firstling is ever sacrificed. Now, however, are we firstlings !

We all bleed on secret sacrificial altars, we all burn and broil in honour of ancient idols (chap. lvi, sec. 6).

There is an old illusion—it is called good and evil. Around soothsayers and astrologers hath hitherto revolved the orbit of this illusion.

Once before did one *believe* in soothsayers and astrologers ; and *therefore* did one believe, " Everything is fate : thou shalt, for thou must ! "

Then again did one distrust all soothsayers and astrologers ; and *therefore* did one believe, " Everything is freedom : thou canst, for thou willst ! "

O my brethren, concerning the stars and the future there hath hitherto been only illusion, and not knowledge ; and *therefore* concerning good and evil there hath hitherto been only illusion and not knowledge ! (chap. lvi, sec. 9).

Your marriage-arranging : see that it be not a bad *arranging !* Ye have arranged too hastily : so there followeth therefrom—marriage-breaking !

And better marriage-breaking than marriage-bending, marriage-lying ! Thus spake a woman unto me : " Truly, I broke the marriage ; but first did the marriage break—me ! "

The badly-paired found I ever the most revengeful ; they make every one suffer for it if they no longer run singly.

On that account want I the honest ones to say to one another : " We love each other : let us see to it that we maintain our love ! Or shall our pledging be blundering ? "

" Give us a set term and a set marriage, that we may see if we are fit for the great marriage ! It is a great matter always to be twain."

Thus do I counsel all honest ones ; and what would be my love to the superman, and to all that is to come, if I should counsel and speak otherwise !

Not only to propagate yourselves onwards, but *upwards*—thereto, O my brethren, may the garden of marriage help you ! (chap. lvi, sec. 24).

Everything goeth, everything returneth ; eternally rolleth the wheel of existence. Everything dieth, everything blossometh forth again ; eternally runneth on the year of existence.

Everything breaketh, everything is integrated anew ; eternally buildeth itself the same house of existence. All things separate, all things again greet one another ; eternally true to itself remaineth the ring of existence (chap. lvii).

" . . . Do not talk further," answered his animals once more, " rather, thou convalescent, prepare for thyself first a lyre, a new lyre !

" For behold, O Zarathustra ! For thy new lays there are needed new lyres. . . . For thine animals know it well, O Zarathustra, who thou art and must become : behold, *thou art the teacher of the eternal return*—that is now *thy* fate ! That thou must be the first to teach this teaching —how could this great fate not be thy greatest danger and infirmity !

" Behold, we know what thou teachest : that all things eternally return, and ourselves with them, and that we have already existed times without number, and all things with us " (chap. lvii).

To show to what extent the sexual instinct in Nietzsche had "mounted into the brain," it is only necessary to quote from the Zarathustrian Yea and Amen Lay.

Oh, how could not I be ardent for Eternity and for the marriage-ring of rings—the ring of the return ?

Never yet have I found the woman by whom I should like to have children, unless it be this woman whom I love : for I love thee, O Eternity !

For I love thee, O Eternity ! (chap. lx).

When the swords ran among one another like red-spotted serpents, then did our fathers become fond of life ; the sun of every peace seemed to them languid and lukewarm—the long peace, however, made them ashamed (chap. lxiii).

"How poor indeed is man !" thought Zarathustra in his heart ; " how ugly, how wheezy, how full of hidden shame ! They tell me that man loveth himself. Ah, how great must that self-love be ! How much contempt is opposed to it ! Even this man hath loved himself—a great lover me thinketh he is, and a great despiser.

" No one have I yet found who more thoroughly despised himself : even *that* is elevation. Alas, was this perhaps the higher man whose cry I heard ?

" I love the great despisers. Man is something that hath to be surpassed " (chap. lxvii).

" Ye higher men "—so blinketh the populace —" there are no higher men, we are all equal ; man is man, before God—we are all equal ! "

Before God ! Now, however, this God hath died. Before the populace, however, we will not be equal. Ye higher men, away from the market-place !

Before God ! Now, however, this God hath died ! Ye higher man, this God was your greatest danger.

Only since he lay in his grave have ye again arisen. Now only cometh the great noontide, now only doth the higher man become master !

Have ye understood this word, O my brethren? Ye are frightened : do your hearts turn giddy ? Doth the abyss here yawn for you ? Doth the hell-hound here yelp at you ? Well ! Take heart, ye higher men ! Now only travaileth the mountain of the human future. God hath died : now do we desire—the Superman to live.

The most careful ask to-day : " How is man to be maintained ? " Zarathustra, however,

asketh, as the first and only one : " How is man
to be *surpassed* ? "

The Superman I have at heart ; that is the
first and only thing to me—and *not* man : not
the neighbour, not the sorriest, not the poorest,
not the best.

O my brethren, what I can love in man is that
he is an over-going and a down-going. And also in
you there is much that maketh me love and hope.

In that ye have despised, ye higher men, that
maketh me hope. For the great despisers are
the great reverers.

In that ye have despaired, there is much to
honour. For ye have not learned to submit
yourselves, ye have not learned petty policy.

For to-day have the petty people become
master : they all preach submission and humility
and policy and diligence and consideration and
the long etcetera of petty virtues.

Whatever is of the effeminate type, whatever
originateth from the servile type, and especially
the populace mishmash : that wisheth now to
be master of all human destiny. O disgust !
Disgust ! Disgust !

That asketh and asketh and never tireth :
" How is man to maintain himself best, longest,
most pleasantly ? " Thereby—are they masters
of to-day.

These masters of to-day—surpass them, O
my brethren—these petty people : they are the
Superman's greatest danger !

Surpass, ye higher men, the petty virtues, the petty policy, the sand-grain considerateness, the ant-hill trumpery, the pitiable comfortableness, the "happiness of the greatest number!" (chap. lxxiii, secs. 2 and 3).

This crown of the laughter, this rose-garland crown : I myself have put on this crown, I myself have consecrated my laughter. No one else have I found to-day potent enough for this.

Zarathustra the dancer, Zarathustra the light one, who beckoneth with his pinions, one ready for flight, beckoning unto all birds, ready and prepared, a blissfully light-spirited one :

Zarathustra the soothsayer, Zarathustra the sooth-laugher, no impatient one, no absolute one, one who loveth leaps and side-leaps : I myself have put on this crown !

Lift up your hearts, my brethren, high, higher ! And do not forget your legs ! Lift up also your legs, ye good dancers, and better still if ye stand upon your heads !

There are also heavy animals in a state of happiness, there are club-footed ones from the beginning. Curiously do they exert themselves, like an elephant which endeavoureth to stand upon its head.

Better, however, to be foolish with happiness than foolish with misfortune, better to dance awkwardly than walk lamely. So learn, I pray you, my wisdom, ye higher men : even the worst thing hath two good reverse sides,—

—Even the worst thing hath good dancing legs : so learn, I pray you, ye higher men, to put yourselves on your proper legs !

So unlearn, I pray you, the sorrow-sighing, and all the populace-sadness ! Oh, how sad the buffoons of the populace seem to me to-day ! This to-day, however, is that of the populace. . . .

Ye higher men, the worst thing in you is that ye have none of you learned to dance—to dance beyond yourselves ! What doth it matter that ye have failed !

How many things are still possible ! So *learn* to dance beyond yourselves ! Lift up your hearts, ye good dancers, high, higher ! And do not forget the good laughter !

This crown of the laughter, this rose-garland crown : to you, my brethren, do I cast this crown ! Laughing have I consecrated ; ye higher men, *learn*, I pray you—to laugh !

While the four parts of *Zarathustra* are complete in themselves as they now stand, Nietzsche intended to add a fifth and a sixth part. This plan, however, was not carried into effect ; but several notes of his in connection with it were collected and published by Mrs. Foerster Nietzsche. Not only are they valuable as a guide to the sections Nietzsche intended to add, but they also serve to elucidate the four parts already published.

Some particulars regarding the superman are

furnished by Mr. Karl Heckel,* a deep student of this side of Nietzsche's philosophy. He traces Nietzsche's conception of the higher being from 1870 onwards, showing how Nietzsche had first looked upon the genius as the man best qualified to realise his aim. But the Bayreuth fiasco upset his calculations in this regard.

In the foreground of Nietzsche's picture of the future, the genius had hitherto stood out prominently above all men as the ideal to be attained ; but this highest of all values now experienced a sudden downfall. What the world called genius appeared to Nietzsche to be merely caricature. But he felt the discord in the existence of the greatest ones even more acutely than the mental and physical lameness of the world in general. " Cripples " was his name for those who had too much of one thing and too little of another. . . . If he formerly, as a follower of Wagner, believed in the absolute power of passion, the praise of Apollo now succeeded to the high value that was set upon the Dionysian and its glorification of the gloomy depths in the spirit of man. With this there begins a new epoch in Nietzsche's view of life. Upon the *Dawn of Day*, sparkling with its unspoken thoughts, follows the *Joyful Wisdom*, shining

* *Die Zukunft*, October 3rd, 1908 ; translated and adapted by the present writer in *The New Age*, May 20th and 27th, 1909. I quote from this translation by kind permission of the editor of *The New Age*.

on all things with the radiance of noon, and forcing
us to believe in the faultless beauty of art. . . .

It was already Nietzsche's wish that the
Good European should be distinguished for his
bravery of head and heart, and he now expected
of the higher man that his superior virility
should urge him on to attain to the greatest
possible power over things—that he should discharge his strength. In the place of the old
imperative " thou shalt," he brought forward a
new one, the " I must " of the super-powerful
man, the creator. This instinct is not to be
looked upon as blind ; there should be a motive
for every action. It is not to be regarded as unrestrained ; for the commander should have
control over his powers. But neither is it to be
thought yielding or compliant ; for the creator
of new values must not be influenced by humanitarian ideals. The master virtue, the breeding
virtue, is that which can overcome even pity for
the sake of the far-off goal.

Even when in this way we have united a few
of Nietzsche's disconnected thoughts, it is clear
that we have advanced within reach of a
new manly ideal. We forget to inquire about
" happiness," for we are quite satisfied with the
conviction : a gigantic strength in man and in
mankind desires to discharge itself. The quality
and powerfulness of this strength determines
the value of a person. We must not think this
strength homophonous ; there are so many

conflicting desires and impulses in man.   We recognise that innumerable instincts are fighting against one another, and we call the man strong who rigorously suppresses them all.   On the other hand, we look upon the *highest* man as the one who combines within himself the greatest versatility in the greatest relative strength of each quality.   The man who achieves this synthesis is master of the world.

   . . . Can we doubt for a moment that he did not picture the superman as a degree of excellence readily attainable by every one ; but rather as the highest possible summit of an imaginary picture of life ?   His command never runs : " Become a superman " ; but : " Contribute your share to the formation of a culture which will one day enable the superman to be begotten," " Act as if you wished the superman to be begotten out of yourself." . . .

   The problem that concerned him was not what kind of a being should succeed to man in the course of ages ; he looked upon it as his life's task to answer in a new way the question : " Which type of man shall be reared ?   Which type of man will be more valuable, more amiable, and more sure of himself ? "   We find in all his writings the varied, ever-differently expressed answer to this question, and we find the exhortation to conquer weakness by strength, and to oppose a manly ideal to the effeminate morality of our age.

Many people are inclined to ask, and have asked : " What will the superman do when he comes ? " And the only answer that can be given is this : The superman is to be first and foremost a creator of values ; and we on our lower plane of life can form no conception of the values he will create. We can only say that the superior qualities of the superman will enable him to create better values than we do. Moses opened the house of bondage ; but Joshua entered the Promised Land. No doubt many Israelites wanted to know from Moses what they were going to do when they arrived—to which he probably replied, in Biblical language, " Wait till you get there, and see."

CHAPTER VIII

LATER WORKS : " BEYOND GOOD AND EVIL "—
" THE GENEALOGY OF MORALS "—" THE WILL
TO POWER "—" THE ANTICHRIST "—" THE
TWILIGHT OF THE IDOLS "—WAGNER ONCE
MORE—" ECCE HOMO "

IT is a rough-and-ready, but by no means inaccurate criticism of *Beyond Good and Evil*
to say that it tells us in prose what *Zarathustra*
tells us in poetry. Many quotations from this
work have already been given ; but, as in the
case of all Nietzsche's writings, except his early
philological essays, the subjects treated are so
diverse that the student must undertake the
pleasing task of reading the entire book, if he
wishes to become acquainted with the philosopher's point of view. The following extracts
may be taken in conjunction with those already
given :

Why Atheism nowadays ? " The father "
in God is thoroughly refuted ; equally so
" the judge," " the rewarder." Also his " free
will " : he does not hear—and, even if he did,
he would not know how to help. The worst

is that he seems incapable of communicating himself clearly; is he uncertain? This is what I have made out (by questioning and listening at a variety of conversations) to be cause of the decline of European theism; it appears to me that though the religious instinct is in vigorous growth—it rejects the theistic satisfaction with profound disgust (Aph. 53).

It is a curious thing that God learnt Greek when he wished to turn author—and that he did not learn it better (Aph. 121).

When a woman has scholarly inclinations, there is generally something wrong with her sexual nature. Barrenness itself conduces to a certain virility of taste; man, indeed, if I may say so, is " the barren animal " (Aph. 144).

Comparing man and woman generally, one may say that woman would not have the genius for adornment, if she had not the instinct for the *secondary* rôle (Aph. 145).

In contrast to *laisser-aller*, every system of morals is a sort of tyranny against " nature " and also against " reason "; that is, however, no objection, unless one should again decree by some system of morals, that all kinds of tyranny and unreasonableness are unlawful. What is essential and invaluable in every system of morals is that it is a long constraint. In order to understand Stoicism, or Port-Royal, or Puritanism, one should remember the constraint under which every language has attained to strength and freedom—the metrical constraint, the tyranny of rhyme and rhythm. How much trouble have the poets and orators of every nation given themselves ! —not excepting some of the prose-writers of to-day, in whose ear dwells an inexorable conscientiousness—" for the sake of a folly," as utilitarian bunglers say, and thereby deem themselves wise—" from submission to arbitrary law," as the anarchists say, and thereby fancy themselves " free," even free-spirited. The singular fact remains, however, that everything of the nature of freedom, elegance, boldness, dance, and masterly certainty, which exists or has existed, whether it be in thought itself, or in administration, or in speaking and persuading, in art just as in conduct, has only developed by means of the tyranny of such arbitrary law ; and in all seriousness, it is not at all improbable that precisely this is " nature " and " natural "—and *not laisser-aller !* Every artist knows how different from the state of letting himself go, is his " most natural " condition, the free arranging, locating, disposing, and constructing in the moments of " inspiration "—and how strictly and delicately he then obeys a thousand laws, which, by their very rigidness and precision, defy all formulation by means of ideas (even the most stable idea has, in comparison therewith, something floating, manifold, and ambiguous in it). The essential thing " in heaven and earth " is apparently (to repeat it once more) that there should be long *obedience* in the same direction ; there thereby results, and has always resulted in the long run, something which has made life worth living ; for instance, art, virtue, music, dancing, reason, spirituality —anything whatever that is transfiguring, refined, foolish, or divine. The long bondage of the spirit, the distrustful constraint in the communicability of ideas, the discipline which the thinker imposed on himself to think in accordance with the rules of a church or a court, or conformably to Aristotelian premises, the persistent spiritual will to interpret everything that happened according to a Christian scheme, and in every occurrence to rediscover and justify the Christian God—all this violence, arbitrariness, severity, dreadfulness, and un-reasonableness, has proved itself the disciplinary means whereby the European spirit has attained its strength, its remorseless curiosity and subtle mobility ; granted also that much irrecoverable strength and spirit had to be stifled, suffocated, and spoilt in the process (for here, as every-where, " nature " shows herself as she is, in all her extravagant and *indifferent* magnificence, which is shocking, but, nevertheless, noble). That for centuries European thinkers only thought in order to prove something—now-adays, on the contrary, we are suspicious of

every thinker who " wishes to prove something "
—that it was always settled beforehand what
was to be the result of their strictest thinking,
as it was perhaps in the Asiatic astrology of
former times, or as it is still at the present
day in the innocent, Christian-moral explanation
of immediate personal events " for the glory
of God," or " for the good of the soul " :—this
tyranny, this arbitrariness, this severe and
magnificent stupidity, has *educated* the spirit ;
slavery, both in the coarser and the finer sense,
is apparently an indispensable means even of
spiritual education and discipline. One may
look at every system of morals in this light :
it is " nature " therein which teaches to hate
the *laisser-aller*, the too-great freedom, and
implants the need for limited horizons, for
immediate duties—it teaches the *narrowing
of perspectives*, and thus, in a certain sense,
that stupidity is a condition of life and development. " Thou must obey some one, and for
a long time ; *otherwise* thou wilt come to grief,
and lose all respect for thyself "—this seems
to me to be the moral imperative of nature,
which is consequently neither " categorical," as
old Kant wished (consequently the "otherwise"),
nor does it address itself to the individual (what
does nature care for the individual !), but
to nations, races, ages, and ranks, above all,
however, to the *animal* " *man* " generally, to
mankind (Aph. 188).

Corruption—as the indication that anarchy threatens to break out among the instincts, and that the foundation of the emotions, called " life," is convulsed—is something radically different according to the organisation in which it manifests itself. When, for instance, an aristocracy like that of France at the beginning of the Revolution, flung away its privileges with sublime disgust and sacrificed itself to an excess of its moral sentiments, it was corruption : it was really only the closing act of the corruption which had existed for centuries, by virtue of which that aristocracy had abdicated step by step its lordly prerogatives and lowered itself to a *function* of royalty (in the end even to its decoration and parade-dress). The essential thing, however, in a good and healthy aristocracy is that it should *not* regard itself as a function either of the kingship or the commonwealth, but as the *significance* and highest justification thereof—that it should therefore accept with a good conscience the sacrifice of a legion of individuals, who, *for its sake*, must be suppressed and reduced to imperfect men, to slaves and instruments. Its fundamental belief must be precisely that society is *not* allowed to exist for its own sake, but only as a foundation and scaffolding, by means of which a select class of beings may be able to elevate themselves to their duties, and in general to a higher *existence* : like those sun-seeking climbing plants in Java—they are called Sipo Matador—which encircle an oak so long and so often with their arms, until at last, high above it, but supported by it, they can unfold their tops in the open light, and exhibit their happiness (Aph. 258).

In *The Genealogy of Morals* Nietzsche brings the master-morality more and more into prominence. The book consists of three essays, each of which is practically complete in itself. The first deals with the valuations " good and evil " and " good and bad," representing master and slave morality respectively. The second essay starts with the theory that debt was the basis of the origin of sin. The third essay endeavours to answer the question : What do ascetic ideals mean ?—ascetic ideals standing for the ideals of slave morality, especially poverty, chastity, humility, and so on. The last essay is undoubtedly the most important, and deals with the whole problem of the decadence caused by Christianity. Section 14 of the first essay has already been quoted (p. 69 foll.).

The knightly-aristocratic valuations presuppose a powerful corporality, a vigorous, rich, superabundant health, together with everything necessary for its maintenance—war, adventure, the chase, dancing, sports, and in general all that calls for strong, free, and cheerful activity. The valuations of the priest-

caste have, as we have already observed,
different presuppositions—so much the worse
for this caste in case of war ! The priests, it
is well known, are the *worst enemies*—and why ?
Because they are the most impotent (I, 7).

That the lambs should not be too well disposed towards the big birds of prey need not
surprise us ; but this fact does not give us any
excuse for blaming the big birds of prey for
flying away with small lambs. And if the lambs
say to one another : " These birds are wicked,
and whoever resembles a bird of prey as little
as possible—whoever is the opposite, rather,
a lamb—is not such a one good ? " we cannot
say a word against such an ideal, even though
the birds of prey look at it with mocking eyes,
and say to themselves : "*We* have no grudge
against them, these good lambs, we even love
them ; for nothing is sweeter to the taste
than a tender lamb." To exact of strength that
it should not manifest itself as strength—
that it should not be a will to overcome, to
subdue, to master—is as ridiculous as to exact
of weakness that it should manifest itself as
strength. A quantum of power is an equal
quantum of impulse, will, activity (I, 13).

The two antithetical values " good and
bad " " good and evil " have fought a terrible
battle on earth, a battle that has lasted thousands of years ; and though the latter, generally
speaking, succeeded long ago in getting the

best of the fight, there are not wanting places
even now where the struggle is still undecided.
It might even be said that the struggle was in
the meantime transferred to higher regions,
and has for this reason become deeper and more
spiritual : so that there is to-day no more distinctive characteristic of a " higher nature,"
or a more spiritual nature, than to be dual in
this sense, and to be still a battle-ground for
these antitheses. The symbol of this battle,
written down in letters which have always remained legible through the long course of
human history, is " Rome against Judea,
Judea against Rome." Hitherto no greater
event has taken place than *this* struggle, *this*
question, *this* deadly antithesis. In the Jew
Rome was conscious of something like anti-
naturalness, its antipodal monster, so to speak ;
in Rome the Jew was considered as " proved
guilty of hatred of the human race," and justly
so, in so far as we have a right to connect the
welfare and future of mankind with the unconditional sovereignty of aristocratic values.
On the other hand, the feelings of the Jews
against Rome ? A thousand indications enable
us to understand what they were ; but it is
sufficient to recall the Apocalypse of St. John
—that vilest of all the written outbursts which
revenge has on its conscience (I, 16).

" Autonomous " and " moral " are mutually
preclusive terms (II, 2).

The curve of man's capacity for feeling pain seems to swerve downwards with uncommon rapidity and suddenness whenever the upper ten thousand or ten million are left behind. For my own part I have no doubt that, in comparison with one single painful night of one hysterical woman of culture, the sufferings of all animals so far operated on to' obtain answers to scientific questions, are as dust in the balance (II, 7).

It is absurd to speak of right and wrong *per se: in itself* the act of injuring, violating, exploiting, annihilation, cannot be " wrong," since life *essentially*—that is to say, in its fundamental functions, presupposes injury, violation, exploitation and annihilation : indeed, we cannot conceive of life without this characteristic (II, 11).

It is self-evident what " state " means—any company of blond beasts of prey, a conquering and mastering race, which, being organised for war and possessing the power of organisation, unhesitatingly lays its powerful talons upon some population, greatly its superior in numbers, perhaps ; but as yet formless and wandering about without fixed habitation. This is what gave rise to the " state " on earth : the foolish theory which would ascribe its origin to an " agreement " is, I think, superseded. The man who can command, who is a master by nature, whose deeds and gestures are violent—what are agreements to him ! Such beings cannot be reckoned with, they appear like a fate, without cause, reason, indulgence, pretext : they are there, like a flash of lightning ; too terrible, too sudden, too convincing, too " different," to be even hated (II, 17).

Undoubtedly the most important work published after Nietzsche's death is *The Will to Power*. The second enlarged edition, arranged in accordance with Nietzsche's own plan, consists of four books : European Nihilism ; A Criticism of the hitherto Highest Values ; The Principles of a New Valuation ; Breeding and Training. (A later fragment, the *Antichrist*, is dealt with separately.) The whole range of human thought comes under review in the two volumes of this wonderful work. " What is Nihilism ? " asks Nietzsche at the start, and then answers : " The devaluation of the highest values." This is the meaning he attaches to the word nihilism throughout the book. And he goes on to tell us : " Nihilism stands at our very door. What I am about to tell you is the history of the next two hundred years. I describe what is coming, what must inevitably come, *the rise of Nihilism*." Then follows the most epoch-making work since the Nouvum Organon. *The Will to Power* does not readily lend itself to quotation ; but *The Antichrist* is an integral part of it, and from this we shall now quote.

What is good ? Everything that increases the feeling of power, the will to power, power itself, in man.

What is bad ? All that proceeds from weakness.

What is happiness ? The feeling that power is increasing, that resistance is being overcome.

Not contentment, but more power ; *not* peace, but war ; *not* virtue, but valour (virtue in the style of the Renaissance, *virtù*, virtue without moralic acid).

The weak and helpless must go to the wall : first principle of our love for humanity. And we shall help them to go.

What is more harmful than any vice ? Pity for the weak and helpless—*Christianity* (Aph. 2).

THE CHRISTIAN CONCEPTION OF GOD.—God as the God of the sick, God as spider, God as spirit—is one of the most corrupt divine conceptions ever realised on earth ; it represents perhaps even the lowest level in the descending evolution of the divine type : God degenerated so far as to be *in contradiction* to life, instead of being its glorification and eternal *affirmation !* To declare war against life, nature, will to live, in the name of God ! God as the formula for all the slandering of " the world," for all the lies about the " beyond " ! Nothingness deified in God, the will to nothing sanctified ! (Aph. 18).

Already the word " Christian " is a misunderstanding—at bottom, there was only one Christian, and he died on the cross. . . . In fact, there have never been Christians. The " Christian "—whoever has called himself a Christian for nearly two thousand years, is merely a self-misunderstanding (Aph. 39).

One does well to put on gloves when reading the New Testament. The neighbourhood of so much impurity almost forces one to do so. We should not choose to be connected with the " first Christians " any more than with Polish Jews—not that we would reproach them in the least. Both of them have an unwholesome smell. I have searched the New Testament in vain for a single sympathetic trait : I found nothing in it which could be called free, kind, frank, loyal. Humanity has not taken its first steps in this book—instincts of *purity* are lacking. There are only *bad* instincts in the New Testament ; and there is not even the courage of these bad instincts. There is only cowardice, closed eyes, self-delusion. Any book is pure after one has read the New Testament : for example, after having read through St. Paul, I read with great delight that charming, wanton mocker, Petronius, of whom we could say what Boccaccio wrote about Cesare Borgia to the Duke of Parma : *è tutto festo* (Aph. 46).

The order of castes, the highest and most dominant law, is but the sanction of a natural order, a natural law of the highest degree of importance, which it is beyond the power of an arbitrary will, a " modern idea," to upset. In every healthy society we distinguish three physiological types which gravitate in different directions, interdependent, each having its hygiene, its own department of labour, its own feelings of perfection and mastery (Aph. 57).

Nietzsche then proceeds to describe these three different castes—first of all the superior ruling caste, the creators of values; secondly, the caste which relieves this class of all drudgery and detail work—lawyers, merchants, tradespeople, etc. ; and thirdly, the lowest caste of all, reserved for the roughest work in the community, who require a religion (resembling Christianity, perhaps) to enable them to forget (" to make them unconscious—this is the aim of all holy lies "). Nietzsche concludes the aphorism by saying :

What do I most cordially detest among the riff-raff of the present day ? The socialistic riff-raff, the disciples of Chandâla, who undermine the workman's instincts, pleasures, and feelings of contentment, and inspire him with disgust at his narrow existence—who make him envious and teach him revenge. Injustice is not to be sought in unequal rights ; but always in the pretension to " equal " rights. . . . What is bad ? I have already said : All that proceeds from weakness, envy, *vengeance*—the anarchist and the Christian spring from the same source (Aph. 57).

The other works need not concern us for very long. Nietzsche's formal poetry, though containing many beautiful passages, is just enough to fill a small volume, and must be read in its entirety in conjunction with his complete works to be truly appreciated. Parts of *The Twilight of the Idols* have already been quoted. This book, like *The Dawn of Day* and the *Human*, is made up of aphorisms from a single page to three or four pages in length. The value of the book cannot be determined from a few passages, however carefully chosen ; but I give the following as being most characteristic. The sub-title of the work, it may be remarked, is " How one philosophises with the hammer " —Nietzsche taps certain moral concepts, and finds that they ring hollow.

To live in solitude one must be either an animal or a god, says Aristotle. He left out the third instance—one must be both—a *philosopher* (I, 3).

Posthumous men—myself, for example—are not so well understood as men who conform to the spirit of their age ; but they are *heard* better. To speak more clearly : we are not understood at all . . . *hence* our authority (I, 15).

MY IMPOSSIBILITIES.—Seneca, or the toreador of virtue. Rousseau, or the return to nature *in impuris naturalibus.* Schiller, or the Morality-Trumpeter of Säkkingen.* Dante, or the hyena that versifies among the tombs. Kant, or "cant," as intelligible character. Victor Hugo, or the Ocean Lighthouse of nonsense. George Sand, or *lactea ubertas*, in other words, the milch cow with the "fine style." Michelet, or enthusiasm in shirt-sleeves. Carlyle, or the pessimism of a bad digestion. John Stuart Mill, or the wounding clearness. The Brothers de Goncourt, or the two Ajaxes struggling with Homer. Music by Offenbach. Zola, or, "the joy of stinking" (IX, 1).

In the pamphlets *The Case of Wagner* and *Nietzsche contra Wagner*, Nietzsche states his reasons for turning away from the musician. The latter pamphlet is merely a series of selections from his own works to justify the attitude he took up. The first-named pamphlet is quite a new work, however, and merits quotation.

No one was more dangerously connected with Wagnerism than I, no one ever defended himself more rigorously against it, no one

* This refers to a poem by Scheffel.

rejoiced more when free from it ! A long story ! Do you wish a word to describe it ? —If I were a moralist, who knows what I should call it ! A self-conquest, perhaps. But the philosopher has no love for moralists, nor does he care for fine phrases.

What does the philosopher exact from himself first and last ? To overcome his age in himself, and to become " ageless," " timeless." With what, then, must the hardest battle be fought ? With that by which he is a child of his age (Preface).

Has it ever been remarked that muisc sets the mind *free* ? That it lends wings to thought ? And that the more one becomes a musician, the more one becomes a philosopher ? (sec. 1).

The danger for artists and men of genius lies in women : adoring women are their ruin. No one, almost, has sufficient character not to let himself be corrupted—" saved "—when he finds himself treated like a God : he immediately *condescends* to women. Man is cowardly before every eternal feminine ; and the dear little women know this. In many cases of female love—and perhaps just in the most celebrated cases—love is nothing but a refined form of parasitism, the nestling of one's self into a strange soul, sometimes even into a strange flesh—how often, alas, at the cost of the host ! (sec. 3).

The artist of decadence—that is the term.

And now I am beginning to speak seriously. I am far from wishing to be a harmless onlooker when that *décadent* is ruining our health—and our music as well! Indeed, is Wagner really a man? Is he not rather a disease? Everything he touches falls ill—*he has made music ill* (sec. 5).

Wagner is the modern artist *par excellence*, the Cagliostro of modernity. In his heart we find bound up, in the most seductive fashion possible, what is necessary for every one to-day —the three great stimulants of exhaustion: the brutal, the artistic, and the innocent (idiocy) (Sec. 5).

What is literary decadence characterised by? By the fact that the spirit dwells no longer in the whole. The word attains the sovereign power and springs out of the sentence, the sentence grows in volume and obscures the meaning of the page, the page acquires life at the cost of the whole—the whole is no longer a whole (sec. 7).

There is an æsthetic of decadence and an æsthetic of classicism—the " beautiful in itself " is a chimera, like all idealism. In the narrow spheres of the so-called moral values, there is no greater contrast to be found than that between the master-morality and the morality of Christian valuations: this latter has grown up from the most morbid of all possible roots (the New Testament shows us exactly the same

z

physiological types as Dostoiewski's novels) ; the master-morality, on the other hand (" Ro-man," " Pagan," " Classical," " Renaissance ") is the indication of a perfect constitution, of *ascending* life, of will to power as principle of life.   Master-morality is *affirmative* as instinc-tively as Christian morality is *negative* (" God," the " beyond," " abnegation "—negations pure and simple).   The first communicates its super-fluity to things : it transfigures, adorns, *ration-alises*, the world.   The latter impoverishes, blanches the cheek, uglifies the value of things : *denies* the world (Epilogue).

Nietzsche's autobiography, *Ecce Homo*, was written at a break-neck pace in the winter of 1888. The first chapters are : Why I am so clever ; Why I am so wise ; Why I write such good books. Under the last heading he enters upon a most interesting and minute analysis of his own pub-lished works, from *The Birth of Tragedy* to *The Case of Wagner*, a few notes from which have already been quoted.   Then comes : " Why I am a Fatality," followed by a poem : " Fame and Eternity."

He abuses the Germans in bitter terms.*

The Germans will in my case also do all in their power to make my destiny bring forth a

* I translated some of this section for *The New Age* (October 24th, 1908), and quote therefrom by permission of Mr. Orage.

mouse. They have already sufficiently com-
promised themselves about me in the past :
I fear they will do it as well in future. Oh, how
I long to be a bad prophet here ! . . . My
natural readers and listeners are even now
Russians, Scandinavians, and Frenchmen—am
I always to be read by foreigners ? The Germans are written down in the history of knowledge with imposing, ambiguous names ; they
have never produced anything but " unconscious " swindlers—(Fichte, Schelling, Schopenhauer, Hegel, Schleiermacher, deserve the word
as much as Kant or Leibnitz : they are all mere
Schleiermachers *). They shall never have the
honour of reckoning as one of them the first
righteous spirit in the history of spirits, the spirit
in which the truth triumphs over the counter-
feit of four thousand years. The German mind
is *my* bad air ; I breathe with difficulty in
the neighbourhood of this instinctive impurity
in psychologicis, which is betrayed by every word,
every look, of a German. They have never come
through a seventeenth century of laborious self-
criticism as the French did—a Larochefou-
cauld, a Descartes, is a hundred times superior
in righteousness to the best Germans—the
Germans have had no psychologist up to the
present. But capacity for psychology is almost
the standard of the purity or impurity of a race
. . . and if one is not pure, how can one be

* Schleiermacher = veil-maker.

deep ? We can never gauge the depth of a German, because, just like women, he has none : that is the explanation. And if a man has no depth, he cannot even be called shallow. What in Germany is called deep is just this instinctive impurity against one's self, about which I am now speaking : they will not see themselves as they are. May I not propose the word " German " as an international coin for this psychological degeneracy ? At this moment, for example, the German Emperor calls it his " Christian duty " to set free the slaves in Africa: we *other* Europeans would call this " German."
. . . Have the Germans ever brought out a book distinguished for its depth ? They have notion of what *deep* means. I have known learned men who looked upon Kant as deep ; at the Prussian court, I fear, Herr von Treitschke is looked upon as deep. And when I occasionally extol Stendhal as a deep psychologist, it has happened to me that German university professors have made me spell out the name for them !

And why should I not go on to the end ? I like to make things clear. It is part of my ambition to be looked upon as a despiser of the Germans *par excellence*. I expressed my distrust of the German character as far back as my twenty-sixth year. The Germans are impossible to me. When I think of a type of man that runs counter to my instincts, a German always

appears. The first means I have of weighing a
man is by knowing whether he perceives rank,
grade, and order between men ; whether he
distinguishes : in this way he is a gentilhomme ;
in every other case he belongs irretrievably to
the open-minded, oh, so good-natured ! tribe of
canaille. But the Germans are canaille—oh,
they are so good-natured ! One lowers one's
self by having dealings with Germans—the
German fraternises at once. . . . With the
exception of my intercourse with some German
artists, especially Richard Wagner, I have not
spent a single happy hour with a German. . . .
Granted that the deepest spirit of all the centuries appeared among Germans, any silly clown
would imagine that his own unbeautiful soul was
of equal importance. . . . I cannot bear this
race, with which one is always in bad company,
and which has not the power to perceive *nuances*
—woe is me ! I am a *nuance*—which is awkward on its feet, and cannot even walk. . . . In
truth, the Germans have no feet ; they have
only legs. . . . The Germans have no conception of how vulgar they are ; but that is the
superlative of vulgarity . . . they are not
ashamed that they are merely Germans ! *

Perhaps the most interesting paragraph in the
volume, however, is that in which Nietzsche
refers to his inspiration.†

* *Ecce Homo*, p. 112 foll.   † *Ibid.*, p. 91 foll.

Has any one at the end of the nineteenth century any distinct notion of what poets of a stronger age understood by the word inspiration ? If not, I will describe it. If one had the smallest vestige of superstition in one, it would hardly be possible to set aside completely the idea that one is the mere incarnation, mouthpiece, or medium of an almighty power. The idea of revelation in the sense that something becomes suddenly visible and audible with indescribable accuracy and certainty, which profoundly convulses and upsets one—describes simply the matter of fact. One hears—one does not seek ; one takes—one does not ask who gives : a thought suddenly flashes up like lightning, it comes with necessity, unhesitatingly—I have never had any choice in the matter. There is an ecstasy such that the immense strain of it is sometimes relaxed by a flood of tears, along with which one's steps either rush or involuntarily lag, alternately. There is the feeling that one is completely out of hand, with the very distinct consciousness of an endless number of fine thrills and quiverings to the very toes ; there is a depth of happiness in which the painfullest and gloomiest do not operate as antitheses, but as conditioned, as demanded in the sense of necessary shades of colour in such an overflow of light. There is an instinct for rhythmic relations which embraces wide areas of forms (length, the need of a wide-embracing rhythm, is almost the measure of the force of an inspiration, a sort of counterpart to its pressure and tension). Everything happens quite involuntarily, as if in a tempestuous out-burst of freedom, of absoluteness, of power and divinity. The involuntariness of the figures and similes is the most remarkable thing ; one loses all perception of what constitutes the figure and what constitutes the simile ; everything seems to present itself as the readiest, the correctest, and the simplest means of expression. It actually seems, to use one of Zarathustra's own phrases, as if all things came unto one, and would fain be similes : ' Here do all things come caressingly to thy talk and flatter thee, for they want to ride upon thy back. On every simile dost thou here ride to every truth. Here fly open unto thee all being's words and word-cabinets ; here all being wanteth to become words, here all becoming wanteth to learn of thee how to talk.' This is *my* experience of inspiration. I do not doubt that one would have to go back thousands of years in order to find some one who could say to me : It is mine also !"

In the midst of some of the most brilliant things Nietzsche ever wrote, we find a certain section of women coming in for no very gentle treatment.*
Woman is unutterably more wicked than man, and more clever ; goodness in woman is a form

* *Ecce Homo,* p. 60 foll.

of degeneration. . . . The struggle for equal rights is a symptom of disease : every physician knows that. A woman, the more womanly she is, battles against rights with all the power at her command : the order of Nature, the eternal *war* between the sexes, sets her by far in the first rank. Have you ears for my definition of love ? the only one worthy of a philosopher. Love : in its means, war ; in its essence, the deadly hatred of the sexes. Have you ever heard my answer to the question, How can a woman be *cured*—" saved " ? Impregnate her ; give her a baby. Woman must have children ; man is only a means : Thus spake Zarathustra. " The emancipation of woman "—this is the instinct of the aberrant ; setting the imperfect woman, incapable of child-bearing, against the true, perfect woman. At bottom, the emancipated women are the anarchists in the domain of the eternal feminine : the shipwrecked, lost, strayed, aberrant beings whose deepest instinct is revenge.

This, and many other equally bitter passages, may be commended to the notice of one-sided English writers and speakers on the question of woman's suffrage. There is, I believe, a schism among our Socialists, theoretical or practical, in regard to the subject of " woman's rights "; and before any further assistance is given to the feminist movement a thorough study of Nietzsche is indispensable.

CHAPTER IX

W E can gather the threads of this teaching together in a few words.

There are no equal " rights "—it is unnatural that there should be. Nietzsche is not the nihilist, the upsetter of values, the anarchist : these are terms of reproach which should be reserved for the real nihilists and upsetters of values—for the Democrats and Socialists, who preach that all men are equal (and, with even greater absurdity, that women should have equal rights with men), and for the Christians, who try to give a divine sanction to the misleading statements of the demagogues by preaching equality before God.

Although many people have given up credence in the Christian faith, they still uphold Christian morality—the table of values established by Christianity. This is clearly illogical ; so Nietzsche provides us with a new and better morality : a morality which sifts the grain from the chaff, and arranges society into three classes, each with its own rights (*v.* p. 333 foll.).

The Superman is a practical aim—not a new race in the Darwinian sense which it would take thousands of years to bring to maturity ; not a species of bliss for us to look forward to after death ; but a real, tangible personality, who could be formed in a few generations, if we carried out Zarathustra's teaching.

We must accept Life ; we must cease from blaspheming the world. We must no longer use " the world " as a term of reproach, as we have been taught to do by Christianity. Hence everything that stimulates Life is to be welcomed. Art stimulates Life to a greater degree than Science ; therefore Art is to be ranked higher than Science—whence it follows that a fine poem or a beautiful picture or a noble piece of sculpture or a charming melody is of much greater value to us than any merely mechanical contrivance which enables an Atlantic liner to travel a few knots an hour faster. Why should one hurry ? Because a few Philistines in the western continent —without art, without even science, of their own—have set the commercial pace ?   An Italian beggar boy, with the instinctive good taste in art shared by all his countrymen, is to be preferred to an American millionaire whose thoughts cannot raise themselves above the fluctuations of the Stock Exchange.

As nearly every Christian (except, perhaps, the Plymouth Brethren) must now admit that the account of Adam and Eve in Genesis is nothing more than a beautiful myth, we must turn to Darwin and his successors for an account of ourselves. A close study of our biological evolution from the ape to man furnishes the best refutation of the ridiculous claims put forward by Democrats and Socialists. It would be childish to think that we had all evolved *equally*, that no man had ever advanced a step in front of his neighbour. On this point the very evidence of our own senses would satisfy any one but the most rabid demagogue : *men are not equal ;* equal rights are an absurdity.

Now, it will in time inevitably be recognised that the distinction between masters and slaves must be made more apparent, must be more generally admitted, than it now is. Instead of the lowest classes in society receiving wages and keeping up their pseudo-independence, they must be trained to submit themselves as property. They will certainly be no worse off than slaves were in ancient communities ; and in most cases they will be better off than they now are. The higher class of workmen would, of course, come into Nietzsche's middle caste of society. Then there will be no unemployed processions of either men or women ; for men's property is not allowed to roam about the streets. At the present day, for example, we do not see horses, cows, dogs, or other domestic animals wandering about unemployed, and there is no reason why the lower classes of men should have to do so. (It is clear, I think, that in our present state of society some animals are more valuable than men, and better treated—animals doing useful work, with men unemployed, would tend to show this : a proof that the game of Christianity is not played according to the rules drawn up by well-known authorities in Greek, and laid down in *the* Book.)

The lower castes may, of course, please themselves by inventing a hell for the higher classes and a heaven for themselves—thus they can gratify their resentment, and nobody will be a penny the worse. They can always be met with the hackneyed but appropriate tag : " You have your joke, and we have your estate." Fulke Greville's lines should be remembered—

> Fire and People do in this agree:
> They both good servants, both ill masters be.*

Nietzsche's sympathies lie with the aristocratically strong, and this may perhaps account for his ill reception in modern England. Having been under the malign influence of Christianity for generations, having become humble and meek and good-mannered, we have tended to become degenerate—most of us, that is. Hence when our teacher grows dissatisfied with our

* *Inquisition upon Fame.*

conduct, brings his fist down on the desk with a crash, and threatens to cane us unless we improve, those of us who have offended begin to quake. This feeling is reflected in the reviews of two or three translations of Nietzsche's books published in this country a decade ago. Every reviewer seemed to have the instinctive feeling that he was *weak*, and that Nietzsche was a strong man ; and forthwith they set about acting the part of Delilahs towards the modern Samson. But behold ! the power of Zarathustra was mighty, and they wist not wherein his strength lay. And Zarathustra waxed wroth, and slew his tens of thousands with the jaw-bone of *The British Weekly*.

The cowardice and fear of strength engendered by Socialism and Democracy pervades to the greatest extent, of course, those countries where Democracy is established to the detriment of the community—for example, Australia and America in particular are always trembling and beseeching some one to deliver them from the Japanese ; for the Japanese are aristocrats with a proper system of castes. No brotherly love in Japan ! China and Russia were not defeated that way.

When Dr. Mügge tells us that Nietzsche's brain resembled a prolate cycloid, and that in metaphysics he was an optimistic voluntarist, with a mystical Dionysian formula of stoical-teleological origin, we feel at first that he is indulging in that species of pleasantry which is tersely described in the vernacular as pulling our leg. We can find no ready-made label to fit Nietzsche properly, and when Dr. Mügge invents these ultra-learned expressions for the benefit of a Philistine public, he is simply flinging rare *aviculæ margaritiferæ* in the path of the *sus*—besides giving what I conceive to be an incorrect view of Nietzsche. Nietzsche was a philosopher, a psychologist, a philologist, and a man of letters, possessing genius in an extraordinary degree. He was not a superman as he conceived the superman ; but he was the superman of his own age—*he combined within himself the greatest versatility in the greatest relative strength of each quality*. But, in addition, he possessed courage—the courage which enabled him to act a man's part in the Franco-German war, and which likewise enabled him to perform the more difficult task of thinking his thoughts out to the bitter end, no matter whither they led him, and also, most difficult task of all, to proclaim his views to a scandalised world.

Reader, if you have overcome the bitterness of the man who knows that science and the

Bible are irreconcilable, who turns drearily
to the world, and sees everything downcast and
tinged with grey, and, above all, if you feel
that you belong to the aristocratically strong,
you may safely neglect systems like Kant's
Categorical Imperative as a substitute for the
religion of your childhood ; but you may turn
with the certainty of attaining practical results
to the philosophy of Friedrich Nietzsche. Take
his three principal doctrines : the distinction
between master and slave morality (his most
important) ; the Superman ; the Eternal Recurrence. The distinction in morality is self-
evident, except to purblind demagogues. The
Superman is a physical and mental possibility,
easily susceptible of realisation. The Eternal
Recurrence has the authority of eminent philosophers of all ages, and is, as " another life "
or a " re-birth," at least as plausible as the heaven
described in the Revelation of St. John. If,
however, you feel, on the other hand, that no
philosophy will suffice to take the place of the
teaching which you considered as " divine " ;
and if you sincerely believe that nothing will
satisfy you but the uplifting of the poor and lowly
and fighting the battle of life in the rank and file
of the weak—then do what Schopenhauer has
told you to do in such circumstances, whether
your teacher be divine or not : go back to your
priests and leave philosophers in peace. And if
you become a Socialist, as you naturally will do,

it may be worth while reminding your fellow-decadents that, in arranging to knock down the barriers which separate European nations and dwell together in an Arcadia of peace and brotherly love, they have generally left Turkey and the Cossacks out of their calculations—and that your awakening may one day be a rude one!

Dixi et animam salvavi.

O my brethren, I consecrate you and point you to a new nobility: ye shall become pro-creators and cultivators and sowers of the future;—

—Verily, not to a nobility which ye could purchase like traders with traders' gold: for little worth is all that hath its price.

Let it not be your honour henceforth whence ye come, but whither ye go! Your Will and your feet which seek to surpass you—let these be your new honour!

O my brethren, not backward shall your nobility gaze, but *outward!* Exiles shall ye be from all fatherlands and forefatherlands!

Your *children's land* shall ye love: let this love be your new nobility—the undiscovered in the remotest seas! For it do I bid your sails search and search!

What of fatherland! *Thither* striveth our

helm where our *children's land* lies ! Thither-
ward, stormier than the sea, stormeth our great
longing !

The sea stormeth. Everything is in mid-
sea. Right away ! On, on, ye old sailor-
hearts ! *

* *Zarathustra*, LVI, secs. 12 and 28.

SHORT BIBLIOGRAPHY

OF MORE IMPORTANT WORKS ONLY

ALBERT, HENRI : several articles in the *Mercure de France* in 1894, 1899, 1900, and 1902.

BARRY, Dr. W.   Heralds of Revolt.

BÉLART, Nietzsches Ethik.

,,   Nietzsches Metaphysik.

,,   Nietzsche und Richard Wagner.

BERNOULLI, C. A.   Overbeck und Nietzsche.

BRANDES, G.   Menschen und Werke.

COMMON, THOS.   Nietzsche as Critic.

O. CRUSIUS.   Erwin Rhode.

DANZIG, S.   Drei Genealogien der Moral.

DUERINGER, A.   Nietzsches Philosophie vom Standpunckte des modernen Rechts.

FOERSTER-NIETZSCHE, E.   Das Leben Friedrich Nietzsche's.

FOUILÉE, A.   Nietzsche et l'Immoralisme.

GAULTIER, J.   De Kant à Nietzsche.

,,   Nietzsche et la Réforme philosophique.

LASSERRE, P.   La Morale de Nietzsche.

LEVY, Dr. OSCAR.   Das XIX Jahrhundert.

,,   ,,   The Revival of Aristocracy.

LICHTENBERGER. H. La Philosophie de Nietzsche.

LUDOVICI, A. M. Who is to be Master of the World?

NAUMANN, G. Zarathustra Commentar.

ORAGE, A. R. Nietzsche : The Dionysian Spirit of the Age.

,, ,, Nietzsche in Outline and Aphorism.

PAPINI, G. Il Crepuscolo dei Filosofi.

PETRONE, L. Nietzsche e Tolstoi.

RICHTER, R. F. Nietzsche, sein Leben und sein Werk.

RIEHL, A. Die Philosophie der Gegenwart.

ROBERTY, E. Friedrich Nietzsche : Contribution à l'Histoire des Idées.

SANZ Y ESCARTIN. F. Nietzsche y el anarquismo intelectual.

SCHELLWIEN, R. Nietzsche und Max Stirner.

SEILLIÈRE, E. Apollon ou Dionysos : Nietzsche et l'Utilitarisme impérialiste.

SERA, L. G. On the Tracks of Life.

STEINER, R. F. Nietzsche : ein Kämpfer gegen seine Zeit.

TILLE, A. Von Darwin bis Nietzsche.

ZEITLER, J. Nietzsches Aesthetik.

ZOCCOLI, E. G. Friedrich Nietzsche : La filosofia religiosa.

INDEX

A

Adam and Eve, myth of, 346
Æschylus, 7 ; compared with
   Wagner, 240
Ænead, *v.* Vergil
Aim, Nietzsche's, 17, 51
Alexandrine Culture, 136
Anarchy, Nietzsche and, 53,
   321 foll.
Antichrist, The, 41 ; quota-
   tions from, 331
Apollo and Dionysus, distinc-
   tion between, 129
Apollonian Period, 120 ; what
   it means, 122
Aristocracy, in France, 325
   foll.
Aristophanes, 7
Aristotle on Homer, 110
Artist, the true, 54 ; discipline
   of, 322
Asceticism, educational, 59
Ascetics, 272
Atheism, 320
Augustus the Strong, 2
Authors, Nietzsche's favour-
   ite, 7

B

Bad, what is, 331
Balfour, A. J., as philosopher,
99 ; compared with Herbert
   Spencer, 100
Barry, Dr. Wm., quoted, 83
Berlin, characteristics of, 33
Beyond Good and Evil pub-
   lished, 38 ; quoted, 58 foll.,
   88, 89, 93, 320 foll.
Birth of Tragedy published,
   19 ; quoted, 121 foll.
Bizet's *Carmen,* 40
Blond beasts, 329
Bonn, 8
Books, men grow tired of,
   210 ; use of, 283
Brandes, Geo., 43
British Weekly, 66 and note,
   349
Brühl, Earl of, 2
Buddha, his shade, 281

C

Carlyle, Nietzsche on, 335
Carmen, Bizet's, 40
Case of Wagner, The, 40 ;
   quoted, 335
Chesterton, G. K., 96
Christianity : "shells to ex-
   plode against," 12 ; Nietzsche becomes estranged
   from, 12 ; virtues of, 64 ;
   denies Life, 65 ; ideals of,
   69 foll. ; if carried to ex-

tremes, 73 and note ; Nietzsche and, 75 ; and Socialism, 101 ; effects of, 103 ; a burlesque of the moral theme, 126 ; condemns art, 127 ; and culture, 195 ; and the State, 216 foll. ; a product of oriental antiquity, 239 ; and despairing men, 272 ; oriental features of, 273 ; and Philology, 273 ; more harmful than any vice, 331 ; a misunderstanding, 332.

Church of England, 74 foll. ; High Church and Romanism, 78 ; and Socialism, 101 ; for the lower classes, 102

Cistercian monks, 4

Common, Thos., quoted, 55

Comte, 120

Composition, teaching of, 151

Cook, Eliza, and Miss Salomé, 34

Corruption in France, 325

Courtney, W. L., 94 and note

Culture, German, 16 ; cardinal principle of, 144 ; and non-culture, 173

Culture, Philistine, v. Philistine

D

Daily News, 66 and note

Dante, Nietzsche on, 335

David Strauss, 170 foll.

Dawn of Day, published, 29 ; quoted, 269 foll.

Decadence, literary, 337

Democracy, 5 ; and v. Socialism

Democritus, 11

Demosthenes and Wagner, 253

Deussen, quoted, 82

Dignity, 273

Diogenes quoted, 226

Diogenes Laertius, 10

Dionysian period, Nietzsche's, 120 ; what it means, 122 ; and Antichrist, 128

Dionysus, 20 ; and Apollo, distinction between, 129

Dogma, extinct, 73

Drama, reinstatement of, 241 ; and music, relationship between, 245 ; its influence, 250

E

Ecce Homo, quoted, 267, 338 foll.

Edda, the, 7

Edition, best, of Nietzsche's works, 106

Educational Institutions, v. Future of our Educational Institutions

Egotism, 56

Eleatics and Kant, 240

Emerson, 7

Empedocles and Schopenhauer, 240

Epicurus, 125

Equality, doctrine of, 277, 345

Eternal Recurrence, 32 ; explanation of, 289 foll. ; teaching of, 311

F

Farrar's *Eric*, 32
Faust, 214
Fichte, 81
Fidelity, a characteristic of Wagner's operas, 233
Financiers in modern society, 248
Foerster, Dr. E., 36
Friedrich-Wilhelm IV, 1
Future of our Educational Institutions, 17; quoted, 144 foll.
Fyfe, Hamilton, *A Modern Aspasia*, quoted, 86

G

Gaiety, German, 251
Gast, Peer, calls on Nietzsche, 3; accompanies him to Venice, 29; care of Nietzsche after breakdown, 44; address at Nietzsche's grave, quoted, 46; his real name, 29, note
Gay Science, v. *Joyful Wisdom*
Genealogy of Morals, 39; quoted, 69 foll., 326 foll.
Genius, definition of, 55; and followers, 165
Germania Club, 5 foll.
Germans, the, characteristics of, 338 foll.
Gervinus and Lessing, 178
God, his needs, 281; death of, 297; Christian conception of, 331

Goethe's man, 212; and Homer, 112; on history, 185
Goncourt brothers, Nietzsche on, 335
Good and evil, an illusion, 309; the battle of, 327
Good, what is, 331
Greeks, the, their ideals and principles, 18; and woman, 89; characteristics of, 125; and the "unhistoric sense," 193
Greek State, the, 142
Greek Woman, the, 142
Greville, Fulke, quoted, 348

H

Happiness; how to increase, 278; how to attain, 282; what it is, 331
Hartmann quoted, 196
Heckel, Karl, quoted, 316 foll.
Hegel, 81; Nietzsche contra, 185 foll.
Heinrich von Stein, 37
Hell invented, 67
Higher men, 312 foll.
History, Use and Abuse of, 23, 185 foll.; what it now is, 237
Homeless Ones, the, 286
Homer and Classical Philology, 14; quoted, 71 and note; summary of, 107; quotations from, 107; the Homeric question, 111; and Hesiod, 142

Horton, Dr., quoted, 73, note
Hugo, Nietzsche on, 335
Human, All-too-human, published, 27; pt. ii., 29
Huneker, James, quoted, 52

I

Ideals, manufacture of, 69 foll.
Iliad, *v.* Homer
" My Impossibilities," 335
Individualities, formation of, 115
Inspiration, 341

J

Jahn, 8
Jesus, 32, 303
Journalism, 147
Joyful Wisdom, 33, 278 foll.

K

Kant, 81; and the Eleatics, 240; Nietzsche on, 335
Knowlson, T. S., 300, note
Koeselitz, *v.* Gast, Peter
Krug, Gustav, 6

L

Landes-Schule, *v.* Pforta
Languages, classical, teaching of, 154, 157; degeneration of, 246
Laughter, sanctified, 314
Leipzig University, 8 foll.; Nietzsche tries to get professorial chair at, 35

Lento, the, 270
Lessing, and German prose, 178; characteristics of, 178
Levy, Dr. O., quoted, vii, viii, 276
Liberality, 282
Liberalism, 80
Lichtenberger, quoted, 63, 227, 255, 292
Life, meaning of, 280
Linguistic instruction, 149, 151; difficulties of, 153
Loneliness, 274
Ludovici, A. M., quoted, 51, 54, 65, 95
Luther, quoted, 146

M

Man, the modern, 191 foll.
Marriage, 309
Masterman, Mr., his ideals, 79
Maurice of Saxony, 4
Metamorphoses of the spirit, 298
Michelet, Nietzsche on, 335
Mill, J. S., Nietzsche on, 335
Mission, our new, 105
Modern times, characteristics of, 211
Montaigne and Shakespeare, 237
Morality, English view of, 30; in England, 56; what Nietzsche means by, 57; master and slave, 61; what it is, 73; campaign against, 270 foll.; master and slave, instance of, 327; master and

Christian, 337 ; summary, 345

Murray, Dr. Gilbert, compared to Nietzsche, 169

Music, Dionysian, 138 ; and drama, 245 ; what it now means, 246–7 ; its effect on thought, 336

Music and Speech, 142

N

Napoleon, and elemental warnings, 45

Naumann, C. G., 37

New Age, 316, note ; 338

New Testament, the ancient *Daily News*, 66 ; and Christians, 68 ; should be read with gloves on, 332

Niebelungen, the, 7

Nietzsche contra Wagner, 41, 335

Nietzsche, Elizabeth Foerster : birth of, 1 ; meets Dr. Foerster, 36 ; returns from Paraguay, 43

Nietzsche, Friedrich Wilhelm : Born 1844, 1 ; Polish descent, 1, 2 ; his appearance, 3, 24, 25 ; is taken to Naumburg, 3 ; juvenile works, 4 ; passion for solitude, 4 ; at Pforta, 4 foll. ; leaves Pforta, 8 ; at Bonn, 8 ; military service, 11 ; accepts chair of classical philology at Basel, 14 ; takes part in Franco-German War, 15 ; lectures on educa-

tion, 17 ; publishes *Birth of Tragedy*, 19 ; early illnesses, 23 ; at Bayreuth, 24 ; rupture with Wagner, 24 ; resigns his professorship, 28 ; travels, 29 foll. ; meets Miss Salomé, 34 ; suffers from insomnia, 35 ; tries to get chair at Leipzig, 35 ; mental breakdown at Turin, 41 ; causes of his madness, 41 ; removes to Weimar, 44 ; final illness, 44 ; death and burial, 45 ; attributes of, 81 ; his sexual feelings, 82, 311 ; and woman, 82 ; compared with ancient writers, 82–3 ; and the German language, 83 ; admires women, 84 ; full views on women, 84 foll. ; his predecessors, 102 ; how influenced by Wagner and Schopenhauer, 256 ; and politics, 268

Nihilism, what Nietzsche means by, 330

O

Odyssey, *v.* Homer

Old Testament, 68

Olympian, the, 123

Outlook, quoted, 53

Overbeck, Prof., 39 ; attends to Nietzsche after breakdown, 42

P

Pain, capacity for feeling, 329

Papini on Spencer, 96 foll.

Pascal, 272

Peace and war, 311

Pessimism, 123

Pforta, Neitzsche goes to, 4 ; leaves, 8

Philistines of culture, 175

Philistinism, English, instance of, 164 foll.

Philology, works on, 10 ; views on, 14 ; protest in favour of, 119

Philosophy, its task, 237

Philosophy in the Tragic Age of Greece, 168 foll.

Pinder, Wm., 6

Pisistratus, 110

Plato, 7 ; quoted, 71, note

Poetry, popular, 112 ; Nietzsche's, 334

Political parties, 275

Politics, Nietzsche and, 78, 268

Polybius, quoted, 188

Pope, Alex., quoted, 17

Populace, the, its pettiness, 313 foll.

Positivism, 120

Posthumous works, Nietzsche's, 106

Pride, 279

Principium individuationis, 129

Productive things always offensive, 182

Protestantism, 75 ; and science, 292

Public Schools, English and German, 149

Punishment, 271

Puritanism, 31 ; educational, 59

R

Reason, living by, 85

Rée, Dr., meets Nietzsche, 29 ; goes to Monaco with him, 33 ; and Miss Salomé, 34

Relationship of Schopenhauer's Philosophy to a German Culture, 168

Religion, Nietzsche's views on, 58 foll. ; what it is, 73 ; influence of, 292

Rhenisches Museum, 10

Ritschl, 8 ; recommends Nietzsche to Bâle University, 13 ; disapproves of *The Birth of Tragedy*, 20

Rohde, Erwin, 9 ; replies to Wilamowitz - Moellendorf, 20 ; letters to Overbeck, 39

Rohn, 10

Roman Catholic Church, 73 and foll. ; what it was and is, 75

Roman Empire, 65

Rome and Judea, 327

Rosebery, Lord, quoted, 79, note

Rousseau's man, 212 ; Nietzsche on, 335

S

Sagacity, little and big, 300

Salomé, Miss A., 34, 35

Sand, George, Nietzsche on, 335

Savants, characteristics of, 217

Schiller, ruined by Philistinism, 180 ; Nietzsche on, 335

Scholarship, German, 171 foll.

Schools, English and American, 18, 19

Schopenhauer, 10 ; actual characteristics of, 21 ; and Apollo, 129 ; his philosophy and German culture, 168 ; as Educator, 199 foll. ; dualism of, 207 ; dangers encountered by, 208 ; his "man," 212 ; and Nietzsche's mental development, 227 ; and Empedocles, 240

Schuré describes Nietzsche at Bayreuth, 24

Science, problem of, 125

Self-confidence, 300

Seneca, quoted, 14 ; Nietzsche's opinion of, 335

Sera, Dr. L. G., quoted, 75 foll.

Sex, prejudices of, 283

Sexuality, English views on, 56 ; and the Roman Catholic Church, 77

Shakespeare, 7

Sils-Maria, 32 foll.

Socialism and Socialists, Nietzsche's views on, 53 ; and genius, 93 ; their adoration of mere reason, 93 ; intellects which would succeed under, 94 ; spread of in Church of England, 101 ; consequences of, 103, 268

Society, Nietzsche's ideal, 333

Socrates, 93, 94 ; irony of, 125 ; daimonion of, 134 ; his death

an ideal death, 136 ; influence of on modern life, 136

Specialisation, 146, 305

Spencer, Herbert, 96 ; Papini on, 97 foll.

Spirit, metamorphoses of, 298

Stanislaus Leszcynsski, 2

State, the Nietzschian, 333 foll.

Stendhal, quoted, viii, 5

Strachey, St. Loe, New Way of Life, 79

Strauss, David, 22, 170 foll.

Systems, 80

T

Tacitus, 7

Tasso, quoted, 248

Theognis, 11

Thoughts out of Season, published, 22 ; quoted, 170 foll.

Tragedy, v. Birth of Tragedy

Translations of Nietzsche's works, 51

Truth and Lying in an Amoral Sense, 168 foll.

Twilight of the Idols, 41 ; quoted, 105, 334

U

United States of America, 19

University philosophers, why not dangerous, 226

Use and Abuse of History, 185

V

Vergil and decadence, 103

Virtues, Christian, 64

W

Wagner, Richard : Nietzsche first hears his music, 5 ; visits him, 20 ; actual characteristics of, 22 ; in Bayreuth, 24 ; quarrel with Nietzsche, 28 ; the *Ring*, 24 ; and Nietzsche's mental development, 227 ; at Bayreuth, 230 foll. ; mental struggles of, 236 ; as philosopher, 238 ; and Æschylus, 240 ; gradual development of, 249 ; his artistic greatness, 253 ; as musician, 254 ; as man of letters, 254 ; his dignity, 255 ; the Cagliostro of modernity, 337

Wagnerism and Nietzsche, 335

War, 311

Wilamowitz-Moellendorf, attacks *Birth of Tragedy*, 20 ; second pamphlet against it, 21

Will Power, 114

Will to Power, 38 ; quoted, 276, note ; 330

Winckelmann, ruined by Philistinism, 178

Wolf, F. W., his Homeric researches, 107

Woman-haters, 274

Women, Nietzsche on, 84 foll. ; and the Greeks, 89 ; and scholarly inclinations, 321 ; a danger to artists, 336 ; rights of, 344

Workmen, status of, 347–8

Works, period of Nietzsche's, 120

World, the, justified only as æsthetic phenomenon, 122 ; Luther on, 190

Z

Zarathustra, "incipit," 105 ; quoted, 296 foll.

Zola, Nietzsche on, 335

WILLIAM BRENDON AND SON, LTD.
PRINTERS, PLYMOUTH

Featured Titles from Westphalia Press

Peasant Art in Sweden, Lapland and Iceland
by Charles Holme

This particular work offers a carefully chosen selection of both the decorative and fine arts of Sweden, Iceland, and the northern most region of Finland. A comprehensive survey, it includes paintings, jewelry, textiles, metalwork, carving, furniture and pottery.

The Rise of the Book Plate: An Exemplative of the Art
by W. G. Bowdoin, Introduction by Henry Blackwel

Bookplates were made to denote ownership and hopefully steer the volume back to the rightful shelf if borrowed. They often contained highly stylized writing, drawings, coat of arms, badges or other images of interest to the owner.

The Art of Table Setting, Ancient and Modern
by Claudia Quigley Murphy

The arrangement of a table in terms of cutlery, arrangement, serving style, and timing of courses has changed a great deal over time and now is enjoying renewed interest. The History of the Art of Tablesetting was written by a true expert in the field, Claudia Quigley Murphy.

Understanding Art: Hendrik Willem Van Loon's
How To Look At Pictures by Hendrik Willem Van
Loon, Introduction by Daniel Gutierrez-Sandoval

Hendrik Willem van Loon was a Dutch-American professor, journalist, prolific writer, and illustrator. His most famous work, "The Story of Mankind" earned him the prestigious John Newbery Medal.

The Etchings of Rembrandt: A Study and History
by P. G. Hamerton

Philip Gilbert Hamerton (1834-1894) was an Englishman who was devoted to the arts in numerous forms. Due to the praise, Hamerton stuck with art criticism, and went on to write other works. He also wrote novels, biographies, and reflections on society.

Lankes, His Woodcut Bookplates by Wilbur Macey Stone

Julius John Lankes was born in Buffalo, New York in 1884, and became a prolific woodcut print artist, as well as an author and professor. As a child, he enjoyed working with the scraps of wood his father brought home from the lumber mill where he was employed. Lankes had a lifelong interest in art.

Los Dibujos de Heriberto Juarez / The Drawings of Heriberto Juarez, Edited by Paul Rich

That the drawings here are from life in México is not surprising because Juárez is constantly, and at times impishly, putting art into life and getting art from life. He doesn't think of art as something that is done just in a studio or for that matter kept in museums and looked at on Sundays.

The History of Photography: Carl W. Ackerman's George Eastman by Carl W. Ackerman, Introduction by Daniel Gutierrez-Sandoval

The life of George Eastman is very much a part of the history of contemporary photography. Founder of the Eastman Kodak Company, Eastman was an enthusiastic photographer himself who became instrumental in bringing photography to the mainstream.

Famous Stars of Light Opera by Lewis C. Strang, Introduction by Matthew Brewer

Strang's attempts to quantify the humorous elements of each performer, as well as quotes from the performers themselves attempting to explain their own success, are an interesting exercise in attempting to explain the inexplicable.

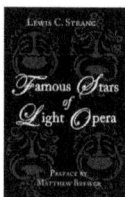

The Historic Codfish by George H. Proctor, Samuel D. Hildreth, William Frank Parsons

There may be 160 representatives in the Massachusetts legislature, but there is only one codfish. The nearly five-foot carving hanging from the ceiling is the third reminder of the importance of fishing to the state. The first was burnt in a 1747 fire and the second destroyed during the Revolution. The present fish was enshrined in 1784.